THE COURT-MARTIAL OF JESUS

THE COURT-MARTIAL OF JESUS

*A Christian Defends the Jews
Against the Charge of Deicide*

WEDDIG FRICKE

Translated from the German
by Salvator Attanasio

GROVE WEIDENFELD
New York

Copyright © 1987 by Weddig Fricke
Translation copyright © 1990 by Grove Weidenfeld

All rights reserved.

No part of this book may be reproduced, stored in a retrieval system, or transmitted in any form, by any means, including mechanical, electronic, photocopying, recording, or otherwise, without prior written permission of the publisher.

Published by Grove Weidenfeld
A division of Wheatland Corporation
841 Broadway
New York, NY 10003-4793

Published in Canada by General Publishing Company, Ltd.

Originally published in German by Mai Verlag

Library of Congress Cataloging-in-Publication Data

Fricke, Weddig, 1930–
    [Standrechtlich gekreuzigt. English]
    The court-martial of Jesus : a Christian defends the Jews against the charge of deicide / Weddig Fricke ; translated from the German by Salvator Attanasio.—1st ed.
        p. cm.
    Translation of: Standrechtlich gekreuzigt.
    Includes bibliographical references.
    1. Jesus Christ—Trial. 2. Jesus Christ—Historicity. 3. Jesus Christ—Passion—Role of Jews. 4. Jesus Christ—Passion—Role of Romans. 5. Passion narratives (Gospels)—Criticism, interpretation, etc. 6. Passion narratives (Gospels)—Controversial literature. 7. Passion narratives (Gospels)—Controversial literature. 8. Christianity and antisemitism—Biblical teaching. I. Title.
BT440.F75 1990
232.96'2—dc20   89-78489
                                                               CIP

ISBN 0-8021-1094-0

Manufactured in the United States of America

Printed on acid-free paper

Designed by Irving Perkins Associates

First Edition 1990

10 9 8 7 6 5 4 3 2 1

CONTENTS

	Preface	vii
	Introduction	3
Part I	THE PERSON	
One	The Sources and Their Historicity	9
Two	The Biblical Jesus	22
Three	In Search of the Historical Jesus	42
Four	How, When, and Where Born	62
Five	Forebears and Family	77
Six	Jesus' Strangeness Endures	83
Part II	THE FACTS	
Seven	The Passion Story	95
Eight	The Romans, Not the Jews	109
Nine	The Alleged Trial Before the Sanhedrin	149
Ten	Transgressions of Jesus Not Mentioned in the Indictment?	181
Eleven	Suffered Under Pontius Pilate	189

Twelve	The Procurator and the Jews	202
	Epilogue	219
	Notes	223
	Bibliography	277
	Index	283
	Index of Biblical Verses	295

PREFACE

A legal case in which I was professionally involved as an attorney prompted me to write this book. From 1970 to 1974 I was the court-appointed defense counsel for a Nazi criminal tried before the Freiburg assize court. The accused, who in 1942 had been a policeman in the Jewish ghetto of Czestochowa, was charged with maliciously shooting and killing eight Jews. Seated in the dock was a respectable master locksmith, an upright citizen and family man, the very picture of a kindly grandfather. He had committed the criminal acts as a young man, thirty-two years earlier. Eyewitnesses testified to his crime, his personal responsibility and guilt were established, and he was sentenced to life imprisonment on a multiple murder charge.

What is shocking in such a trial is the scenario of horror that unfolds in the courtroom as witnesses recall the events. Equally shocking is the realization that this utterly unassuming defendant could have committed his crimes only within the wider context of a perverted sense of justice, for which he was no more responsible than those who now had to deal with his crime.

Whereas an ordinary murderer, by violating public law and

order and the social principles on which it is based, willfully places himself beyond the pale of the state and society, a policeman who shot eight ghetto Jews in 1942 because they violated some petty regulations could well have believed that his action conformed to the precepts of state and society. The distinction between a state in which crimes occur and one in which crime is declared a virtue comes into play precisely in such a circumstance.

As defense counsel I was obliged to confront historical "anti-Semitism"—actually, it would be more accurate to speak of "anti-Judaism"—a phenomenon that reached an apogee of horror under Hitler but that is much older and by no means limited to Germany.

Historical anti-Judaism is deeply ingrained in all countries within the Christian cultural orbit. In tracing it back to its source, one inevitably comes to—regrettably, this must be said—the authors of the New Testament. Their thesis, namely, the guilt of the Jews in the death of Jesus and their supposed self-damnation as related in Matthew 27:25–26, over the centuries became a legal title sanctioning discriminatory treatment, expulsion, and slaughter of Jews. Whenever "Christians" gave vent to their hatred of Jews, they cited the Gospels—those of Matthew and John in particular—in support of their actions.

This initial insight prompted me to study the sources in greater depth and, finally, to succumb to the fascination exerted by the historical personality of Jesus of Nazareth. Thus did this book come into being.

I would like to thank all those who encouraged me to pursue this project, and whose suggestions and proddings led me to work further on the manuscript, which often remained in the drawer for long stretches of time because of the daily demands of my profession.

My special thanks go to my friend Georg Thamm. In long evening conversations he not only advised me knowledgeably but also assisted by reading manuscripts and verifying quotations. His many hints and suggestions led me to further findings. Thanks are also due to Elke Lenski, who as a fledgling legal assistant typed the manuscript, often after hours and on weekends, and who managed always to preserve her cheerfulness even when pages had to be retyped many times over to incorporate stylistic corrections. I also thank all those who in the interest of historical honesty have contributed to the dissemination of this book.

Freiburg
November 9, 1986

THE COURT-MARTIAL OF JESUS

INTRODUCTION

Up to now lawyers have seldom concerned themselves with the person of Jesus of Nazareth and the circumstances of his violent death. This is surprising inasmuch as lawyers, more than most, should feel challenged to adopt a point of view about Jesus. For according to tradition, his trial is one of those—and indeed the most momentous—in which an innocent person was sentenced to death and executed.

But we cannot adopt a point of view on the trial proceedings without first looking at the biographical information on the accused—as far as it is available—and then subjecting it to a critical appraisal, taking into account certain facts of his environment. Accordingly, as is customary in a modern criminal trial, I have begun with a section concerning the "person" before dealing with the proceedings.

No attempt can be made here to depict the course of Jesus' life or to undertake a playback, as it were, of the Jerusalem trial in order to revise the verdict. A legal analysis would be doomed *a priori* to fail because it is doubtful whether a trial, in the sense of a contemporary criminal proceeding, ever in fact took place.

In the final analysis, none of the three theories—the only historically relevant ones—about the circumstances leading to Jesus' crucifixion can be conclusively verified: not the one holding that the Jewish establishment wanted to rid itself of the troublesome prophet from Galilee and handed him over to the Romans; nor the one according to which Jesus was in fact a Zealot resistance fighter against the Roman occupation and was apprehended and executed as such; nor finally the theory to which the greatest probability is attributed here, which holds that Jesus was sentenced and crucified by the Romans as a suspected rebel in a military-type summary proceeding* because they misunderstood the essentially pacifist character of his public activity.

The Gospels give only scant information regarding the course of Jesus' life and its sudden end with his arrest and execution. It is easier by far to show where Gospel reportage appears to conflict with objective criteria and thus requires correction. The fact that nowhere outside the Gospels is any trial of a prominent personality said to have taken place in Jerusalem around the year 30 of our era leads me to conclude that the event that transpired on Golgotha could not have been viewed as sensational or memorable, at least not by contemporaries.

Neither Paul nor the Gospels nor the other authors of the New Testament are particularly interested in a biography of Jesus. Indeed, the unusual dearth of information gave rise over the years to doubts that Jesus even existed as a historical personality. Only as a result of the findings of so-called historical-critical research on Jesus has this skepticism been definitively overcome.

The Gospel accounts were concerned with the proclamation of the Christian message in the Roman Empire. Hence they were biased from the outset as to the question of guilt for Jesus' death. For example, the Roman procurator Pontius Pilate, described in the historical sources as especially cruel and anti-Jewish, is presented as a mild presiding judge who supposedly moved heaven and earth in a futile attempt to free the accused Jesus arraigned before his court.

---

*In other words, the criminal proceedings against Jesus could be compared to a trial held before a court-martial. I am aware that the comparison is historically weak. It can be argued that a court-martial is an institution created by the military penal code to try military personnel exclusively. Nevertheless I consider it useful for the purpose of underlining the extreme "summary" character of the trial of Jesus.

The particular points the reader will encounter in this book can also be found elsewhere. Indeed, no opinion or conjecture expressed here has not already been voiced in the broad spectrum of theological discussion. But as far as I know, there has as yet been no overall synthesis of the kind attempted here. The method of this book also differs from those of other publications.

As a lawyer I found it tempting to undertake a kind of "cross-examination of the witnesses" concerning the person and the trial of Jesus. The argumentative form of presentation I have chosen, frequently citing precisely those sources that are unquestionably anchored in the Christian faith or have special value for the Christian-Jewish dialogue, should make the reader aware that the Jesus portrayed by the Church and from the pulpit differs in a number of decisive ways from the Jesus who emerges from the historical record insofar as it can be established.

Although all views of the historical Jesus are necessarily colored by the philosophical or religious biases of those who hold them, I have taken great pains here not to touch on questions of personal faith. Christians who may be inclined to subscribe to my arguments will be able to hold unreservedly to the central message of Christianity for the individual: that Jesus of Nazareth is the Christ who died and rose from the dead. However, I do oppose a faith that denies the findings of historical research and can therefore be considered naive. History teaches how easily naive faith can degenerate into fanaticism and persecution. This book is properly understood not in theological but in juridical-historical terms.

Part I

THE PERSON

One

THE SOURCES AND THEIR HISTORICITY

Authors and Canon

Anyone seeking biographical facts about Jesus Christ almost literally gropes in the dark. Not nearly as much is known about him as, say, about Alexander, Caesar, or Augustus; we can only speculate as to how this or that event may—perhaps—have transpired. It is much easier to determine what is legend in the known accounts of his personality and actions.[1]

Jesus himself left behind no written testimonial for posterity. He is not portrayed in the literature of his time.[2] The only source is the New Testament. Yet no one who reported about Jesus in the New Testament had ever met him, not even Paul, the one man who was actually a contemporary of Jesus. The Franciscan scholar Dautzenberg expresses a view more or less shared by theologians for some time: "No Gospel was written by an eyewitness."[3]

The authors of the Gospels—all belonging to a later generation—are unknown historical figures. None of them is identical to any of the apostles of the same name who were called disciples of

Jesus. Even the author of the two letters of Peter, though he presents himself as the disciple Simon Peter and an eyewitness to the events he relates, is not identical to the disciple Simon Peter in the Gospels and Acts. The unknown author of both letters merely appropriated the name Peter so as to enhance his authority and impart more weight to his words.[4] The same applies to the letters of James and Jude. The names were probably chosen in homage to the family of Jesus. At any rate, the authors of these letters are not the James and Jude mentioned in Mark 6:3 as brothers of Jesus.

In the ancient world the notion of literary property was unknown, and numerous writings were composed under the names of important personalities who most certainly were not the authors of the works attributed to them. For example, most of the psalms of David and the words of Solomon have as little to do with David or Solomon as Moses had to do with the Books of Moses.

When the author of the Gospel of John declares, "This disciple is the one who vouches for these things and has written them down, and we know that his testimony is true" (John 21:24), he is just as misleading as the author of the Petrine Letters. The intention is to convey the idea that the evangelist John is identical to John the so-called beloved disciple. The passage in which John is said to have stood at the foot of the cross and shared Jesus' last moments (John 19:35) serves to buttress the erroneous assumption that the beloved disciple and the evangelist are one and the same. In reality, the events described in the Gospel of John occurred about eighty years before it was composed. Thus, the author would have to have been around a hundred years old had he really been present at the scene.

The disciples,[5] and in fact all those who may have surrounded Jesus during his short public ministry, were simple people but knew the rudiments of reading and writing. Although Jesus takes pains to make himself understandable to simple people and makes no special intellectual demands on his audience, it is precisely the disciples who often seem to have trouble following him. Their questions as to how this or that parable or saying should be understood must often have tried the master's patience severely.

> "Do you not understand this parable? Then how will you understand any of the parables?" (Mark 4:13)
> "Do you not yet understand? Have you no perception? Are your minds closed? Have you eyes that do not see, ears that do not hear?" (Mark 8:17–18)

Like Peter, most of the disciples were probably Galilean fishermen. Apart from the fact that there is no written testimony about them, it is inconceivable that any of them would have been capable of the theological formulations expressed in the New Testament. In Acts 4:13 Peter and John are explicitly called "uneducated laymen"—further proof that the Petrine Letters were not composed by the disciple Peter, nor the Gospel of John by the disciple John.

The Gospels and the other New Testament accounts were written in Greek; at any rate, there is neither philological proof nor reasonable ground for assuming that they were originally written in Hebrew or Aramaic and that the texts we know are only Greek translations.

In Jesus' time Greek was the language of the educated strata in Palestine. Whether Jesus had mastered Greek we do not know, but according to Salcia Landmann, "We can take it for granted that the Galilean villager Jesus would know as much Greek and Latin as an East Galician miracle worker rabbi would know Polish or Ruthenian—that is, a few words that would suffice for a sketchy understanding of the simplest everyday questions."[6]

Jesus himself and his closest followers spoke Aramaic, a language closely related to Hebrew. We may assume that it was a rather heavily accented Aramaic, typical of Galilee. Indeed, Peter is said to have been recognized as a Galilean and thus as a follower of Jesus precisely because of this accent: " 'You are one of them for sure! Why, your accent gives you away' " (Matt. 26:74).

There is absolutely no documentation about what Jesus said in the intimacy of his private circle about his family or the course of his life. In most of the New Testament—for example, Paul's letters—Jesus himself is never quoted. Only the Gospels purport to quote him directly. His words were then presumably translated into Greek, the universal language of the time. It was then necessary to translate them back into Aramaic for the adherents of the fledgling Jesus movement who spoke that language. Finally, the sayings were committed to writing in the form of the Gospels as we know them, for a public that was at home with the Greek language.

Jesus' sayings, as we read and understand them in the Gospels, are grounded not in his Semitic but in our European linguistic world. It is generally known now that members of different linguistic families not only speak differently but also think differently. Jesus and his disciples, as members of a Semitic language family, thought in different categories than did speakers of Indo-European languages.

The oldest testimonies about Jesus that have come down to us are Paul's letters, the first of which were presumably sent in A.D. 50 from Corinth to Salonika, the community of the Thessalonians. Paul, of course, neither deals with the earthly person of Jesus nor evinces the slightest interest in it. He reports on the crucified and risen Christ, the Christ of faith and preaching, but not on the historical person Jesus of Nazareth.

Scholars are in broad agreement on the chronological sequence of the Gospels, but the precise date of their origin is not known. According to prevailing opinion, the Gospel of Mark originated around A.D. 70 (except for the last half of the concluding chapter, which was supposedly written about a hundred years later); Matthew originated in the 80s (with a concluding chapter written about a hundred and fifty years later); Luke, shortly thereafter, around A.D. 90; John, ten to thirty years later, around or after the turn of the century.[7] The Acts of the Apostles, written by the author of the Lucan Gospel, originated around A.D. 95.

The conquest of Jerusalem and the destruction of the Temple (A.D. 70) are mentioned in both Mark 13:2 and Luke 19:43–44. In Matthew the report of the fallen capital is embedded in the parable of the wedding feast (22:7–8).

The Apocalypse, or Revelation, of John, the last book in the New Testament, is also regarded as the latest canonical document. A small minority opinion, however, places it much earlier, on the grounds that the mystical number 666 mentioned in Revelation 13:18 is an arcane symbol for "Nero Caesar."[8]

Neither the Gospels nor the other writings of the New Testament are preserved in their original version, nor are the first transcripts extant. We have only transcripts of transcripts of transcripts. No one can prove that these transcripts do not contain interpolations reflecting later Church doctrine. The oldest transcripts of the Synoptic Gospels that have come down to us, no longer written on papyrus but on parchment, date back to the third and fourth centuries. The New Testament as it exists today corresponds to its condition at the time it was being spread in eastern Christendom around A.D. 380.[9] A papyrus fragment of Chapter 18 of John's Gospel dating from the first half of the second century was found in the Egyptian desert in 1933.

The Johannine Gospel was definitely not written by a single

author. We do not know whether the other Gospels are also the work of several authors. These authors must be considered more or less educated theologians. Whence they came, where they primarily lived and composed their works, remains unknown. Only the oldest Gospel, Mark's, is frequently assumed by scholars and also in Church tradition to have been composed in Rome.

The Gospels have come down to us anonymously; they received the names they now bear from the Church Fathers some time in the second century. The reasons for the attribution are not known, except perhaps in the case of John's Gospel, where we may assume that it was so called because in it John alone is designated the disciple "whom Jesus loved."

The Gospels and the letters of Jesus' wandering followers were repeatedly transcribed, and for this reason alone deviations inevitably crept in. A further source of error lies in the fact that the pious chroniclers' accounts of Jesus were largely based on oral narratives. If it is also borne in mind that the whole event transpired in the Near East and that the "informants" were mostly of humble origin—and furthermore, were people who became followers of Jesus after falling under the spell of those who firmly and passionately believed in his resurrection—the difficulty of separating fiction from fact is self-evident.

In the three hundred years between Jesus' death and the elevation of Christian doctrine to the status of state religion, a welter of doctrinal opinion developed. A manuscript discovered in Istanbul in 1966, which provides information on the first Christian centuries, reports that there were about eighty different versions of the Gospels. Some were preserved but were considered apocryphal and therefore were not accepted into the New Testament.

Just what from the profusion of different drafts and writings could be viewed as binding, and what not, was a problem confronting the first Pauline communities. From time to time "choices" or "emendations" had to be made, more or less arbitrarily. Papias, an early Christian bishop, describes around A.D. 140 a meeting of Church Fathers at which the existing texts were placed at the foot of the altar. Since there was no longer any way to distinguish between authentic and inauthentic texts, the Fathers prayed that the authentic books would rise up and place themselves on the altar. According to Papias this actually happened. Unfortunately, he neglects to mention which books they were.

The so-called Old Testament, then as before, was viewed as a "sacred" book in the strict sense of the word. The orally transmitted sayings of Jesus enjoyed the same authority. Next to them, but of far less importance, were the numerous gospels and other writings that had not yet been arranged in order of precedence. What was to be considered "catholic" and what "heresy" was contested for a long time and occasioned the controversy within the Church. Hundreds of competing teachers professed to proclaim the "true teaching of Christ" and accused the others of being frauds.[10] The quarrel among Christians was conducted with a vehemence far greater than that with the pagans, toward whom tolerance was the policy as long as the Church had no power.

In a process that lasted more than two hundred years, some gospels eventually became accepted into the so-called New Testament, even though many of them had been contested for a long time. Others fell victim to the controversy within the Church: one Church authority might have wanted to accept a certain writing but failed to have his way. For example, Tertullian and Origen wanted the Hebrew and Egyptian gospels to be canonized. (At an earlier canonization it had been decided that only Luke's Gospel—after it had been "purged" of its Judaisms—and ten likewise "purged" letters of the apostle Paul were to be considered canonical.) This was precisely the demand, later to be condemned as heresy, of the Church teacher Marcion, surely the most important Christian disputant of the second century.[11]

Not until A.D. 383 was an end put to the confusion when Pope Damasus I commissioned his secretary Hieronymus (St. Jerome) to revise the ancient Latin Bible translation. The result was another Latin work, the Vulgate, containing the twenty-seven writings that henceforth represented the canon of the New Testament. From then on they were also regarded as the writings of the apostles, books inspired by the Holy Spirit and thus of divine origin. Any questioning of their content was *a priori* forbidden. The four Gospels in particular were approved on the basis of a peculiar argument: There are four points of the compass, and furthermore, according to the prophet Ezekiel, there are four animals attached to the chariot of the Almighty God.

Only in the wake of the Enlightenment was any theological question raised, tentatively, as to whether the New Testament was the exclusive work of God. It came to be viewed—in the words of Johann Gottfried Herder—as "a book written by humans for humans." To be sure, only Protestant theologians could officially argue the question. For Catholics the dogma of divine inspiration of the New Testament texts was reaffirmed at the First Vatican Council in 1870. To this day no discussion on this subject has been sanctioned by the ecclesiastical magisterium.

Good News Should Be Proclaimed

The authors of the New Testament are not really interested in historical fact: their concern is quite different. They want to proclaim the Good News *(eu-angelion)*, primarily the Pauline message of the risen Christ whose death on the cross took away the sins of humankind (2 Cor. 5:19). The evangelists in particular want to spread the Good News as Jesus himself proclaimed it, namely the message of the approaching kingdom of God (Mark 1:15).[12]
The problem of the historicity of Jesus' sayings is compounded by the fact that no one teaching has its origin in Jesus. Since the discovery of the Dead Sea Scrolls in 1947 at the latest, this must be taken as fact.[13] Even Helmut Thielicke, a rather conservative theologian, insists that Jesus "hardly spoke a word that could not already be read, in rabbinical literature before him, substantially in the same form."[14] Hans Küng[15] cites Barth, Bultmann, and Tillich, who are even more skeptical; they do not consider any one of Jesus' sayings as handed down to us to be historically beyond doubt. But according to their religious conviction, true faith manifests itself precisely in historical uncertainty. Küng himself does not share this view. In agreement with the conception now prevailing[16] he sees in the Gospels not only pure testimonials of faith but also sources of historical information that raise questions about the historical Jesus.
A distinction must be made between the words that Jesus could have really spoken *(ipsissima verba Jesu)* and those that were only put in his mouth. What is reportage of an event and what interpretation, preaching of the post-paschal communities? And where does even interpretation give way to exegesis and transfiguration? For example, according to Mark 15:34 and Matthew 27:46, Jesus died with a despairing cry, "My God, my God, why have you deserted me?" These two evangelists do not disguise the utter despair of a man who believes himself forsaken by his God. But the author of the hellenized Lucan Gospel, somewhat later, already views things differently. There the last words no longer reflect

despair, but a stoical acceptance of death: "Father, into your hands I commit my spirit" (Luke 23:46).

In John's Gospel, finally, where all that was human has now largely entered into the divine nature of the preached Christ, neither despair nor humble acquiescence are in evidence. Here Jesus ends his earthly life with the triumphant cry, "It is accomplished" (John 19:30).[17]

In reading the Gospels it must always be borne in mind that they are concerned not with historical truth, but with a truth[18] relating to the welfare and salvation of humankind. Küng[19] compares the Gospels to a play of Shakespeare. Neither seeks to present exact history; rather, they proclaim a message and the dawn of a new age. Viewed thus, a legend can be an altogether more important truth than a historical account. The story of the Good Samaritan is probably the most beautiful example.[20]

Trends and Transformations in the Earliest Christianity

The authors of the New Testament cannot be considered neutral witnesses. At best they report hearsay, and even this isn't true of the two John evangelists. The earliest Christian accounts contain "no biographical material worthy of the name."[21]

From the beginning the "stories" told about Jesus of Nazareth were accounts related by people for whom Jesus was much more than just the memory of a deceased person to whom they had been close. Each of the narrators had an entirely personal experience of salvation because of him. At all events, it may be assumed that those who had known Jesus in person thought and reported about him differently than did Paul and the evangelists later. Since Paul, the "Jewishness" of Jesus has become almost incidental and instead the impression has deliberately been given that Jesus was in constant conflict with Jewry, or at least with a specific Jewish group, the Pharisees. Yet it can be assumed that the early Christian community still considered and portrayed him without reservation as a "Jew in body and soul."

Superimposed on the texts of the New Testament is the spiritual intent to portray Jesus from the perspective of his resurrection and apotheosis as the Redeemer (the kerygmatic character of the Gospels). Between the Jesus of faith and the historical Jesus yawns the so-called Easter tomb.

The extraordinary dearth of information on the man from Nazareth indicates that even the earliest Christian communities had no special interest in biographical details about him. His historical figure was systematically disembodied—following the Pauline lead—and gradually transformed into the "divine Christ." From the outset the image depicted Jesus not as he had been, but as the community required for its faith.[22] Certain stages of this progression can be discerned in the Gospels, corresponding to the order in which they were written. These can be identified as follows: carpenter's son in Mark; son of David in Matthew; prophet and Savior in Luke; Son of God in John—and then God Himself at the Councils of Nicaea (A.D. 325) and Chalcedon (A.D. 451).[23]

The Gospel accounts are not independent of one another; the authors of the Matthew and Luke Gospels based theirs on the Marcan Gospel. Both expanded the Marcan text by one-third, so that they have jokingly been called the "second and third enlarged edition of the Gospel of Mark." The Gospels of Mark, Matthew, and Luke are called the Synoptic Gospels because they are similar in their arrangement and choice of materials; they present one general view and can be read together. But in many points they do differ from one another.

John's Gospel is of a completely different character and betrays nothing of its Palestinian origin. It is an exclusively Christological treatise; theologically it is designated as the "Pneumatic" Gospel.

Most New Testament scholars are of the opinion that at least Matthew and Luke used a source—perhaps written, possibly Aramaic—for their accounts, which they subsequently amended in keeping with their Pauline concept of the faith. This so-called *logia* source (generally simply designated "Q" by scholars) is lost; it probably fell victim to ecclesiastical censorship. It is assumed to have been a collection of certain sayings ascribed to Jesus that were later elaborated and amalgamated in, for example, the Sermon on the Mount.[24]

The Passion story, in particular, was probably transmitted very early, perhaps still during the terms of office of Caiaphas and Pilate, before A.D. 37. The subject of this early Passion story was Jesus' bitter way to the cross under Pontius Pilate. It did not contain the "religious trial" before the Sanhedrin.[25]

The historical editing and adaptation is especially clear in relation to the Passion. The Synoptic Gospels contain elements from different transmissions of the Passion story. The Gospels of Mark and Matthew relate that the authorities were reluctant to have Jesus arrested in Jerusalem, lest during the Passover feast, which drew huge crowds, such a step might lead to a popular uproar in protest against his arrest. "For they said, 'It must not be during the festivities, or there will be a disturbance among the people'" (Mark 14:2).

In Luke the Romans sometimes appear as foes of the Jesus faith and the Jewish people.[26] There must have been an original version according to which Jesus' execution on the cross was felt as a national tragedy by the people of Jerusalem: A huge crowd of people followed him to the site of the execution, bemoaning and lamenting his fate. Jewish women tried to soothe his agony with an anaesthetic drink, and the simple people beat their breasts when the execution was carried out:

> Large numbers of people followed him, and of women too, who mourned and lamented for him. But Jesus turned to them and said, "Daughters of Jerusalem, do not weep for me; weep rather for yourselves and your children...." And when all the people who had gathered for the spectacle saw what had happened, they went home beating their breasts. (Luke 23:27–29, 48)

Mark handles the same theme—albeit somewhat toned down—by reporting that on the way to the execution site Jesus was "offered wine mixed with myrrh, but he refused it" (Mark 15:23). In Israel as David Flusser[27] remarks, it was customary to make this compassionate gesture to a condemned person on his last walk. The drink supposedly anaesthetized him and eased his suffering.

The Marcan and Lucan passages can be ascribed to the same source. They conflict with an important tenet of the Gospel accounts: that the Jewish people, in an outburst of passionate hatred, had demanded Jesus' execution. Luke further relates, and historical knowledge confirms, that Pilate was an especially cruel man who would not have been upset by the mass slaughter of Jewish pilgrims: "It was just about this time that some people arrived and told him about the Galileans whose blood Pilate had mingled with that of their sacrifices" (Luke 13:1). This passage probably also goes back to a source; it contradicts other sections of the Gospels that portray Pilate as a good-natured fellow who made several attempts to save Jesus' life.

This double layering can be seen in many other Gospel passages. Thus Matthew's Gospel is characterized on the one hand by an overall anti-Jewish tendency, yet on the other it constantly stresses that Jesus and his deeds fulfill the words of the Old Testament prophets. What is striking in Luke is a pronounced pro-Roman overall tendency; for example, he maintains that the Romans actually had nothing whatsoever to do with Jesus' violent death (Luke 23:25–26; Acts 2:36; 5:30). Yet Jesus is presented as the expected warrior Messiah who will drive the Romans out of the country (Luke 1:68–71; 24:19–21), and his execution is described as a major calamity for the people.

To sum up, it has yet to be established that an original version of Jesus' life and death once existed in which even more was contained that later, after the victory of the Hellenic Pauline teaching, corresponded to the current state of the story.

Those members of the first Christian community who had had close personal contact with Jesus and had reported truthfully on their master no longer had any editorial influence on the writings after the destruction of Jerusalem. Nor did they remain in Jerusalem much longer. At the outbreak of the Jewish War against the Romans in A.D. 66 they fled to Pella in eastern Jordan;[28] having become pacifists meanwhile, they refused to bear arms.[29] These Jewish Christians, basing themselves on the authority of Jesus' brother James, lived according to the ideal of poverty even when displaced, called themselves "Ebionites" ("the poor"), and were faithful to Jewish law. They were unaware of the teachings of the virgin birth and the divinity of Christ, both having originated only after Jesus' death. For this reason the Ebionites were banned as heretics in the course of the second century, their memory erased from Church history.[30] At all events, at the time the Gospels and Acts came into being, Pauline theology had already triumphed over the faith entertained by the early Christian community in Jerusalem. It became the prevailing opinion among the followers of Jesus.[31]

The hallmark of the Pauline teaching lies in judging Jesus' life not in terms of what he effected or how, but from the perspective of his death. The evangelists also do exactly this, and combine Jesus' death with the notion of an Israel unrepentant since time immemorial, whose stubbornness of heart was manifest in the killing of the prophets.[32]

Completely Pauline, for example, are the so-called baptismal mandate[33] and missionary mandate contained in the Gospels of Mark and Matthew: "Go, therefore, make disciples of all the nations; baptize them in the name of the Father and of the Son and of the Holy Spirit" (Matt. 28:19); ". . . since the Good News must first be proclaimed to all the nations" (Mark 13:10).

Both mandates were inserted into the Gospels in order to justify Paul's missionary travels. Furthermore, the baptismal mandate is a clear transformation of Pauline thought into dogma. It is derived from the doctrine of the Trinity, which was first formulated by Tertullian in the third century and was prescribed in the fourth century at the Councils of Nicaea and Constantinople.[34] The missionary mandate literally contradicts the historical situation in which Jesus wanted to spread his message: "I was sent only to the lost sheep of the House of Israel" (Matt. 15:25). To Jesus, it was not even a matter of indifference whether pagans also profited from his message; he expressly forbade the disciples to take it to non-Jews: "Do not turn your steps to pagan territory, and do not enter any Samaritan town; go rather to the lost sheep of the House of Israel" (Matt. 10:5–6).

This standpoint is all the more noteworthy given that Jesus knew that his biblical faith in no way forbade him from turning to the pagans. The God of Israel turned to all men, as said in the 1 and 2 Kings and by the prophet Isaiah.[35]

In modern terms, some sayings of Jesus must even be called explicitly chauvinistic. For example, he says that non-Jews "babble" when they pray and calls them dogs and pigs: "Do not give dogs what is holy; and do not throw your pearls in front of pigs" (Matt. 7:6). As a proud Israelite, he even went so far as to set a national boundary around the precept to love one's neighbor. When a non-Jewish woman implores him to heal her sick daughter, she hears these bitter words from the mouth of Jesus: "The children should be fed first, because it is not fair to take the children's food and throw it to the house dogs" (Mark 7:27–28).

The "children" are the children of Israel; the "dogs" here are the non-Jews. Ben-Chorin[36] writes, "Only after the deeply mortified woman, concerned about her sick daughter, resorts to this parable: 'Ah, yes, sir,' she replied, 'but the house dogs under the table can eat the children's scraps,' is he overcome by her faith: 'For saying this, you may go home happy; the devil has gone out of your daughter.'" The Gospels mention only one pagan, the servant of the Roman centurion, upon whom Jesus unreservedly bestows his healing powers (Matt. 8:10–13; Luke 7:9–10).[37]

In short, it is precisely in the Gospels and the multilayered history of their origin that traces of the historical Jesus can still be glimpsed under the Pauline whitewash.

Two

THE BIBLICAL JESUS

A Survey of the Four Gospels

The oldest of these texts, the Gospel of Mark, originated directly after the destruction of Jerusalem and the plundering of the Temple by the Romans in A.D. 70. The so-called priority of Mark was established historically and theologically in the mid-nineteenth century. Mark had created the framework of the narrative, as it were, to which the other evangelists then adhered. The prevailing assumption is that the Marcan Gospel was composed in Rome.

Whether Mark was a Jewish or pagan Christian is a subject of controversy; at all events, he was friendly to the pagans. There are some indications that he was a Galilean. His Gospel, although written for pagan Christian readers,[1] has a pronounced Galilean cast. This also applies to the concluding chapter, the so-called Mark-postscript,[2] which originated much later, presumably in the middle of the second century. Even the risen Christ betakes himself first to Galilee.[3] Another indication of Galilean origin is the frequent use of expressions from the Aramaic linguistic world, some of them graphic expressions that have a correspondingly "indelicate" ring in Greek.

The sociologist Anton Mayer undertook the task of demonstrating Jesus' proletarian origin on this basis, citing the lower-class parlance peculiar to this earliest Gospel. Thus, for example, we are told in Mark 7:20 that Jesus used the coarse word *aphedron* without embarrassment. Mayer writes,[4] "Aphedron is neither a toilet nor a latrine and not at all a WC. Speaking with all due respect, it is the 'shithouse' of the proletarians that not even a classical writer of the ancient world would have dared to name." A possible explanation for the occasional coarse expressions is that the evangelist Mark had a soldierly past. Strikingly often, he speaks in terms derived from Roman military life. That could also suggest that he may have been a Roman citizen.

In Mark (unlike in Matthew and Luke who at least allege a virgin birth), there is not the slightest suggestion that Jesus could be a supernatural figure. According to Mark's portrayal, Jesus' only peculiarity is that the spirit of God descended upon him in the form of a dove as a sign of divine favor after he had let himself be baptized by John the Baptist. Only after that point in the narrative, and then only sporadically, is the epithet "Son of God" used. Except for the heavenly voice (Mark 1:11; 9:7–8), only two men possessed by unclean spirits address Jesus thus (Mark 3:12; 5:7). At the very end of the Gospel the expression is also used by Jesus' executioner, the Roman centurion (Mark 15:39). The main forms of address in Mark are "Master" and "Rabbi."

The Gospel of Matthew, probably composed a decade after Mark's, is written in correct Greek, albeit not as elegant as that of the Lucan Gospel, which was written at a still later point in time. The author of Matthew was a Jewish Christian who probably lived in Syria. He reports that Jesus' fame had "spread throughout Syria" (4:24), and that from his location Judea lies "on the far side of the Jordan."

A misleading assertion occasionally espoused, that Matthew was the tax collector who joined Jesus' disciples, arose because this tax collector, otherwise called Levi ("Jewish"), bears the name Matthew in Matthew's Gospel, and also because in Acts 1:13 another early Christian apostle named Matthew is mentioned in connection with the band of disciples who are said to have foregathered on the Mount of Olives[5] after Jesus' death. The evangelist Matthew himself never states that he belonged to Jesus' disciples, nor does Paul mention any disciple named Matthew who engaged in any special activities in connection with the proclamation of the Good News. Only James, Peter, and John are designated as apostles in Paul's letters.

The Gospel according to Matthew is the favorite Gospel of the Catholic Church, and for an obvious reason: Only there is it pointedly stated that Jesus bestowed a privileged position on a single disciple, Simon Peter. The other evangelists confine themselves to saying simply that Jesus had given the disciple Simon the appellation Peter, which means "rock."

> Simon son of Jonah, you are a happy man! Because it was not flesh and blood that revealed this to you but my Father in heaven. So now I say to you: You are Peter and on this rock I will build my Church. And the gates of the underworld can never hold out against it. I will give you the keys of the kingdom of heaven; whatever you bind on earth shall be considered bound in heaven; whatever you loose on earth shall be considered loosed in heaven. (Matt. 16:17–19)

Since time immemorial popes have quoted this passage, in which Peter is even granted full divine authority, in order to establish their own authority as his successors. For this reason Matthew's Gospel (instead of Mark's) begins the New Testament. Catholic sources also claim that Peter came to Rome at the close of his life and suffered a martyr's death in the persecution of Christians under Nero. In reality, nothing further is known about Peter's fate. It is not impossible that he, like the Zebedees John and James, was hanged as a Zealot by King Agrippa in A.D. 44.

It can no longer be seriously disputed that the passage in Matthew 16:17–19 is a later Christological interpolation. This assertion is based on the idea that it could never have occurred to the Jew Jesus to establish a church[6] of his own. Nor do the other evangelists know of any privilege bestowed upon Peter, something they surely would have reported if it were historically accurate. The absence of Peter's preeminence from the original text, moreover, is made clear by the fact that Jesus reprimands the disciple Peter in an extraordinarily sharp tone only four verses later: "Get behind me, Satan! You are an obstacle in my path, because the way you think is not God's way but man's" (Matt. 16:23). This reprimand cannot be reconciled with Peter's alleged preeminence, and certainly not with the bestowal of the so-called Power of the Keys.[7]

In Matthew's Gospel, more clearly than in the other synoptics, it is emphasized that Judaism, except for the community of converts, is mired in sin. Its leaders—the traditionalist Pharisees—are called hypocrites, blind fools, adders, brood of vipers, and children of hell. Only Matthew's Gospel contains the two pericopes that through western history have been repeatedly served as "legal grounds" for the persecution of Jews, namely, the "repudiation of Jesus" and the "self-damnation of the Jews": "I tell you, then, that the kingdom of God will be taken from you and given to a people who will produce its fruit" (Matt. 21:43); "And the people to a man shouted back, 'His blood be on us and on our children!'" (Matt. 27:25–26).

Paradoxically, in view of his otherwise sharp rejection of Israel, it is precisely Matthew who determined to mesh the New and the Old Testaments. He seeks to convey the idea of so-called scriptural proof: With the coming of Jesus and his deeds, what the Bible has promised Israel has been fulfilled. The formula reads, "This was to fulfill what the Lord had spoken through the prophets"; it is used constantly. (In this, Matthew is no different from those fundamentalists of modern Judaism who know exactly which biblical verse foretells the Balfour Declaration, the establishment of the state of Israel, or the Six Day War.)

A further aim of the evangelist Matthew is to bear witness to Jesus as the promised Messiah. This is expressed in the epithet "Son of David," which appears with special frequency and which at that time would have been interpreted as a Messianic attribute. The detailed genealogy of Jesus in this Gospel's introduction, the prominence given to Bethlehem as his birthplace, and the typical Messianic fate of flight (in this case, to Egypt) are examples of this concern. Nevertheless it is interesting that Jesus is presented not as the militant Messiah so longed for at the time of the Roman yoke, but specifically as a Prince of Peace (Matt. 21:4–5).

Luke, whose Gospel was composed in the penultimate or last decade of the first century, was perhaps Greek, presumably non-Jewish, and a theologically educated scholar, a pagan Christian. He lived in Greece or Asia Minor and had traveled, widely, as attested by his detailed knowledge of localities. The Lucan Jesus is no longer the one who lived on earth, but the one who, although he had once lived, in the meantime had since found acceptance in heaven. Luke is the only one of the New Testament authors to portray the ascension of Jesus (Luke 24:50–52; Acts 1:9–11). Simonis[8] calls him the "great storyteller" among the evangelists, in whom the figure of Jesus has become "consciously literary." The Hellenistic world in which Luke lived may have been the reason why this author more than the other evangelists shows a special predilection for the miracles that Jesus allegedly worked.

It is cheerfully asserted, primarily by the Church, that Luke was a physician. Of this there is no proof, and at most a very slight indication: Illnesses are more exactly described by Luke than by the other evangelists, and Jesus' successes as a healer are set in bolder relief. Where Mark criticizes doctors because a hemorrhaging woman has spent all her money to pay their fees, Luke tones down the criticism—perhaps out of professional solidarity? (Mark 5:25–26; Luke 8:43). In the Letter to the Colossians 4:14 Paul refers to Luke as "my dear friend, the doctor." Exegetical research, however, shows that this Luke is not the author of the Gospel.

The author of the Lucan Gospel is also the author of the Acts of the Apostles (Acts 1:1), so the Lucan Gospel cannot be considered in isolation. It is one component of a two-fold theological work. The account begins and ends in the Temple (Luke 1:5–10; and 24:53). Jesus' fate is seen in association with the fate of Jerusalem.[9]

As Mayer stresses,[10] Luke is considered "the most distinguished New Testament author," one who addressed himself "to a refined reading public, to the propertied bourgeois stratum": "He is fond of choosing words according to their social prestige. To the extent that a word, even from a distance, smells of the lower depths, he avoids it. . . . Luke presumably would not object to being called the first Christian gentleman." There is frequent talk in his Gospel of "leading men," "distinguished origin," and "royal dignity." In the parable of the prodigal son, the father can afford to slaughter a calf.

On the other hand, the Lucan Gospel has an overtly sociocritical slant. The contrast between the poor and the rich is frequently emphasized. In the parable of the great banquet (Luke 14:15–24), it is the poor and the crippled, the blind and the lame who are invited—but this parable, like that of the wicked husbandmen, has an anti-Jewish bias. The distinguished guests, who are invited first, are the people of Israel; Israel, however, is rigid and does not accept God's invitation. In his wrath God then turns to the poor, the crippled, and the blind, from then on the pagans are God's guests. The so-called original communism of the first Christian communities is mentioned only in the Lucan Acts (4:32–37). Even the Magnificat intoned by Mary has the character of a class struggle:[11] "He has pulled down princes from their thrones and exalted the lowly. The hungry he has filled with good things, the rich sent empty away" (Luke 1:52–53). Jesus is pointedly presented as the child of poor people; the mother cannot even find a decent place for the confinement, so a dark stable is the birthplace. Perhaps it really was so; one would hardly make up the idea of a cow-shed out of nowhere. But Luke knows how to touch sentimental chords. The miserable birth becomes a manger idyll. This is precisely why the German public so loves the Christmas story in Luke's Gospel: Mary, who wraps the infant Jesus and lays him in the manger, flanked by Joseph, an ox, and a donkey.[12]

Mary is the one who achieves a prominent position in the Lucan Gospel. In the fourth century, this inspired veneration of Mary (which was then strengthened in the wake of the Counter-Reformation) became the basis for a full-fledged Marian cult. It also served as a lyrical foundation for a "cult of the mother of God." "He [the angel Gabriel] went in and said to her, 'Rejoice, so highly favored!' And Mary said: 'My soul proclaims the greatness of the Lord and my spirit exults in God my savior' " (Luke 1:28–29, 46–47).

Otherwise Mary plays an insignificant role in the Gospels. The chance meetings between Jesus and his mother, if they are referred to, tend to be shown negatively.[13] Paul obviously considers Mary so negligible that he does not even mention her name, although he presumably met her in Jerusalem (Acts 1:14). But in Luke too, there is a striking passage that shows an outright disrespect toward his mother. When she is praised by a woman in the crowd, Jesus himself immediately demurs: "Now as he was speaking, a woman in the crowd raised her voice and said, 'Happy the womb that bore you and the breasts you sucked!' But he replied, 'Still happier those who hear the word of God and keep it!' " (Luke 11:27–28). Likewise, only Luke's Gospel mentions the fact that not only male disciples were among Jesus' following:

> Now after this he made his way through towns and villages preaching, and proclaiming the Good News of the kingdom of God. With him went the Twelve, as well as

certain women who had been cured of evil spirits and ailments; Mary surnamed the Magdalene, from whom seven demons had gone out, Joanna the wife of Herod's steward Chuza, Susanna, and several others who provided for them out of their own resources. (Luke 8:1–3)

There were several other women besides the three who were named; probably even more women than men were among Jesus' closer associates.[14]

The author of the Gospel of John—which probably originated only after the turn of the first century—has nothing to do with the so-called beloved disciple John who like his brother James is called a son of Zebedee ("son of thunder"). The latter, like his brother, was said to have been beheaded by King Herod Agrippa in A.D. 44 as a martyr, possibly a Zealot.[15]

The Johannine Gospel is characterized by an all-pervasive and fundamental anti-Judaism. Surprisingly, it nonetheless contains the famous phrase that Jesus is said to have addressed to the woman at Jacob's well, ". . . for salvation comes from the Jews" (John 4:22). But that phrase expresses nothing more than the conviction that the Messiah will come from the people of Israel,[16] which was never at issue.

This, of course, indicates that a multiplicity of views is contained in the Johannine Gospel also; despite its fundamental and total anti-Jewish tendency, it reverses itself and often depicts the Jews as especially enthusiastic followers of Jesus.[17] They even wanted to make him their king (John 6:14–15).

According to John's Gospel, Jesus insults and damns his fellow Jews whenever he happens to run into them. He asserts that they have no understanding whatsoever of God (5:37–38), and at times behaves as if they were foreigners to him. He speaks of "your law" (John 10:34) or "their law" (John 15:25), and of "the Jewish feast" (John 7:2). He curses even those Jews "who believed in him" (John 8:31): "The devil is your father, and you prefer to do what your father wants. He was a murderer from the start" (John 8:44).

Lapide[18] formulates it graphically:

An eskimo whose knowledge of Christianity is based exclusively on the Fourth Gospel, on the basis of such texts perforce concludes that Jesus for some reason must have fallen into the evil society of traitorous, non-believing, and bloodthirsty Jews whose hatred was bound to lead to his death sooner or later. The idea that this Jesus and "the Jews" could have had anything, even the least thing, in common, would necessarily be inconceivable to him.

Jesus alone is the Good Shepherd. The Jews cannot know God, since God is known only through Christ.[19] The Jews are incapable of perceiving the meaning of Holy Scripture because they reject the Christological exegesis.[20]

The evangelist John did not live in Palestine, but in some Hellenic locality, presumably in Asia Minor. Although it cannot be excluded that he himself was a Diaspora Jew, the arrangement of the Gospel is quite un-Jewish. It is strongly influenced by a specific Gnostic branch of early Christianity (later harshly opposed by other sects), which the Protestant theologian Hans Conzelmann described as "a monstrous *mixtum compositum* of Iranian, Babylonian and Egyptian ideas."[21] The prevailing opinion among scholars is that the evangelist died before his work was completed. Colleagues or other authors not only embellished and edited it but also completed it by adding Chapter 21. Some theologians think John completed the Synoptic Gospels; others contend that he wanted to supplant them, while a third view holds that John did not even know the Synoptic Gospels and that the parallels to them in his work are the product of a common Christian tradition.[22]

The synoptics' Jesus, in the manner of a Jewish rabbi of the time, explains God's precepts in the form of parables and sayings and proclaims the approaching kingdom of God in language calculated to be understood easily by the people and to find its way into many hearts. In the Johannine Gospel, Jesus speaks in long, repetitious monologues revolving around his own person. It is hard to imagine that the actual Jesus could have spoken thus to his fellow countrymen:

> I am the living bread which has come down from heaven. Anyone who eats this bread will live for ever; and the bread that I shall give is my flesh, for the life of the world. . . . I tell you most solemnly, if you do not eat the flesh of the Son of Man and drink his blood, you will not have life in you. Anyone who does eat my flesh and drink my blood has eternal life, and I shall raise him up on the last

day. For my flesh is real food and my blood is real drink. He who eats my flesh and drinks my blood lives in me and I live in him. As I, who am sent by the living Father, myself draw life from the Father, so whoever eats me will draw life from me. This is the bread come down from heaven; not like the bread our ancestors ate: they are dead, but anyone who eats this bread will live for ever. (John 6:51–58)

Aside from some allegorical portrayals like that of the Good Shepherd, and the figurative speech of the fruit-bearing branches, not a single parable is to be found in this Gospel.

John's Gospel provides even less biographical information about Jesus than do the others. It would be sheer chance if what is alleged to be a saying of Jesus, even in the Synoptic Gospels, was actually uttered by him; but it is completely out of the question that any authentic saying or message of Jesus is to be found in the Johannine Gospel.

In John Jesus is no longer the figure in the synoptics, the rabbi from Galilee in whom the people see a prophet and the apostles divine the Messiah. The Johannine Jesus has no human weaknesses and undergoes no penitential baptism, no temptation through Satan, no fear and trembling in Gethsemane. Also omitted is the shout of pain on the cross handed down by Mark and Matthew. The descent from the royal House of David is no longer of interest. Instead an omniscience is conferred upon Jesus that is otherwise peculiar to God. This Gospel was written, says its author, "so that you may believe that Jesus is the Christ, the Son of God."

Of the four, John's Gospel is undoubtedly the one at the highest intellectual level. It is, moreover, the favorite Gospel of Martin Luther:

> the one tender, true, chief
> Gospel and far, far preferable
> to the other three.[23]

Here events are presented within a theoretical framework. They are viewed with detachment so that meaning can be extrapolated. In contrast to the other Gospels, John provides historical settings and explains political calculations. This is just the Gospel to answer questions about how this or that event fits credibly into the whole. A remarkable example is 18:14, where the high priest Caiaphas sets forth the pragmatic political argument that it is fitting and proper to denounce Jesus to the Romans in the interests of the Jewish people as a whole.

THE APOSTLE PAUL REPORTS

Paul is certainly the towering personality among the authors of the New Testament. Although he is not mentioned in any historical writings, there is no doubt that he existed. According to an official count, thirteen letters comprise his legacy, of which at least seven are considered authentic: the letter to the Romans, the two letters to the Corinthians, the letters to the Galatians and to the Philippians, the first letter to the Thessalonians, and the letter to Philemon.[24] The remaining Pauline letters are probably by collaborators of the apostle who used Paul's name to lend more weight to their letters.

Luke's Acts of the Apostles contain detailed references to Paul himself, but no references to the letters. It must be concluded they had not reached a very broad audience at the end of the first century.[25]

Paul was born in A.D. 10. Hence he was still quite a young man at the time of Jesus' execution. He was probably a student in Jerusalem at exactly that time, but he never got to know Jesus personally. From the account in Acts 22:3 it can be inferred that Paul came from an orthodox family residing in the city of Tarsus in Cilicia, in present-day Anatolia. He possessed Roman citizenship, and was very familiar with Hellenic philosophy and religion; Tarsus proclaimed itself the most Grecian of the cities in Asia Minor.

Paul remained a Diaspora Jew: "I made myself a Jew to the Jews. . . . To those who have no Law, I was free of the Law myself . . ." (1 Cor. 9:20–21). The Greek world was his missionary territory, it was there that he achieved success as the "apostle to the Gentiles."[26] Ben-Chorin describes him as "a Roman citizen of the Jewish faith and of Hellenic culture," and contrasts him to Jesus, whom he designates as "a hundred percent and naught but Jew, a Jewish national and a complete Jew whom we would call a sabra today."[27]

As befitted a proper Jew regardless of educational level and social position, Paul had at first learned a trade: He was a tent-maker (harness maker). Subsequently he received a theological and legal education in Jerusalem under Rabbi Gamaliel and became a Pharisee. He readily referred to his Pharisaism when it seemed useful to him. Thus, for example, when he was summoned to the Sanhedrin in A.D. 60 to answer charges of illegal conduct: "Brothers, I am a Pharisee and the son of Pharisees" (Acts 23:6). In reality this allusion was only formally correct. Paul had indeed enjoyed a rabbinical education; his epistolary style bears the stamp of Pharisaism. Yet as a Hellenist and because of his bias toward the pagans he was fundamentally in opposition to the Pharisees.

A tragedy of a special kind lies therein because with Paul a process begins that forms the basis not only of the Church's later rigor, but also of a crass anti-Judaism.[28] Paul pillories his own Jewish descent—the expression of a split personality?—and characterizes what made him an orthodox Jew as rubbish (Phil. 3:8). Some of the apostle's slanderous remarks, directed to his fellow Jews who did not belong to the Jesus sect, were so sharp that they have the fateful ring of a "final solution" mentality:

> For you, my brothers, have been like the churches of God in Christ Jesus which are in Judea, in suffering the same treatment from your countrymen as they have suffered from the Jews, the people who put the Lord Jesus to death, and the prophets too. And now they have been persecuting us, and acting in a way that cannot please God and makes them the enemies of the whole human race . . . but retribution is overtaking them at last. (1 Thess. 2:14–16)

In the final analysis it remains incomprehensible how a man who feels a close bond to the people of Israel, and sees them in the allegory of the good olive tree whose roots nourish the pagans to be converted, can write so disparagingly about Jews. "One must see the Jewish self-hatred and the love of Israel in Paul's utterances in order to picture the excruciating schizophrenic ordeal to which this man was prey," analyzes Ben-Chorin.[29] It would be an immense relief if the anti-Semitic sallies, specifically those in the Letter to the Thessalonians, should be proven to have been falsified. It cannot in fact be excluded that such shameful utterances were put in the apostle's mouth subsequently, through "revision" of his letters by the Church Fathers, who were in the main hostile to Jews. At any rate, statements of utterly opposite character penned by Paul exist, statements of reconciliation and unequivocal avowal of Judaism:[30]

> Both Jew and pagan sinned and forfeited God's glory, and both are justified through the free gift of his grace by being redeemed in Christ Jesus. (Rom. 3:23–24)[31]

> I would willingly be condemned and be cut off from Christ if it could help my brothers of Israel, my own flesh and blood. They were adopted as sons, they were given the glory and the covenants; the Law and the ritual were drawn up for them, and the promises were made to them. They are descended from the patriarchs and from their flesh and blood came Christ who is above all, God for ever blessed! Amen. (Rom. 9:3–5)

> I, an Israelite . . . could never agree that God had rejected his people, the people he chose specially long ago. (Rom. 11:1–2)

Several years after Jesus' death, Paul espoused the new faith of Jesus' followers. In the Letter to the Galatians 1:17–20 the apostle reports that after he had become a follower of Jesus he had made several journeys between Damascus and Arabia, and had only thereafter journeyed to Jerusalem to meet Peter. In Jerusalem he also made the acquaintance of Jesus' brother James. Just when this meeting with the first Christians occurred cannot be exactly determined. At all events it was a very brief encounter, from which one may conclude that Paul and Peter did not especially like each other from the outset. The fortnight they spent together was presumably marked by friction, so much so that it bred further personal discord between them. The members of the Jerusalem community probably mistrusted a man who had suddenly declared himself a follower of Jesus. Moreover, his "past" gave rise to skepticism and prompted the suspicion that he could be a spy of the Sanhedrin or the Roman military administration. Not until fourteen years later did Paul meet Peter again (Gal. 2:1–9); following this encounter, the two split permanently.

The report in Acts 15:1–35 that Peter and James had sided with the Pauline standpoint is an apologetic attempt to cover up their differences as much as possible. Thirty years later, when the Jewish-Christian wing had lost even the slight influence it had previously enjoyed, no one wanted to emphasize the discord between Paul and the original Christian community. But the fact remains that a split within Christianity had developed at the outset: Hebraists against Hellenists. On the one side stood the Israelites of the original community, strict observants of Mosaic Law, led by James and Peter; on the other, the Diaspora Jews, Greek-speaking and sharing the Greek culture, led by Stephen and then Paul. The Catholic holy day of Peter and Paul can only be interpreted as an expression of a posthumous reconciliation.

As he reports in several letters (e.g., Gal. 1:13) Paul had at first participated in the persecutions to which the members of the Jesus sect were subjected by the Jewish authorities.[32] The stoning of Stephen before the gates of Jerusalem, according to Acts 7:45 ff., is an example. It is questionable, however, whether the stoning was by order of the Jewish authorities or simply an outbreak of mob fury for which the causes are now unknown.

"Paul" was the apostle's surname as a Roman citizen; his real Jewish name was Saul (pronounced "Scha-ul"). The assumption that he discarded his Jewish name and called himself Paul after his conversion to Christianity is erroneous; Paul never really converted to Christianity in the sense of rejecting the old religion and founding a new one.[33]

Paul does not base his report on Jesus on, for example, the testimony of the pioneer apostles in Jerusalem (whom he sometimes mockingly calls "super-apostles"), but on a direct revelation through the risen Christ: "The fact is, brothers, and I want you to realize this, the Good News I preached is not a human message that I was given by men, it is something I learned only through a revelation of Jesus Christ" (Gal. 1:11–13). He makes no secret of the fact that he did not see the historical Jesus with bodily eyes but saw Christ with spiritual eyes, as by a revelation of God (Gal. 1:16). He speaks of a meeting with the risen Christ only figuratively: After Christ had risen "on the third day in accordance with the scriptures," Paul says:

> He appeared first to Cephas and secondly to the Twelve. Next he appeared to more than five hundred of the brothers at the same time, most of whom are still alive, though

some have died; then he appeared to James, and then to
all the apostles; and last of all he appeared to me; it was
as though I was born when no one expected it. (1 Cor.
15:5–8)

Nowhere does Paul declare that Jesus the risen Christ met him
in the flesh. The only passage that, in context, might lead one to
this conclusion is in Acts, which came into being thirty years after
his death: the mystical experience at Damascus, which is portrayed
three different times (9:1–9; 22:6–11; 26:12–18). Saul had set out for
Damascus, allegedly to organize the persecution of Christians ordered by the Jewish authorities. Jesus, from heaven, is said to have
asked him why he was persecuting him. Thereupon Saul converted on the spot and expressed the wish to meet the followers
of Jesus in Jerusalem:

> Meanwhile Saul was still breathing threats to slaughter
> the Lord's disciples. He had gone to the high priest and
> asked for letters addressed to the synagogues in Damas-
> cus, that would authorize him to arrest and to take to
> Jerusalem any followers of the Way, men or women, that
> he could find.
>   Suddenly, while he was traveling to Damascus and just
> before he reached the city, there came a light from heaven
> all around him. He fell to the ground and then he heard
> a voice saying, "Saul, Saul, why are you persecuting me?"
> "Who are you, Lord?" he asked, and the voice answered.
> "I am Jesus, and you are persecuting me." (Acts 9:1–6)

Aside from the fact that in Acts Saul is said only to have heard
a voice and not to have beheld the risen Christ, the account of
meeting with the risen Christ at Damascus does not hold up under
historical scrutiny for several reasons. First of all, Paul cannot
have journeyed to Damascus at the behest of the Sanhedrin in
order to persecute the Jesus-followers and drag them back in
chains to the Jerusalem tribunal. In those years, organized communities of Jesus-followers could be found only in Jerusalem, some
perhaps in a few outlying communities and maybe in Galilee, but
definitely not in faraway Damascus.[34] Paul himself was responsible for founding communities outside Palestine. On the other
hand, it is highly questionable whether the jurisdiction of the
Jerusalem authorities in Roman-occupied Judea extended as far as

Damascus. Besides, the Sanhedrin intervened only in cases where a Jewish culprit had drawn attention to himself by special agitation, and the normal sentence was not death but flogging.

It is especially unlikely that Paul, having undergone an experience unparalleled in its sheer drama, would have failed to describe the experience in many of his letters, the more so as he was much inclined to recount his personal experiences to the communities. True, he does mention journeying to Damascus during the period in question (Gal. 1:17). But he does not mention any persecution of Christians, or the event we know as the "Damascus Experience."[35]

Moreover, one dating of Paul's alleged vision of the risen Jesus conflicts with the New Testament reportage. Mark and Luke report that Jesus made an appearance as the risen Christ only on one day, Easter Sunday. Matthew extends the duration of the appearance to the time it took the risen Christ to get from Jerusalem to Galilee; John does not give any duration. According to the Acts of the Apostles, the appearances lasted forty days.[36]

No specific teaching of Jesus plays any role in the Pauline accounts. Only in the description of the Last Supper does Paul let the Nazarene speak for himself, and only three or four times does the apostle refer to "the Lord's words."

The simple name Jesus is used by Paul 15 times in all; the title "the Christ," on the other hand, crops up 378 times. Jesus' life interests him not at all, only his death: "Even if we did once know Christ in the flesh, that is not how we know him now" (2 Cor. 5:16). Paul does not inquire into the circumstances that led to Jesus' violent death; his message deals exclusively with the "crucified Christ." Precisely this concept explains the process of transfiguration. It begins with Paul and thereafter forms the real foundation of his preaching: "During my stay with you, the only knowledge I claimed to have was about Jesus, and only about him as the crucified Christ" (1 Cor. 2:2–3).

Paul is even less interested in a biography of Jesus than were the other evangelists. The only facts that he reports are these: Jesus was a loyal Jew; he was born not of a virgin, but of a normal woman (Gal. 4:4); he had several siblings (Rom. 8:30); he was always obedient to God (Phil. 2:8); he held a Last Supper after which he was betrayed (1 Cor. 11:23–24); he was exposed to slanders; and he was crucified (Gal. 2:19; 3:13).[37] The Passion story—the central event of the Gospels—remains untold; Paul reveals only an insignificant detail about the Passion, and even that is narrated not by himself but by one of his pupils: ". . . Jesus Christ who spoke up as a witness for the truth in front of Pontius Pilate" (1 Tim. 6:13).

Jesus of Nazareth crucified on Golgotha would hardly recognize himself in the mirror of the Pauline proclamation. The carpenter's son from Galilee, who had called on his people of Israel to reconcile itself with God, was from now forward himself the Redeemer of the whole world. "One could in this sense imagine Jesus of Nazareth eavesdropping on Paul's preaching in order to learn about the Messiah mystery of the pre-existent Christ."[38]

Jesus allegedly said about himself that he had come to fulfill the Law:

> Do not imagine that I have come to abolish the Law or the Prophets. I have come not to abolish but to complete them. I tell you solemnly, till heaven and earth disappear, not one dot, not one little stroke, shall disappear from the Law until its purpose is achieved. Therefore, the man who infringes even one of the least of these commandments and teaches others to do the same will be considered the least in the kingdom of heaven; but the man who keeps them and teaches them will be considered great in the kingdom of heaven. (Matt. 5:17–19)

According to Jesus (Mark 10:18) "No one is good but God alone." Jesus had not attempted to found a new faith, least of all to be the founder of a worldwide religion. He felt he was sent: ". . . only to the lost sheep of the House of Israel" (Matt. 15:25).

Paul changes all this. He no longer turns to the Jews, but to the pagans with a message. Also abandoned is the idea that God, despite his inaccessibility, is actually so near that he can be addressed as "Father" or even "Abba," as the Psalms, the prophets, and Jesus himself taught. Access to God, so Paul teaches, requires a mediator: Christ Jesus.[39] As the Lamb of God, Jesus takes the sins of all humankind on himself and thus makes possible justification before the Last Judgment. Paul reinterpreted Jesus of Nazareth who died on the cross in a way that is unique in human history. The Protestant theologian Zahrnt[40] has designated him the "spoiler of the Gospel of Jesus." And the Protestant theologian Overbeck states,[41] "All the beautiful things of Christianity are woven together in Jesus, all the unbeautiful in Paul."

Since Paul, it has been more or less "officially" allowed to tell what amount to "holy lies," for the glorification of God and that to which the Church dedicates its proclamation. To Paul it is all the same whether Christ is proclaimed sincerely or not (Phil. 1:18). Although he often affirms that he is telling the truth (Rom. 9:1; Gal. 1:21), he stresses that lying is an absolutely legitimate means for achieving a desired goal: "You might as well say that since my untruthfulness makes God demonstrate his truthfulness and thus gives him glory, I should not be judged to be a sinner at all" (Rom. 3:7–8). In the two-thousand-year history of the Church, the "pious lie" has become an almost endearing notion, or at least one to be understood tongue in cheek. Ignatius of Loyola stipulated, "In order that we may progress with sureness in all, we must always cling to the concept that once the hierarchic Church declares that white is black, it is black even if it appears white to our eyes."[42]

Paul was strongly attacked, and not only by the earliest apostles. From the outset he was definitely the most controversial figure. The Church Fathers Papias, Justin, and Tertullian rejected him. The author of the Letter of James distanced himself from him. The rallying cry "Back to Jesus—away from Paul" has lost nothing of its actuality in our day. Its purpose is obvious in view of the fact that the apostle who gave us the first written Christian testimonies completely disregarded Jesus of Nazareth as a historical personality.

To Paul, the greatest theologian of all times, is due the credit for being the founder of Christianity.[43] His teaching certainly diluted the monotheism of the Jews, and hence of Jesus; but in principle he did not dissociate himself from the faith that there is but one God and Creator. For good reasons, I would like to leave the last word not to a Christian author, but to two Jewish scholars:[44] Franz Rosenzweig: "It was Paul who brought the Hebrew Bible to the farthest islands, wholly in the sense of the prophet Isaiah," and Pinches Lapide: "It is Paul, in the final analysis, to whom we are indebted for the fact that the one God faith was able to conquer the Occident."

Witnesses and Theories Concerning the Resurrection

Not a single New Testament witness claims to have seen the resurrection of Jesus as such. And even if such a witness had existed, the question of his or her credibility would remain. After all there were witnesses who (under oath) confirmed to Livia, Augustus' widow, that they had seen the deceased emperor journey to heaven.[45]

From the outset the question as to where Jesus betook himself after he rose from the dead was especially problematic. Neither Paul nor Mark, Matthew, or John answer this question. Luke alone comes up with an answer—an all too pragmatic one of course. In both his Gospel (Luke 24:50–52) and in Acts (1:9–11), he relates an edifying story of a visible ascension.[46] The questioners could believe or not believe, but they had an answer.

Luke's report was apparently too pale and irrelevant to most of the early Christian communities; they did not include it in their creed. The belief in the ascension of Christ[47] only got the upper hand in the fourth century, but then became so powerful that it found its way into the Apostles' Creed.[48]

In Jesus' lifetime nobody gave a thought to the notion that the master would rise from the dead before the end of time. Otherwise Mary Magdalene, Mary, Mary the mother of James, and Salome would not have been "frightened out of their wits" upon beholding the empty tomb (Mark 16:8) and the disciples would have reacted less skeptically to Mary Magdalene's report. The evangelist John, clearly and bluntly, sets the kerygmatic content of the ascension in bold relief: "Till this moment they had failed to understand the teaching of scripture, that he must rise from the dead. The disciples then went home again" (John 20:9–10).

The many hypotheses proposed in this connection indicate the difficulty of the concept of Jesus' resurrection from the dead. One opinion being voiced in some quarters is that Jesus did not die on the Roman cross, but lived to an old age in India, where he enjoyed some influence.[49] An older theory contends that when Jesus was taken down from the cross he was not yet dead—a fact supposedly overlooked by the Roman centurion—and that Joseph of Arimathea and his helper, unnoticed by the Roman guard, took him away and nursed him back to health. Thus arose the assumption that he had risen from the dead.

In the middle of the last century the Heidelberg exegete H. E. G. Paulus[50] reconstructed events as follows: Jesus survived the ghastly ordeal. He put on a garment that the gardener lent him. But his weakness forced him to remain nearby in the garden. When Mary Magdalene spotted him, he forbade her to touch him because his body was still too sensitive to pain. By afternoon he had recovered sufficient strength to set out on the walk to Emmaus. Later he even ventured as far as Galilee. But all this did not help his recovery; he died later of tetanus.

A special story was invented by the bishop's son Marcion, whom Egon Friedel views as the most important theologian of the second century: As God, Jesus absolutely could not have suffered or died. On the other hand, since the narratives of Jesus' Passion were still circulating among the faithful, Marcion and his numerous followers spread the following speculation,[51] which was handed down by the Church Father Ireneus. Simon of Cyrene not only carried Jesus' cross but in some miraculous way was substituted for him, crucified in the place and person of Jesus. Meanwhile the real Jesus, who made himself scarce in the crowd, laughed as he witnessed the execution of his double.[52] Marcionism flourished for a long time; not until centuries later did it cease to play a role in the consciousness of the faithful. The Pauline teaching of the resurrection of Jesus finally established itself at the Council of Nicaea in A.D. 325.

The resurrection of Jesus is accepted *a priori* by the faith. Yet all that can be verified historically is that the first proclaimers of the Gospel believed in the resurrection, as voiced by Peter in his Pentecost sermon: "God raised this man Jesus to life, and all of us are witnesses to that" (Acts 2:32).[53]

The account of an event is not to be equated with the event itself. The account is colored by the author's attitude and the intention behind his story. Bornkamm writes,[54] "The event of the resurrection of Jesus Christ from the dead . . . is excluded from historiography." From the outset faith in the resurrection, not any attempt to furnish proof, was the point of the predication. "The important thing for faith is not that Jesus was bodily resurrected, the historical fact as such, but that for me he is the Risen One," is how Bultmann formulates it.[55] And Küng[56] writes, "What happened is not nothing. But what happened bursts through and goes beyond the bounds of history. It is a transcendental happening out of human death into the all-embracing dimension of God." Despite all attempts at reinterpretation, Paul must have thought no differently. Like all believing Jews up to the present day, he recited the hymn of praise of the Eighteen Petitional Prayers, "Praised be Thou, Yahweh, who makes the dead living."

Paul describes the resurrection as "a mystery," a transformation of the physical into a spiritual existence:[57] "Or else, brothers, put it this way: flesh and blood cannot inherit the kingdom of God; and the perishable cannot inherit what lasts forever" (1 Cor. 15:50–51). According to Pauline understanding, the resurrection is not Jesus' personal fate; it would not be understood as a personal resurrection. It means that the Spirit of the Lord enables man to overcome evil and thereby to defy death.[58] "Now this Lord is the Spirit, and where the Spirit of the Lord is, there is freedom" (2 Cor. 3:17–18). The Pauline faith in the resurrection is like the ascension vision of the disciples, as Paul himself attests (1 Cor. 15:5–8). In both cases it involves a spiritual vision not accessible to the bodily eye.

Three

IN SEARCH OF THE HISTORICAL JESUS

The Chroniclers Are Silent

The historians of the first century confined themselves to a few insignificant lines in dealing with Christians. No non-Christian (i.e., neutral) sources report anything about Jesus of Nazareth. This is all the more astonishing inasmuch as a whole series of authors have written in great detail about the situation in Palestine at that time, among them the Roman Pliny the Elder (A.D. 23–79) and the Jewish writer and philosopher Philo of Alexandria (c. 20 B.C.–A.D. 50). Philo especially deserves great credit for mediating between the Jewish tradition and the Greek culture, as well as for his courageous appearance before Caligula. Philo was in constant touch, so to speak, with the tense situations amid which Jesus' activity would have taken place; but nowhere in his writings does the Nazarene turn up. Pliny publicly ridicules the unjustified executions ordered by Pilate, but makes no mention of Jesus' execution.

Pliny the Younger also merits mention. In A.D. 111, in his capacity as pro-consul in Bithynia, he referred to the rapid growth of the new faith in a letter to the emperor Trajan. There is no mention of Jesus in his writings. Nor is Jesus mentioned in the writings of the historian Justus of Tiberias (though only fragments are preserved). Justus was a contemporary of Jesus who lived in the same area.

The same applies to the writings of the Essenes discovered in 1947. This sect maintained an important monastery in the Jewish desert at Qumran, a few kilometers from the northwestern shore of the Dead Sea. There is no mention of Jesus of Nazareth in the Qumran scrolls, which originated at the time Jesus is said to have been active and were composed close to the scenes of his activity.

The texts found in Qumran contain passages that correspond in content, and even sometimes verbatim, to passages from the New Testament. The relationship to the Sermon on the Mount is clear. Brotherhood was considered a religious duty by the Essenes; love of one's neighbor, a moral precept. Essenes were forbidden to swear oaths and were instead enjoined to say only "yes, yes" or "no, no." Poverty, humility, and asceticism were their ideals. They believed in the immortality of the soul. The center of their ritual was the baptismal bath, which they viewed as a purification from sins. The precept to love the enemy is anchored in the Essene canon—and in the Old Testament, for that matter:[1] "No one will I requite with evil, I will pursue men with good for with God is judgment over all that lives."

Stretching a point, one could say that there is no Christian tenet that is not already present in the writings of the Essenes. For them, the Jerusalem Temple embodied the "Old Covenant." They wanted to conclude a "New Covenant" with God so that he could again become reconciled with the people of Israel and free them from bondage. According to the Gospels, Jesus concluded the New Covenant, or New Testament, as Martin Luther translated it, following St. Jerome.

Given these numerous and surprising parallels, the question of a connection between Jesus and Essenism (possibly through John the Baptist) obviously arises. That Jesus finds no mention of any kind in the writings of the Essenes can only be explained by the general obscurity surrounding the Nazarene in his lifetime and up to the end of the first century. The converse is also true: The important religious group of the Essenes, reported on in great detail by contemporaries, receives no mention in the New Testament.² It was hoped that the finds at Qumran would provide information on the personality of Jesus; unfortunately they have yielded nothing in this respect.

The few indirect references to Jesus in neutral sources are not of much use because they were written almost a hundred years after his death, at a time when Christianity had already become a mass movement. It is neither sensational nor surprising to read in these sources that Christians viewed the founder of their religion as a Messiah, or that he was crucified by the procurator Pontius Pilate. Nor do these relatively late mentions provide any concrete particulars because they are so vague; and this very vagueness leads inevitably to the conclusion that Jesus' public activity took place in obscurity and that this obscurity persisted in the decades that followed.³

For example, Tacitus describes in his *Annals,* around A.D. 115, a persecution of Christians said to have taken place about fifty years before, under Nero:

> In order to remove the imputation [that the fire had been set on his orders], he determined to transfer the guilt to others. For this purpose he punished, with exquisite torture, a race of men detested for their evil practices, by vulgar appellation commonly called Christians.
>
> The name was derived from Christ, who in the reign of Tiberius, suffered under Pontius Pilate, the procurator of Judaea. By that event the sect, of which he was the founder, received a blow which, for a time, checked the growth of a dangerous superstition; but it revived soon after, and spread with renewed vigour, not only in Judaea, the soil that gave it birth, but even in the city of Rome, the common sink into which every thing infamous and abominable flows like a torrent from all quarters of the world. (*Annals,* xv 44)⁴

This great Roman historian, eighty years after Jesus' death, has naught else to report. The slight importance that Tacitus accords the mention of the presumed founder of Christianity is evident from the fact that he speaks not of Jesus of Nazareth but of "Christ" from whom Christians derive their name. Evidently the "ordinary" name Jesus was not known to him. Numerically it must still have been a very small Christian community that existed in Rome at the time of Nero. That their existence came to the emperor's attention is surprising, and even more so is the fact that he viewed them as a group that had cut itself off from Judaism. People of Jewish faith were not persecuted by Nero; indeed his influential wife Poppaea Sabina converted to Judaism. This prompted many conjectures that the passage in the *Annals* does not stem from Tacitus but is a later interpolation.[5] No writer before Tacitus had ever asserted that Christians had been persecuted under Nero.

In A.D. 120, the Roman historian Suetonius mentioned a certain "Chresto" in his book *Vita Claudi*, as the instigator of the uprisings in Rome under Emperor Claudius (who reigned A.D. 41–54). This mention, however, can hardly be linked to Jesus. First, there were no Christians in Rome during the reign of Claudius, the Christian community in Rome was founded later than those of Antioch and Alexandria, at the end of the 50s at the earliest. Secondly, emergent Christian communities took great pains not to create disturbances, as Paul expressly commanded in his Letter to the Romans (13:1 ff.). Thirdly, Suetonius assumes that the instigator of the uprisings under Claudius is still alive and residing in Rome, which does not apply to Jesus. Fourthly, Suetonius' report obviously refers to rebellious Jews, not Christians.

A further potential source that merits mention here is a private letter that the Syrian Mara bar Sarapion sent to his son studying in Edessa. A passage of it reads as follows:

> What benefit did the Athenians derive from their killing of Socrates? . . . Or the Sumerians from the burning of Pythagoras? . . . Or the Jews from the execution of their wise king, since from that time onwards the kingdom was taken away from them. For justly God took revenge for those three wise men.[6]

It is extremely difficult to date this letter. Aufhauser leaves the date open between A.D. 73 and 160. Whether the writer meant Jesus by the reference to the "wise king" is questionable. Even if this were the case, he obviously did not know his name, yet Socrates and Pythagoras were known to him. No historical value can be attributed to the letter in regard to Jesus' person since Pilate and the Romans receive not a single mention—quite aside from the fact that we do not know whether the letter stems from a Christian or a non-Christian source.

Jesus is mentioned by name by the famous Roman philosopher and politician Celsus (Kelsos) around the middle of the second century. What Celsus writes, however, is anything but neutral: It is quite obviously based on Talmudic slanders of Christians that had been written and circulated since the end of the first century.

> Celsus says expressly (orig. C.C.I: 28) that Mary had been divorced by her husband, a carpenter by trade, for adultery; that she gave birth to Jesus secretly; that poverty forced him to earn his living in Egypt as a day-laborer; that he learned magic there; and that he then returned and by virtue of this skill publicly declared himself God.[7]

In the Talmud, a collection of texts and commentaries that constitutes the written Jewish civil and religious law, there is an account of a rabbinical discussion that took place around A.D. 95. There Jesus is characterized as a fool; his mother "Miriam, the hair-braider, was unfaithful to her husband, her paramour was called Pandera." According to Craveri,

> Nevertheless, some students have taken the trouble to investigate the possible accuracy of the Talmudic tradition. There appears to be in Bingerbrück, Germany, the gravestone of a Roman soldier born in Sidon in Phoenicia, whose name was Tiberius Julius Panther and who belonged to a cohort garrisoned in Palestine about A.D. 90. The authority of the Talmud was such among the fathers of the Church themselves that for a long time they found it necessary to explain the presence of this embarrassing fellow in the life of Jesus.[8]

Whether one can conclude that, at the end of the first century, Jesus' historical existence was not in doubt even in the Talmud is a question that I should like to leave open; the slanders could be of a fictitious character. More importantly, in Jesus' actual lifetime he does not appear in Jewish writing; specifically, no mention is made of his alleged conflicts with the Pharisees. Salcia Landmann writes,[9] "Even debates with 'heretics' after all were entered unabridged into the Talmud. . . . The fact is that Jesus is not mentioned with even one syllable, although the writings report on wholly unimportant personalities and episodes in great detail."

Josephus Flavius (A.D. 37–94) was the most important writer of his time. In his historical works, *Antiquities of the Jews* and *History of the Jewish War,* written after the destruction of the state of Israel, he deals extensively with events in Palestine at precisely the time of Jesus.[10] The slightest disturbance of the peace, every uprising, every just or unjust death sentence that had some kind of political importance was described by Josephus in great detail. The violent encroachments of the procurator Pilate, especially on the Jewish people, are listed and presented individually.[11] All the influences and spiritual trends of that time are described in great detail. Yet Josephus Flavius makes no mention of any Christian communities, nor does he report on Jesus of Nazareth as a historical personality.

The first Christian community outside Palestine was at Antioch, a Roman city in Asia Minor that had a large Jewish population. Paul had founded the community around the middle of the 40s. The "brethren" who gathered there were called Christians. The designation crops up here for the first time (Acts 11:26); hence it is of Pauline origin. The Hebrew sect in Jerusalem was called the Nazarene sect (Acts 24:6). The community of Alexandria was created around a decade after the Antioch community, and several years later one was established in Rome.

Obviously no importance whatsoever was attributed to Jesus or his followers in the forty years between his death and the end of the Jewish war. After all, Josephus had no reason to ignore Jesus intentionally (or Paul, who is not mentioned either). Altogether, he mentions about twenty persons who bear the name Jesus, around half of them contemporaries of our Jesus. One is a prophet Jesus "son of Ananos." He says this Jesus prophesied the fall of the Temple and for this he was arrested by the Jews and handed over to the Romans. The Romans reportedly flogged him mercilessly, after which they released him because they concluded that he was a madman.[12]

The name Jesus—in Hebrew Josua, Jesua, or Jehousa—has several meanings such as "God helps" or "God will redeem." At that time it was as common as William or Otto would be later. Later the name Jesus was heard less often; the Jews probably disliked it too much to want to pass it on to their children. And in the young Christian communities there was a reluctance to give another person the name Jesus; the healing name was supposed to glow in an untouchable uniqueness. If one had to refer to another person of this name, then his name was changed. Thus Paul, in the Letter to the Colossians 4:11, renames a coworker called Jesus "Jesus Justus."

As a matter of fact the Nazarene Jesus does turn up once in a work of Josephus, the *Antiquities of the Jews* completed around the year A.D. 90. Here Josephus reports on the high priest Ananos,[13] who was removed by King Agrippa II because he had Jesus' brother James sentenced at a summary hearing and executed: "He assembled the Sanhedrin of judges and brought before them the brother of Jesus who was called Christ, whose name was James, and some others (or some of his companions); and when he had formed an accusation against them, as breakers of our law, he delivered them to be stoned" (*Antiquities of the Jews*, xx, 9:1). The relative clause joined to the mention of the name Jesus, "who was called Christ," attests to the fact that this name was common. In exegetic studies it is generally assumed that the relative clause in the Josephus text is a later interpolation: Only Christians could have had an interest in highlighting Jesus' Messianic status.[14]

In contrast to the Nazarene Jesus, John the Baptist is an unimpeachable historically verified personality, known and described with honor. In *Antiquities of the Jews* Josephus reports:

> Now some of the Jews thought that the destruction of Herod's army came from God, and that very justly, as a punishment of what he did against John, that was called the *Baptist*; for Herod slew him, who was a good man, and commanded the Jews to exercise virtue, both as to righteousness towards one another, and piety towards God, and so to come to baptism. (xviii, 5:2)

What would one give to find—with no possible question as to its authenticity—a single sentence like this concerning Jesus anywhere in the historiography of that time!

As long as the young Christian Church had not secured tolerance or acceptance from the government but had to struggle for success, recognition, and, initially, sheer survival, it could not give much thought to the fact that its founder was a historically unknown personality. There were more important things to be done. In the fourth century, however, the bishop and Church Father Eusebius cultivated a strategic and successful alliance with the Emperor Constantine—a mutually beneficial entente. Then the historical lacunae surrounding the central figure of the Christian faith were borne in upon the young state Church in the process of establishing itself. Eusebius had meanwhile been promoted to the post of Constantine's court theologian (Jacob Burckhardt calls the bishop the "first thoroughly disreputable historian of antiquity"[15]). He wrote a Church history for the emperor around A.D. 320 in which he inserted what he claimed was an excerpt from Josephus' *Antiquities of the Jews.* Constantine could now read the following sentences, whose ostensible author was still highly esteemed in the empire:

> Now there was about this time Jesus, a wise man, if it be lawful to call him a man; for he was a doer of wonderful works, a teacher of such men as receive the truth with pleasure. He drew over to him both many of the Jews and many of the Gentiles. He was the Christ. And when Pilate, at the suggestion of the principal men amongst us, had condemned him to the cross, those that loved him at the first did not forsake him, for he appeared to them alive again the third day, as the divine prophets had foretold these and ten thousand other wonderful things concerning him. And the tribe of Christians, so named for him, are not extinct to this day. (xviii, 3:3)

That these sentences (the so-called Testimonium Flavianum) constitute a forgery, and a rather crude one at that, is no longer doubted by any serious researcher as far as I know. Josephus would have had to be a Christian to write such a passage; but he was not a Christian. Though he was in the service of the Romans, he had remained loyal to the Jewish faith and did not believe Jesus was the Messiah.[16] A tiny minority of authors (Klausner, for example) do consider it credible that the explicit mention of Jesus stems from Josephus, possibly even the positive comment that Jesus had been a wise man and the sentence, "And when Pilate, at the suggestion of the principal men amongst us, had condemned him to the cross." If one follows this minority view, one must also maintain that at the end of the first century, when Christianity had already become widespread in many regions, the historical significance of Jesus of Nazareth amounted to nothing more than this inclusion, by name only, in a major chronicle.

Josephus Flavius came from an aristocratic Jerusalem family. His father was a priest (and thus a member of the Sanhedrin) when the trial of Jesus allegedly took place. Josephus himself was first a Pharisee. At the outbreak of war in A.D. 66 he was a Jewish commander in chief in Galilee. After the Romans captured the

Jotapata fortress he was taken prisoner and brought before his Roman counterpart, the old veteran warrior Vespasian.[17] Josephus knew how to win the victor's favor and soon received Roman citizenship—Vespasian had meanwhile become emperor. Soon thereafter he received Vespasian's first name and pagan name, "Titus Flavius." As surname he chose his Jewish name and gave it a Latin ending. As a Roman citizen, therefore, he was called Titus Flavius Josephus, whereas his Jewish name was Joseph ben Matitjahu ha-Kohen.

Josephus would certainly have heard, from his father or relatives and friends of his parents, if a prominent personality in Jerusalem in the last year of Tiberius' reign had figured in a sensational and unprecedented double trial before the Jewish Sanhedrin and the Roman tribunal, and had been sentenced to death and executed. Nor does Nicodemus, a member of the Sanhedrin of whom much has been preserved,[18] waste a single word on a trial in which he was allegedly closely linked to the executed defendant (John 19:39). Together with another member of the Sanhedrin, Joseph of Arimathea, he is said to have taken pains to see that Jesus received a dignified burial.

Another known, and likewise silent, member of the Sanhedrin was Gamaliel the Wise, Paul's teacher, of whom several writings are extant. According to the synoptics Gamaliel, like Nicodemus, had voted for the death sentence for Jesus. All members of the Sanhedrin except Joseph of Arimathea, whose vote is reported only by Luke (23:51), approved the death sentence.

Finally, Paul himself is silent.[19] He writes nothing about the trial, although he was a law and theology student in Jerusalem at exactly the time when the event allegedly took place and he attended the lectures of a member of the court that supposedly sentenced Jesus to death.

According to Gospel accounts, the execution was accompanied by unique occurrences:

> From the sixth hour there was darkness over all the land until the ninth hour. . . . At that, the veil of the Temple was torn in two from top to bottom; the earth quaked; the rocks were split; the tombs opened and the bodies of many holy men rose from the dead, and these, after his resurrection, came out of the tombs, entered the Holy City and appeared to a number of people. (Matt. 27:45, 51–54)

That, of course, is not a historical account, but a legendary message intended to warn of imminent threat and disaster. The alleged solar eclipse never took place, if only because at full moon the moon cannot stand between the sun and the earth.[20] The tear in the curtain of the Temple is to signify that from that moment onwards God no longer chose to dwell in the Temple and had forsaken Jews. Current Christian ideology concludes that because the Jews rejected Jesus God no longer dwells in the Temple of Jerusalem. He has passed over to the Christians and dwells in Christian churches.

But no solar eclipse or other natural disaster occurred. And members of the Sanhedrin like Nicodemus or Gamaliel would surely have told a student like Paul or a committed historian like Josephus about a trial of Jesus of Nazareth if it had been a noteworthy event and not just a summary military proceeding such as was customary at that time.

> Jewish history in the period of the Messianic uprisings had seen the crosses rise forest-like—it viewed the three crosses on Golgotha as an insignificant episode that it never registered in its annals, just as Tacitus deemed it undeserving of mention in his Roman history. One crucified Jew more or less made no difference to the procurators and emperors or their historians.[21]

The lack of any report by Pilate in the imperial archives was perceived by the Church, after it became a state church, as a void to be filled. Just as a citation from Josephus in relation to Jesus' life and activity was invented and passed off as authentic, the so-called *Acta Pilati* ("Acts of Pilate") were invented to deal with Jesus' death and resurrection; they are a palpable forgery.[22]

Pilate had simply found nothing extraordinary to report to Rome regarding a man called Jesus of Nazareth. Even theologians came to terms with this fact a long time ago. No doubt theologians like Dibelius, Rahner, or Küng would immediately confirm the unimportance of the trial from the procurator's viewpoint. Most theologians, however, are once again attempting to gloss over this fact.

Anatole France, in his short story *The Procurator of Judea*, tells of a meeting of the aged Pontius Pilate with his friend Lamia. They chat about old times in the baths of Baiae. Lamia talks about a lover who had left him.

"A few months later I learned by chance that she had joined a small group of men and women who followed a young Galilean who wandered about and worked miracles. He was from Nazareth and was called Jesus. Later he was crucified for some crime, I no longer know what it was. Do you remember this man, Pilate?" Pontius Pilate wrinkled his brows, and rested his hand on his forehead as though he were trying to recall something. Then, after a brief pause, he murmured: "Jesus, Jesus? From Nazareth? No, I don't remember anymore."[23]

There had been many Roman military governors in Palestine, Syria, Gaul, and Germany. They are all documented, but only specialists know their names. Such would also have been the case with Pontius Pilate, a grey mouse among grey mice, if he had not been assigned such a towering place by the small band of proclaimers of the Gospel. The Protestant theologian Goguel observes, "Pilate . . . would have been very much surprised if he had been told that the 'poor little Jew' who appeared before him on that day would cause his own name to be handed down in an immortal story."[24] And the Catholic theologian Kolping views the execution of Jesus as "an insignificant episode in the official history of the Roman Empire which would have been forgotten if it had not become the astonishing foundation of the faith in Christ professed by the post-Easter Church."[25]

Whatever one may think about the scarcity of mentions of Jesus, one thing stands firm: even if he did become a prominent personality in his own lifetime, having come from the provinces, hardly any of his contemporaries could have imagined that the emergence of this Galilean would become a world-transforming event.

The Historical Jesus Research

People like Frederick the Great, Napoleon, and Goethe—admittedly mostly for the purpose of keeping up with a fashionable intellectual trend of their time—expressed doubts as to the historicity of Jesus. The dearth of reports of Jesus in contemporary writings and the incontrovertible facts that no unbiased record exists and that the sources we do have are contradictory are cited by all researchers. It is a puzzling assignment and one that even the shrewdest detective would find well-nigh impossible.

Not until the Age of the Enlightenment were any studies along these lines possible. Before that, since the New Testament was thought to have been inspired by the Holy Spirit, any doubters were subject to criminal proceedings. Only naive faith was considered true faith. So deeply entrenched was this notion that its aftereffects are still felt today. Trying to question firm opinions about the earthly Jesus is like treading gingerly on an exceptionally thorny path. Even theologians note with pain the great mistrust among Christian churchgoers of recognized and well-documented findings of historical criticism.[26] "There is," as Zahrnt[27] formulates it, "not only a stubborn unbelief, there is also a stubborn belief."

Küng, more than anyone else, in lectures and writings speaks out against the widespread naiveté in matters of faith and tries to reduce faith in Jesus and historical knowledge about Jesus to a common denominator.

> Naiveté in matters of faith is not evil, but at least dangerous. Naive faith can miss the true Jesus and lead us with the best intentions to false conclusions in theory and practice. Naive faith can lead the individual or a community to become blind, authoritarian, self-righteous. On the other hand, a knowledge of history can reveal new prospects to the Christian believer, and give him insight and satisfaction, can inspire him in a variety of ways. Enlightenment—as history proves—can avert religious fanaticism and intolerance. Only faith and knowledge combined, a faith that knows and a knowledge that believes, are capable today of understanding the true Christ in his breadth and depth.[28]

The first phase of research into the life of Jesus, the so-called literary-critical phase, turned against the dogmatic Christ image of the Church. Goethe made the following short poetic contribution in his *West-East Divan:*

> Jesus felt pure and gave thought
> Only to the one, sole God when all was still,
> Anyone who of him God wrought,
> offended his holy will.

Lessing's *Fragments of H. S. Reimarus*, published in 1773, managed to achieve scientific relevance. The literary-critical phase tried to find the historical Jesus in order to present him as he is, in order to situate him in the present as teacher or Savior. Later Albert Schweitzer was to summarize the failure of this effort as follows:

> It loosened the bonds by which he had been riveted for centuries to the stony rocks of ecclesiastical doctrine, and rejoiced to see life and movement coming into the figure once more, and the historical Jesus advancing, as it seemed, to meet it. But he does not stay; He passes by our time and returns to His own.[29]

The dominant thesis of life-of-Jesus research at the end of the nineteenth century and the beginning of the twentieth held that Jesus of Nazareth never existed and that his figure was an invention, based upon a misinterpretation of those who first proclaimed the Christian faith. It was not that a historical person had been deified through faith, but rather that myth, through faith, brought a historical person into being.[30]

The German, English, French, and American scholars who proposed the thesis of the nonhistoricity of Jesus included Arthur Drews, Bruno Bauer, David Friedrich Strauss, John M. Robertson, Emile Burns, and William Benjamin Smith.[31] According to these scholars, ancient symbolic ideas were concentrated in the person, history, and parables of Jesus. Addressing himself to this viewpoint as a committed Christian, Albert Schweitzer[32] wrote, "Modern Christianity must now reckon—has always had to reckon—with the possible surrender of the historical existence of Jesus." He also came out against any solution that would distinguish between the historical and the Jesus of faith but would present the latter in a guise that suits his historicity just as little as does the old cliché.

> The Jesus of Nazareth who came forward publicly as the Messiah, who preached the ethic of the Kingdom of God, who founded the Kingdom of Heaven on earth, and died to give his work its final consecration, never had an existence. He is a figure designed by rationalism, endowed with life by liberalism and clothed by modern theology in historical garb.

Schweitzer does, in the final analysis, accept the historicity of Jesus, but for reasons more resigned than assertive: If all the findings are critically analyzed, it is more probable that Jesus lived than that he did not. But Schweitzer regards the question as to whether Jesus actually lived as of only secondary importance for the faith.

Confirmed Circumstantial Evidence

Today, as far as I know, no scholar of standing doubts Jesus' historicity. Scholars, principally American, English, French, and Scandinavian, have taken the enquiries of the literary critical phase of life-of-Jesus research as a basis. They have tried to go beyond resignation in dealing with the historical Jesus, and to tread new paths. Their starting point was a conviction that the writings pointed too explicitly to one central personality to have had an imaginary figure as a foundation. Moreover, it must have been a personality whose life and death coincided almost exactly with the initial proclaimers of the Christian message. For example, Peter's sermons in Acts contain elements of an ancient tradition that makes no mention of any "Lord" or "Risen One," but simply of "Jesus" or "Jesus of Nazareth." And if there were no real personal reference to a Jesus of Nazareth it would be inconceivable, for example, that the authority of James as the Lord's brother would have been recognized by Paul, particularly as he felt that the greatest credit for the proclamation of the faith was due to him (1 Cor. 15:10). Why accept a brother of the Lord if the Lord had never existed as a person?

To summarize, the descriptions of events in the Gospels would have assumed another tone if a made-up figure had been at their center. The praise would have been vastly more inflated; any weaknesses of the figure would have been suppressed. The death would not have been that of a man, lonely and tormented, but of a hero whose spirit and unshaken faith in eventual victory triumphed over his physical destruction. Accordingly, the New Testament as a whole would be a brilliantly polished work; but precisely the opposite is the case. Ernst Bloch writes, "The stable, the carpenter's son, the visionary among simple people, the gallows at the end, this is taken from historical stuff, not the golden stuff beloved of legend."[33]

The so-called literary-historical (also known as "form criticism" and "history criticism") method was founded by Ernst Käsemann and is recognized today by almost all historians researching Jesus. It is an indirect method and has two significant points of departure, different but related to each other.

The procedure for the first point of departure (the "cross-section" principle) is as follows: Take the non-Christian historical writing of the era that describes all the conditions, events, and figures who played any role whatsoever, especially during the presumed lifetime of Jesus and at the time of his public activity. Compare these to any Gospel passages that mention—even only briefly or in passing—the same conditions, events, or figures by non-Christian authors. Then check the "news reports" contained in the New Testament.

If confirmed historical findings are meshed with the Gospel accounts, one can determine with some accuracy which Gospel descriptions are based on historical truth and which must be considered legendary or propagandistic. If an evangelist truthfully described a concrete, verified historical event there is no reason to assume that his description of Jesus in the situation does not likewise rest on historical truth. Had Jesus been a phantom, the evangelist would have described him abstractly, not in relation to a concrete situation or historical event. The account is all the more credible if the event is of a wholly neutral character and hence cannot be used to enhance Jesus' image.

A further question from this standpoint is whether the Gospels contain any statements concerning Jesus that are neither a legacy of Jewish culture in general nor expressions of an early Christian faith. If even one such fact can be encountered, an *a posteriori* conclusion of confirmed historicity is to some extent warranted.[34] Jesus' liking for good food,[35] his socializing with prostitutes and sinners, and indeed the mere fact that he associated with women, are examples of such facts.

Just as convincing and much more fruitful is the second point of departure, which supplements the first. This proceeds from the following premise: It is firmly established that the evangelists and those ecclesiastics who supplemented and amended their work had a two-fold purpose. They sought on the one hand to present Jesus as the Christ sent by God, invested with divine authority and power plus the capacity to perform miraculous deeds: "These are recorded so that you may believe that Jesus is the Christ, the Son of God" (John 20:31). Secondly, they wished to prove that the coming of Jesus was an exact fulfillment of promises made by the prophets. In Matthew the following passage and variations on it appear repeatedly: "Now all this took place to fulfill the words spoken by the Lord through the prophets." A third intention was to portray Jesus as in constant conflict with Jewish Pharisees, to attribute as much responsibility for Jesus' death as possible to the Jews, and to tone down the role of the Romans in his death.

With this in mind, everything in the texts that does not concern either Jesus' alleged authority and divine power or the thesis that his emergence fulfilled prophetic promises automatically gains in historical veracity. Passages that omit any antagonism between Jesus and Judaism, or in which he clearly confesses his Jewish faith (possibly linked to a critical or hostile attitude to Rome)—or, going one step further, that show Jesus' crucifixion on the Roman cross being deplored by the Jewish population—likewise gain credibility. Some examples follow:

1. The Gospels agree that Jesus had been baptized by John the Baptist. This involved the so-called penitential bath during which those who confess their sins undergo a ritual immersion in water to wash them away, make a vow of conversion, and undertake thenceforth to live in the fear of God. But if Jesus had been the Christ invested with divine authority, God's only begotten son, he would have had no need to be baptized. That Jesus was baptized by John and joined him as a disciple implies his awareness of his own sin, hardly a divine state. Obviously this incident could not be hidden. Nor could it be said that John had asked for forgiveness of sins from Jesus, not Jesus from John. Such a presentation would not have been possible because the Baptist sects were very strongly represented in the first half of the post-Christian century and were in conflict with the Jesus-followers.[36] Hence any concealment of Jesus' baptism by John or a reversal of the roles could easily have been exposed as a fraud.[37] The baptism of Jesus could be dealt with only with great difficulty. Indeed the Church Father Ignatius opined that the Lord had intended to sanctify the water with his baptism, an argument that Thomas Aquinas was to adopt a thousand years later.
2. As described in the Gospels, Jesus' life was anything but pleasant. Death overtook him as he had just begun to develop his public ministry. His success was modest. Fame was out of the question. In his homeland he was laughed at, repudiated, and

even pronounced crazy.³⁸ The occasional approval he achieved was constantly countered by doubts among his fellowmen, strife and quarrels with those around him, and controversies with the disciples.³⁹ An air of resignation and loneliness hovers over the entire narrative.

These two examples directly contradict the notion of Jesus' glorified status. Furthermore, no Old Testament prophesy holds that a Messiah must undergo a penitential baptism or lead a humble earthly life.

3. The fact that the evangelists frankly describe Jesus' death on the cross is seen as the most convincing proof of Jesus' historicity. They did not consider death on the cross to be an honorable martyr's death; on the contrary, it must have been seen as a scandal of the first rank, the most shameful end that could befall the Messiah. Had Jesus been stoned like the other martyrs, or beheaded like John the Baptist, it would have been much easier to bear. In Jesus' time, crucifixion was viewed as a most dishonorable punishment, as Moses had made clear: "for one who has been hanged is accursed of God" (Deut. 21:23).

Moses, of course, had not been thinking of a crucifixion by Romans or other occupation troops (Persian or Greek) who employed this means of execution. The "accursed" were blasphemers, who were stoned, or other criminals who were strangled; their corpses hung from a beam as a deterrent. In their unshakable loyalty to the written word and the resultant literal mode of thinking, the later Jews heaped curses and other humiliations on people who were tied or nailed to a cross for execution. To add to the desecration, crucified corpses were frequently left unburied, fodder for roaming dogs, hyenas, or bears and birds of prey. For the entire ancient world crucifixion was an offense. From a Roman point of view it was the mode of execution practiced by barbarians, though they themselves employed it on a large scale. Slaves and mercenaries were entrusted with the actual work of execution.

The victims of this "barbaric" mode of execution were also mostly slaves or members of the lower strata of subjugated peoples. If a victim happened to be a Roman citizen, it caused a sensation. Hengel⁴⁰ describes one of these exceptional cases, as reported by Suetonius. The procurator of Spain, Galba, had a disloyal guardian sentenced to death because the latter had poisoned his ward out of greed. The condemned man cited his rights as a Roman citizen, whereupon Galba had him raised on an especially high cross[41] painted white. The procurator of Sicily, Gaius Verres, had a Roman crucified on the Sicilian coast overlooking the Italian mainland in order to underline the utter uselessness of his Roman citizenship.[42] In the provinces, procurators were empowered to crucify both Romans and rebels. Hengel[43] writes: "The executions of rebels and violent criminals were of a military character.... An alleged Son of God who could not save himself in his last hour (Mark 15:31), who, on the contrary, begged for help in bearing the cross, could hardly hold much appeal for the lower orders."

Paul later made a virtue out of necessity, so to speak, in his theology. An erudite Jewish theologian, with good connections, he must have realized that Jesus of Nazareth had been an innocent victim. But he probably took the strategic path: Since Christianity was being proclaimed in the Roman-Hellenic orbit, to people for whom a crucified person was no more than a common criminal, he appeared to share this view. He even cited Moses, for whom a crucified person was "accursed of God," in order to argue more effectively for his own theology: Jesus took the curse of the whole world upon himself through his "shameful" death on the cross, and thereby became the Redeemer of the pagans; i.e., of those to whom Paul and his successors directed their message. In other words, Paul accepts the curse of the cross and the stigma of the gallows—in his famous words, "to the Jews an obstacle that they cannot get over, to the pagans madness" (1 Cor. 1:23). But he argues that this curse has freed men from the curse of God so that Christ appears as the Redeemer precisely through the death suffered on the cross.

> Christ redeemed us from the curse of the Law by being cursed for our sake, since Scripture says: Cursed be everyone who is hanged on a tree. This was done so that in Christ Jesus the blessing of Abraham might include the pagans, and so that through faith we might receive the promised Spirit. (Gal. 3:13–14)

The evangelist John follows the same train of thought. For him too, the hour of the crucifixion is also that of the resurrection (John 3:13; 8:28; 12:32, 34; 17:1, 5). And the Letter to the Hebrews 12:2 states that Jesus "for the sake of the joy which was still in the future ... endured the cross, disregarding the shamefulness of it."

The early Christian Church could not accept the cross as a symbol of the new faith. Blinzler writes, "What really disturbed the community was the fact that the one revered by them as Messiah and Son of God had found an accursed death on a gallows for criminals."[44] The symbol of the young Christian communities was fish, a reference to the beginning, the fishermen, and the Lake of Gennesaret. In addition, the fish had a secret significance: The Greek word for fish is an acronym for the words "Jesus Christ Son of God Savior." The cross found its way only gradually into the liturgy, after Emperor Constantine had long since abolished crucifixion. From the second century onwards the sacrificial lamb was the dominant Christian symbol. At the Quinisextum Synod in A.D. 692, the representation of the Savior as a human figure was demanded; the fifth century had seen figurations of Jesus on the cross, but artists were still reluctant to show him as crucified. Instead, he stood on a small pedestal on the cross, eyes open, arms extended as though in blessing, his head surrounded by the sun disk as a mystical sign of redemption. Not until the eighth century was a dead Jesus on the cross portrayed in Christian art.

The cross furnishes three pieces of evidence that Jesus was a historical character. First, the stigma of crucifixion was not consistent with the attempts to glorify him. Secondly, no prophesy stated that the Messiah would be crucified.[45] Finally, the cross proves that Jesus was not killed by the Jews, but died a patriotic martyr's death as a victim of Rome.

The little inconsistencies, oversights, inaccuracies, and absurdities in the writings of his followers are further evidence of Jesus' historicity.[46] Any writer presenting him as the Messiah is overlooking the fact that this is a national figure of Judaism and can have meaning only for Jewry. He is thus directly undermining the Christological effort to free Jesus from the fetters of Judaism and to present him as the Redeemer of all humankind.

Another example is more telling. Jesus believed steadfastly that the world was coming to an end and that he, along with the disciples and the entire people of Israel, would experience the beginning of the kingdom of God, the *Parousia*. He proved to be mistaken (humorous theologians occasionally refer to the "*Parousia* postponement").[47] This cardinal error was based on a cornerstone of Jesus' teaching, and it is surprising that ecclesiastical censorship did not cover it up.

Fortunately, neither Paul nor the all-embracing ecclesiastical censorship that followed him could completely cover the historical substratum, though they wanted to in an attempt to blot out anything that might mitigate the glorification of the Risen One. A tiny bit of biographical material has survived underneath all the embellishments, through which the person of Jesus can be glimpsed in outline.

Four

HOW, WHEN, AND WHERE BORN

BORN OF A VIRGIN!

Only Matthew and Luke give accounts of Jesus' descent and the circumstances of his birth. Both speak of his conception through the Holy Spirit and refer to Mary as a virgin (Matt. 1:18 ff.; Luke 1:27–28). Neither Mark nor John nor Paul says anything about a virgin birth; and further along in the narrative Matthew and Luke take as a matter of course that Jesus' father was a carpenter (Matt. 13:55) named Joseph (Luke 4:23). The account of the virgin birth was probably not even part of their original narratives, but was added later. Interestingly, the well-known Christmas story of Luke's Gospel does not mention Mary's virginity even once: "So Joseph set out . . . to be registered together with Mary, his betrothed, who was with child" (Luke 2:3–5).[1]

Many other passages of this Gospel present a normal parent-child relationship. It was "the parents" who brought the child Jesus into the Temple (Luke 2:27). Luke (2:33) writes, ". . . the child's father and mother stood there wondering at the things that were being said about him"; and "his parents" betook themselves to Jerusalem every year in celebration of the Passover feast (Luke 2:41).

Only Matthew (1:23) broaches the subject of virginity. He believes it to be the fulfillment of a prophesy of Isaiah: ". . . the maiden is with child and will soon give birth to a son whom she will call Immanuel" (Isa. 7:14). Isaiah's utterance, however, cannot refer to the birth of Jesus. Isaiah was prophesying to the future King Ahaz that his spouse would bear him an heir to the throne (Hezekiab), an event that preceded the birth of Jesus by about seven hundred years. Nor did Isaiah speak of a virgin (which Ahaz's wife no longer was) but of a "maiden," i.e., the newly married queen.

Matthew had the writings of the prophets in Greek translation, since the original Hebrew text was no longer in general use. The Hebrew text uses the word *alma,* maiden. This was confirmed by the finds at Qumran; the scrolls include a complete edition of Isaiah in Hebrew. Because of an error in translation the word *parthenos* (virgin) was used in the Septuagint.[2] Had the prophet meant a virgin he would have used the word *betulla.* Possibly Matthew fell victim to this error, but more probably the error in the Septuagint suited him and he knowingly took it over.

The story of the virgin was unknown to the apostles of the original Christian community. Paul wasted no words on a miraculous birth: "born of a woman" (Gal. 4:5). Nor does Mark mention a virgin birth; he automatically assumes a normal birth. Thus, when Jesus leads the services in the synagogue of his hometown for the first time, the people ask in amazement: "This is the carpenter, surely, the son of Mary . . . ?" (Mark 6:3). Surprisingly, this Marcan text was taken over in John 6:42, by the very evangelist who is otherwise so bent on presenting Jesus as a divine being.

Given that so sensational and unique an event as a virgin birth is not mentioned by the majority of the proclaimers of the Gospel and is even disavowed, and that Jesus never once asserted about himself that he was the son of a virgin, only one conclusion can be drawn: The virgin birth is a legend. This is now also the prevailing opinion among theologians. Küng[3] writes, "Jesus' being God's son is not dependent on the virgin birth. . . . There is no incompatibility between birth from God and human procreation."

Just when the belief in the virgin birth originated can no longer be determined. In Acts 1:14 the only information about Mary is that she joined the followers of Jesus; she played only a minor role in the community. The idea of her virginity would have struck men like James and Peter as an absurdity.

On the other hand, however, the belief in the virgin birth seems to have had some importance before the cult of Mary began. Such notions were fully consistent with the spirit of the times—except in Israel.[4] That the birth of a human being endowed with divine attributes could result from a brief encounter between a god and a virgin was widely accepted throughout the ancient world. In Egyptian mythology the Pharaoh was miraculously begotten; in Greek mythology, gods were wont to enter into "sacred marriages" with the daughters of men, from which such gods as Perseus and Heracles were born. Hence the belief in a virgin mother is not specifically Christian. Alexander the Great was allegedly not the natural son of the Macedonian King Philip II, but engendered by Zeus through a flash of lightning. Why not proclaim something similar for Jesus?[5]

The Marian cult arose under Eusebius and Emperor Constantine, when Christianity became a state religion and the state saw a political need to establish a competitor to the important Isis cult in the Hellenic-Roman orbit.[6] Mother Goddess Mary supplanted Mother Goddess Isis. The Isis temples were transformed into Marian churches, and the temples of Ceres, Minerva, and Venus were also consecrated to Mary after the attributes of those goddesses were ascribed to her. The new goddess could no longer be presented as a carpenter's wife.

From a woman who was not considered worthy of mention among Jesus' followers in the primitive community, from the plain human "woman" who bore Jesus (as Paul designated her), by way of the "mother of Jesus," as John detachedly called her, Mary was transformed into a heavenly being to be venerated like an ancient goddess. This process began in the fourth century and received further impetus from the Counter-Reformation. In 1854 Pope Pius IX proclaimed the dogma of the "Immaculate Conception," whereby Mary's conception was considered stainless so that she remained immune to original sin. And in 1964 Cardinal Wyszynski succeeded in having Pope Paul VI proclaim Mary "Mater Ecclesia," against the Council's will. The "Mother of God" and "Queen of Heaven" was officially placed at the pinnacle of the Church.

To the extent that the presumed virginity of Mary played any role[7] before the emergence of the Marian cult, it was believed only in the Matthean-Lucan sense. Only the conception of the son Jesus, the future Messiah, was important *(virginitas ante partum)*. In Matthew the angel's mission does not extend beyond this. "When Joseph woke up he did what the angel of the Lord had told him to do: he took his wife to his home and, though he had not had intercourse with her, she gave birth to a son; and he named him Jesus" (Matt. 1:24–25). The Christmas story of Luke's Gospel states explicitly, "and she gave birth to a son, her firstborn" (2:7).

In earlier representations Joseph appears young and fresh and beardless. Only as a result of the Marian cult was he completely set aside and given the humble role of a family provider. From then on he is shown exclusively as a kindly old man, bearded, obviously impotent, a celibate spouse.

For three hundred years the Church had evinced no interest in Mary's sexual life later in her marriage.[8] Only the increasing veneration of Mary and the growing cult prompted serious discussion of her virginity. Church teachers such as Tertullian and Ambrose[9] quarreled bitterly over such notions as *vulva reservata* and *uterus clausus*. *Vulva reservata* did not exclude the possibility that Mary had sexual relations later and bore more children. Later, the cult of Mary pushed its idea of *uterus clausus* into general acceptance. From then on it was proclaimed that Mary had never forfeited her virginity, that she is the "perpetual virgin" *(semper virgo)*.[10] This was accepted as dogma at the Lateran Council in A.D. 645. Mary never had any sexual relations, and had no further children. The Church Fathers would not believe what they thought, but thought what they wanted to believe. But a consideration of Mary in the moral context of her own time would lead inevitably to the opposite conclusion. For an Oriental Jewess, marriage and the surrender of virginity were goals as vital as fertility. Sexual abstinence is an invention of the Church in line with the interests of the Roman Empire in the fourth century. Human beings mate; a goddess does nothing of the sort.

Day and Year of Birth

The day of Jesus' birth is unknown. We have the date of December 25 (or the night of December 24–25) in the Church calendar, but this date was certainly arbitrary. Jesus' birthday was not celebrated until the fourth century; before that there was no "Christmas." For three hundred years the Gospel was proclaimed without this holiday.

Ironically, December 25 was originally a pagan holiday. This was the day of the *sol invictus*, the unconquered sun-god, introduced in the third century as an imperial festival to reinforce the idea that the emperor was god.[11] After embracing Christianity, Emperor Constantine turned this pagan holiday into the birthday of the Redeemer.

(In both German and English, the word Sunday demonstrates its derivation. It is the day that the Romans of the Empire had consecrated to the sun-god, *dies dominica*, which was called *dimanche* in French and *domenica* in Italian. The pagan peoples did not observe a day of rest; this is originally a Jewish concept, taken from the creation story in Genesis. It was later adopted by Christians and Muslims.[12]) For centuries, December 25 marked the beginning of the new year; later, for practical reasons, the first day of the following month was chosen.[13]

The Eastern Church also celebrated Jesus' birthday, but observed it on January 6. This date was arrived at in an odd way. Basing themselves on Luke 3:23, which says that Jesus was *about* thirty years old when he began his public ministry, the Church authorities deduced that Jesus was *exactly* thirty when he died, calculating from the day of conception. The day of his death was fixed as April 6th. The date of January 6 allowed for the nine months of pregnancy.

When Quirinius Was Governor of Syria

As regards the year of Jesus' birth, we must acknowledge that if the calendar is correct it is so purely by coincidence. In the sixth century, the Roman monk Dionysius Exiguus fixed the birth of Christ as the starting date of our era. Jesus could have been born a few years after the beginning of our era, but it is far more likely that he was born a few years before.[14]

According to Luke's Gospel, Jesus was born in the year when the Emperor Augustus ordered a census to be taken in Palestine, presumably when Quirinius was governor in Syria.[15]

> Now at this time Caesar Augustus issued a decree for a census of the whole world to be taken. This census—the

first—took place while Quirinius was governor of Syria, and everyone went to his own town to be registered. So Joseph set out for the town of Nazareth in Galilee and traveled up to Judea, to the town of David called Bethlehem, since he was of David's House and line, in order to be registered together with Mary, his betrothed, who was with child. (Luke 2:1–5)

Quirinius is the same Quirinius mentioned in many historical sources, the successor of Quintilius Vara who was crushed by Arminius the Cherischian (presumably in the Teutoburg Forest) in A.D. 9. King Herod the Great ruled all Palestine[16] until his death in A.D. 4. Although he was of course a Roman vassal he had complete authority in his own country. After his death the country was divided among some of his sons, who received the title "Tetrarchs" (four rulers). Phillipus received the northeast: the headwaters of the Jordan and the Golan Heights with the towering Mount Heron. Herod Antipas acquired Galilee, Perea, and a portion of the east Jordan region, including the Dead Sea and the city of Jericho. Archelaus inherited Judea, including the capital Jerusalem. While Archelaus was considered cruel and Herod Antipas sly, Phillipus was judged a good and just ruler. In A.D. 6 Archelaus was deposed by the Romans, and his territory was added to the Roman province of Syria.

The governor of the province was from a senatorial family. He bore the title of *Legatus Augusti* and resided in Damascus. He was the direct superior of the procurator of Judea and his seat was in Caesarea. Whereas the governor of the province had regular legions at his disposal and could deploy them at his discretion, the procurator had only auxiliary troops consisting of half a legion. Of these, four cohorts were stationed in Caesarea and one formed the garrison of the Antonia Fortress in Jerusalem. Heading each cohort was a tribune *(chiliarchos);* the junior officers were called centurions.

Judea had special status, as a kind of autonomous region. This was manifest in the fact that its highest Roman official, the procurator, had to be a knight and was thus equivalent to a proconsul. Coponius was the first procurator, installed by the governor Quirinius in A.D. 6. Pilate was installed as procurator in A.D. 26[17] under the governor Vitellius, who persuaded Emperor Tiberius to dismiss him in A.D. 36.[18]

Quirinius did order a census—not in Galilee, which was ruled by Tetrarch Herod Antipas, but only in Judea, which was directly under Roman rule. Josephus Flavius unequivocally confirms this. It was the only census conducted at that time. This census—the first, according to Luke—took place at the end of A.D. 6 or 7. Its purpose could only have been to give the Roman authorities a listing of all residents so that taxes could be assessed and collected. The Romans wanted a total picture of village populations and income levels; accordingly, no one was to travel lest they go uncounted.

The hypothesis that Jesus was born in A.D. 6 or 7 is not generally accepted since it would mean that he was only twenty-four years old when he was crucified. But the Lucan passage quoted above contains a direct reference to the historical Jesus. Jesus was born a hundred years before Luke wrote his Gospel, so the evangelist must have taken the census as a rough point of reference, simply to indicate the approximate date of Jesus' birth. He also dates the pregnancies of both the mother of Jesus and the mother of John the Baptist in the time of the reign of Herod the Great (1:5–25), disregarding the ten-year interval between Herod's death and the census conducted under Quirinius.

King Herod's Infanticide

The infanticide described in Matthew's Gospel might provide a further clue to the year of birth, but this would mean that Jesus must have been born by 4 B.C., the year of Herod's death.

> After Jesus had been born at Bethlehem in Judea during the reign of King Herod, some wise men came to Jerusalem from the east. "Where is the infant King of the Jews?" they asked. "We saw his star as it rose and have come to do him homage." When King Herod heard this he was perturbed, and so was the whole of Jerusalem. (Matt. 2:1–4)

The Gospel goes on to say that Herod had all male children in Bethlehem up to the age of two butchered as a precautionary measure, and that the Holy Family escaped only by means of a precipitate flight to Egypt. This story must be relegated to the realm of legend. The parallels to other ancient myths, the birth of Oedipus, for example, are all too obvious. Moses is also said to have been miraculously rescued from the wicked Pharaoh. The slaughter of the innocents of Bethlehem was viewed as the fulfillment of the words of the Old Testament prophet Jeremiah, "Thus speaks Yahweh: A voice is heard in Ramah, lamenting and weeping bitterly: it is Rachel weeping for her children, refusing to be comforted for her children, because they are no more" (Jer. 31:15).

There is no known record of the mass infanticide that Herod allegedly ordered in Bethlehem. Any such event would undoubtedly have been recorded by the historians of the time, especially Josephus Flavius, who described Herod and his crimes in great detail. It is also striking that no evangelist except Matthew mentions any such event, although Jesus only narrowly escaped death. Even Luke, the only one to whom Jesus' childhood and adolescence are of any importance,[19] omits it.

Herod, who has gone down in history as an unscrupulous villain despite extraordinary abilities, would certainly have been capable of such a mass slaughter. He had two of his wives and three of his sons executed. Emperor Augustus is said to have quipped that he "would prefer to be a pig than a child in the house of Herod." (This might also allude to the fact that the Jewish religion forbids eating pork, so that Herod would have hesitated more before slaughtering a pig than a human being.)

Herod had his sons Alexander and Aristobulus strangled in 7 B.C., after discovering, just in time, that one of them had planned an insurrection. Conceivably, "This massacre passed into contemporary memory as the Slaughter of the Innocents,"[20] and later the legend spoke of a "mass murder" of children according to which Herod, in connection with the execution of his sons, also had 300 of their followers (mostly youths) lynched by the rabble in Jericho.

Thus if Herod is considered in relation to the birth year of Jesus, the year 7 B.C. offers a point of reference. But Jesus would then have had to have been born four years before the beginning of the modern era, since 4 B.C. is the year of Herod's death.

The Star of Bethlehem

The "star of Bethlehem" mentioned in Matthew can also be used to determine the year of Jesus' birth. There had in fact been a very striking stellar constellation. This phenomenon had already been investigated by the astronomer Johannes Kepler

(1571–1635). About every 800 years a constellation appears in which the planets Jupiter and Saturn appear in the same degree of longitude *(conjunctio Magna)* within the configuration Pisces, so that they appear to be one huge bright star. Kepler had determined that such a conjunction occurred in the year 7 B.C.; the exactness of his calculation has been confirmed by modern science.

The star, of course, did not stand over Bethlehem, much less a particular structure such as a stable. But we can assume that the constellation was particularly visible in the Mediterranean area and in the Near East, and it must have deeply impressed the people living there. Matthew, who has the appearance of the constellation coincide with the birth of Christ, must have met people who talked about the event even though they themselves could not have witnessed it.

If Jesus' birth did coincide with that conjunction of stars, he would have been born in 7 B.C.; this would be consistent with the date of the so-called slaughter of the innocents. But it would mean that Jesus lived to the age of approximately thirty-seven.[21]

The Birthplace

The place of Jesus' birth is as uncertain as the year. From the pulpits it is proclaimed, especially at Christmas, that Jesus was born in Bethlehem, a small village in Judea, though prevailing opinion holds that he was born in Nazareth. Capernaum, on Lake Gennesaret, cannot be ruled out, for several reasons. Unlike Nazareth, Capernaum is known to have existed as a town in Galilee. It also had a synagogue; Jesus spoke there early in his public activity (Mark 1:21). According to Mark 2:1 and 3:20, Jesus "went home again" to Capernaum, where his relatives, i.e., his mother and his siblings, were located (3:21). Matthew 9:1 says Jesus traveled by boat to "his own town," meaning Capernaum, and he asserts that Jesus moved from Nazareth to Capernaum (4:13).

Paul and Mark, the two oldest New Testament authors, never heard Bethlehem given as Jesus' birthplace. Matthew and Luke do accept Bethlehem as the birthplace, but their versions of the circumstances surrounding the birth are contradictory. John also must have heard Bethlehem cited as the birthplace, since the accounts of Matthew and Luke were completed when his Gospel was written. But he distanced himself from them.[22]

That Bethlehem was given so little mention in the New Testament is significant. Being a Jewish town, it would have been a much better quarter from which to proclaim the risen Christ than would a town in Galilee. Isaiah speaks with utter contempt of the "Galilee of the nations [pagans],"[23] and Nazareth was the backwoods of Galilee, so to speak. A Galilean fisherman who was invited to become a disciple asked bluntly, "From Nazareth? Can anything good come from that place?" (John 1:46).

At the Feast of Tabernacles, when some people asserted that Jesus was the Messiah, others shouted, "Would the Christ be from Galilee? Does not scripture say that the Christ must be descended from David and come from the town of Bethlehem?" (John 7:41–43). Paul, Mark, and John accept that Jesus comes from the northeastern province of Galilee, not Judea (Mark 1:9; John 1:45). He was from a Galilean family, born in Galilee, and, apart from being baptized in what is today west Jordan and entering into Jerusalem where he was arrested and executed, he was active only in Galilee. His followers were likewise Galileans.

The reason Matthew and Luke gave Bethlehem, the city of David, as Jesus' birthplace is obvious: Bethlehem is the city in which the Messiah would be born someday, according to the prophets (Mic. 5:1–2). The Messiah had to be a descendant of David. Kolping writes, "The differences between Matthew's and Luke's accounts of the birth suggest that Bethlehem was cited for reasons of dogma, not knowledge."[24] Matthew cites Micah to support his conviction that Bethlehem was the birthplace of Jesus: "for this is what the prophet wrote: And you, Bethlehem, in the land of Judah, you are by no means least among the leaders of Judah, for out of you will come a leader who will shepherd my people Israel" (Matt. 2:6).

There is one flaw, however. Micah is not referring to the well-known Bethlehem, only fifteen kilometers southwest of Jerusalem, but to Bethlehem-Ephratha, a small town northwest of Jerusalem near Rama: "But you, [Bethlehem] Ephratha, the least of the clans of Judah, out of you will be born for me the one who is to rule over Israel" (Mic. 5:1–2).

Luke has Mary and Joseph arrive in Bethlehem from Nazareth, so that the Messiah can come into the world there in fulfillment of the prophesy. Matthew assumes that Jesus' parents have always lived in Bethlehem; consequently, Jesus is born not in a stable but in his parents' house (2:10–11).

Matthew writes nothing about the first weeks of his infancy, merely noting that the family cannot remain in Bethlehem. The same angel of the Lord who barely a year before appeared to Mary in a dream to apprise her of her pregnancy now appears to Joseph in a dream and warns him of King Herod's murderous intentions. Thereupon Joseph decides to flee with his family.

According to Matthew's account, all this happened immediately after Jesus' birth and was related to the adoration of the newborn infant by the Wise Men from the East (which put Herod on the infant's track). Some theologians, relying on the apocryphal gospel "Pseudo-Matthew," date the visit of the Wise Men and Herod's murder campaign two years later. This would imply that Jesus spent his first two years in Bethlehem.

The family flees to Egypt. When it returns to Israel another prophesy is fulfilled: "There was a vine: you uprooted it from Egypt; to plant it, you drove out other nations" (Ps. 80:8). Actually, according to Matthew, the Holy Family returns to Judea after receiving news of Herod's death. Upon arrival, they learn that Herod's son Archelaus has succeeded his father. They fear him also, and return to Galilee where another of Herod's sons rules. But they apparently see no danger in Herod Antipas. Thenceforth the family lives "in a town called Nazareth." So according to Matthew, Jesus and his parents were not from Galilee, but merely traveled there.

Luke's account is entirely different. He states that Joseph had to go to Bethlehem for a mundane reason (the census). The matter assumes significance because Mary was in a late stage of pregnancy and accompanied her husband on the journey. It was as a result of these two coincidences that Jesus was born in Bethlehem, the town of David. Subsequently the couple returned home as quickly as possible. Mary must have been confined to bed for seven days after the birth; the infant was then circumcised and given the name Jesus. Since they were near the Holy City they did not miss the opportunity to visit the Temple in order to perform the ritual acts prescribed by the Mosaic Law.

The ritual waiting periods are described in Leviticus 12:1–8. For forty days after the birth of a son (or twice as long after the birth of a daughter), a woman may not touch anything consecrated or set foot in the Temple.[25] Then she must offer an animal sacrifice, usually a one-year-old lamb. (Luke's mention of the sacrifice of two pigeons is to draw attention to the poverty of the Holy Family.)[26]

Jesus would thus have been barely six weeks old when his parents made the return trip to Galilee with him.

The charming descriptions of the journey from Nazareth to Bethlehem, the birth in the manger, and the return to Nazareth are nothing more than a beautiful legend. Nor does the alleged political background of the nativity story stand up to historical scrutiny, regardless of whether the census ordered by Emperor Augustus took place in Galilee or in Samaria and Judea, the regions added to the province of Syria.

Luke's narrative revolves around events whose real course was quite different from his version. At the time that a census was being conducted in Judea by imperial order, the Roman authorities in Galilee were ruthlessly persecuting the population in order to collect taxes ("the great census"). To do this they employed primarily Jewish help, so-called tax collectors. This provoked a revolt by Zealots, led by Judas of Gamala. The revolt was crushed by the troops of the Roman commander in chief in Syria. A large number of Galilean villages were destroyed, and two thousand followers of Judas of Gamala ended up on the cross—he himself managed to flee.

The boy Jesus, at that time thirteen or fourteen years old, must have been aware of these events. Was his father perhaps one of the partisans who fell into the hands of the legionnaires and were crucified? Lapide does not consider this improbable, and it could also be the reason why there is no trace of Joseph in the Gospel, even during Jesus' childhood. His fate had to be hushed up at all costs so Jesus would not himself come into the Zealot orbit.[27]

But Lapide has also proposed another alternative to the Christian interpretation of the Christmas story, obtained by "brushing it against the Greek text": Joseph set out not on a journey, but in flight. As one who was close to the Galilean patriots and had signaled his opposition to Rome by refusing to pay the tax, he fled with his pregnant betrothed to a cave, a typical hideout for an insurgent. Jesus was born in the cave (not in a manger, as the Vulgate translation erroneously states). If there was indeed a manger, the implication is that the fleeing parents abandoned the infant there, where they could assume that he would be discovered and cared for by shepherds.[28]

Given that Bethlehem is not Jesus' birthplace, that Jesus came from Galilee, that there was a Galilean town called Nazareth, and that—according to the still prevailing exegetical interpretation—

all the Gospels and the Acts associate Jesus with Nazareth (only Paul is completely silent on this point), Nazareth might perforce be regarded as Jesus' birthplace. But in comparison to Capernaum, Nazareth plays no role at all in Jesus' life. Many scholars contend that a locality called Nazareth or one that might have been confused with Nazareth did not exist in Jesus' time, but was invented later. Josephus Flavius had mapped Galilee, so to speak, and identified sixty-three communities, none called Nazareth. Either he overlooked Nazareth, perhaps because it was insignificant, or Nazareth found its way into the Gospels later, at a time when it really existed.

The Nazarite and the Nazar Prophesy of the Branch

The epithet "Nazarene," it is argued, can refer to something besides a person hailing from Nazareth. The original Greek text mentioned Jesus "the *Nazoraios,*" which supposedly became first "the Nazarene" and later "of Nazareth." But *Nazoraios* is actually a dialectical variant of "Nazarite." Schweitzer writes,

> In the time after Paul a quarrel arose among Christians for and against the ascetic way of life. The followers of abstinence were called after the old Jewish Nazarites. . . . In no case did the expressions originally have anything to do with the locality Nazareth, otherwise the name would have read "Nazarethans" or something similar. Since Jesus' ascetic bent naturally made him a Nazarite, he was named accordingly. This phrase is fixed in the Acts of the Apostles. They speak of Christians as Nazorene and also call Jesus a Nazorene. Later the "anti-ascetic groups" endeavored to eradicate Nazaritism within Christianity. For this purpose they created a "new, quasi-historical foundation" for the expression and had Jesus come from a locality Nazareth.[29]

In the Old Testament it is the mighty Samson who is presented as one of the Nazarites (Judg. 13:5–7). They were the "consecrated of God," ascetics, who practiced abstinence in eating and drinking, drank no wine, and would not allow their hair to be cut. This description, of course, would apply less to Jesus than to John the

Baptist, who led an ascetic life in the desert and preached discipline and repentance. Nevertheless it is conceivable that Jesus had been dubbed a Nazarite because he was originally a disciple of the Baptist, had come from his school, so to speak, and succeeded him. Bultmann writes,

> Possibly the Mandaean Gnostic sect which emerged later is a development of this Baptist (John's) sect, and perhaps many of the Mandaean conceptions go back to the beginning of the movement. It is worth noting that the Mandaeans called themselves "Nazarenes," and that Jesus is often so called in the early Christian tradition. Since this epithet cannot be derived from the name of his own village, Nazareth, and since the early Christian tradition has preserved the recollection that Jesus was baptized by John, it might be concluded that Jesus originally belonged to the sect of the Baptist, that the Jesus-sect was an offshoot of the John-sect.[30]

The term Nazarite could also be applied to Jesus' brother James. James was the leading intellect of the original Christian community in Jerusalem,[31] having joined the disciples gathered there awaiting the return of their executed rabbi (Gal. 2:9; 1 Cor. 15:7; Acts 1:14). Eusebius describes him thus:

> He was sanctified from his mother's womb. He drank neither wine nor any other alcoholic beverage, he never ate food from the animal kingdom, and he never let his hair be shorn. He never anointed himself with oil, and never took a bath. No one but he was allowed access to the Sanctuary because he wore not woolen clothes, but a linen garment. He went alone to the Temple, where he could be seen on his knees imploring God's forgiveness of the people; the skin of his knees became as hard as that of a camel.[32]

Thus the designation of Jesus as a Nazarite could possibly be based on his kinship with James and the assumption that both had come from the same town.

There is another explanation for the epithet Nazarite. According to both John 1:45–46 and Matthew 2:23, the prophets had proclaimed that the Messiah would come from Nazareth. This gives rise to suspicion, since the prophets themselves make no mention of Nazareth. Matthew's assumption is all the more astonishing because in the first chapter of his Gospel he explicitly commits himself to Bethlehem, citing the prophet Micah. One might thus conclude that the reference in the second chapter of Matthew is not to the town of Nazareth at all. The same must also apply to the author of the Johannine Gospel. Exegetes have sought to find out which prophets Matthew and John had in mind in connection with Nazareth, and have identified likely passages in Isaiah and Jeremiah: "A shoot springs from the stock of Jesse, a scion thrusts from his roots: on him the spirit of Yahweh rests, a spirit of wisdom and insight, a spirit of counsel and power, a spirit of knowledge and of the fear of Yahweh" (Isa. 11:1–2). The stem of Jesse of which Isaiah speaks is the royal House of David since Jesse is the father of King David. A branch is to originate from this house, it will bear fruit and from this fruit will come forth the Messiah.

The passage from Jeremiah in question reads, "See, the days are coming—it is Yahweh who speaks—when I will raise a virtuous Branch for David, who will reign as true king and be wise, practicing honesty and integrity in the land" (Jer. 23:5).

Ben-Chorin[33] points out that the growth that emerges from a root is called *nezer* in Hebrew, hence the reference is to a shoot. But the word *nezer* also means twig, branch, or offspring. Ezekiel 17:3–4 speaks of a twig (the tender top branch) that a huge eagle breaks off from a cedar in Lebanon in order to carry it to Jerusalem where it takes root. Hence the church hymn reads: "Lo, how a rose ever blooming/From tender stem hath sprung." Thus it is quite possible that the Nazarene received this name in a linguistic detour.

Jesus' actual birthplace—Capernaum, Nazareth, or elsewhere in Galilee—is just as impossible to determine as the day and year of his birth. Küng[34] writes, "The stories as part of the proclamation and as professions of faith are meant to make known *not primarily historical*, but saving truth: the message of the salvation of men in Jesus."

At any rate Jesus was not born in Bethlehem, and no one calls him "Jesus of Bethlehem." Nor was he born—unless by pure coincidence—in the year that began our era, but at the earliest seven years before or at the latest six years after. A more precise determination is not possible.

Five

FOREBEARS AND FAMILY

The names of Jesus' parents are common knowledge; the assumption is that they were called Mary and Joseph. But these names are not conclusively established; only the Gospels of Matthew and Luke name both parents individually. Paul mentions neither the mother nor the father by name; Mark mentions Mary only, and John speaks of Joseph and the "mother of Jesus."

The Genealogies in the Gospels of Matthew and Luke

The Gospels of Matthew and Luke are the only ones to attach importance to a descent from the House of David. The purpose of their genealogies (Matt. 1:1–16; Luke 3:24–38) is to present Joseph as a descendant of King David. But this is illogical; if the descent from David is through Joseph, the thesis of Mary's virginity is no longer tenable.[1]

Some people who appear in the genealogy are completely inconsistent with puritanical Church teaching.[2] For example, a Rahab is mentioned. Rahab is called the "harlot of Jericho" (Josh. 2:1–2). The servants of the aged King David provided him with a damsel when he was constantly cold, to warm him in bed (1 Kings 1:1–3). And King Solomon, finally, a son of David and thus allegedly a forebear of Jesus, was famous not only for the greatness of his wisdom but also for the size of his harem.

David died in 961 B.C. By Jesus' time, there was probably no one who could claim descent from King David. Even a devout Christian probably finds it difficult to imagine Jesus as a prince in disguise. At all events, the legendary character of the genealogies is obvious.[3] The contradictions begin with Joseph's father: In Matthew he is called James, in Luke, Eli.

Family Life and Tensions

In Mark Jesus is simply presented as "the son of Mary"; Joseph is not mentioned. In contrast to Matthew and Luke, Mark makes no effort to prove Jesus' descent from the House of David; and only two passages (10:48 and 11:10) allude to it indirectly. Apart from the absent father, Mark presents a completely normal family situation: Jesus has four brothers and several sisters. When he preaches in the local synagogue, the people poke fun at him: "This is the carpenter, surely, the son of Mary, the brother of James and Joseph and Jude and Simon? His sisters, too, are they not here with us?" (Mark 6:3).[4]

So one of the brothers is called Judas. It is difficult to imagine that anyone would name Jesus' brother Judas if this brother had not really existed. The clear account of Jesus' siblings concurs with Matthew (3:55–56). Jesus' mother must have borne many children in the early years of her marriage, obeying the Mosaic Law "Be fruitful, multiply" (Gen. 1:28).

In any case, it cannot be rationally argued that Jesus was an only child, though this is still maintained by some people. Such assertions are outgrowths of the cult of Mary, who was to be presented as asexually as possible, despite Luke 2:7, where Jesus is called Mary's firstborn.[5] Jesus' brothers and sisters are turned into male or female cousins or other more distant relatives.[6] Apologists point out the Hebrew language does not differentiate among brothers, cousins, and stepsiblings. That is correct; but the evangelists wrote in Greek, which draws these distinctions very clearly. The word *adelphos* used by the evangelists can designate only a blood brother. Rudolph Pesch writes, "Unbiased exegesis allows only the conclusion that in Mark 6:3 the names of the four blood brothers of Jesus and the existence of blood sisters are historically attested."[7]

From Mark we learn that Jesus was a carpenter, or at any rate a craftsman, perhaps a cabinetmaker. Cabinetmakers were esteemed very highly and considered clever. Anyone wrestling with a difficult problem might ask, "Is there a cabinetmaker here, or the son of a cabinetmaker who can answer the question?"[8] Jesus was not an academic, but probably an autodidact; Luke's legend of the twelve-year-old in the temple was probably intended to emphasize this. Otherwise nothing is known of Jesus' childhood and adolescence, aside from a single passage in Luke (2:52) where it is mentioned that he "increased in wisdom, in stature." Nothing much seems to have happened during his childhood.

Many attempts have been made to explain why Mark makes no mention of Jesus' father—a truly striking omission in view of the preeminent position of a Jewish patriarch. But the Catholic theologian Kolping and the Protestant theologian Stauffer consider it conceivable that Mark 6:3 is "defamatory." Both[9] conclude, based on other texts, that the evangelists were trying to counter the accusation that Jesus came from an "immoral union." Stauffer suspects that "all kinds of gossip about Mary" came from the Jerusalem Baptist sect, hence from the followers of John the Baptist.

Despite these alleged attempts on the part of the evangelists, some authors have drawn a very far-reaching conclusion from Mark 6:3: A permanent bond between Mary and Joseph never existed, and Joseph broke off his engagement after Mary informed him of her pregnancy. Hence Jesus was illegitimate. "We were not born of prostitution," Jesus' interlocutors retort (John 8:41). This version finds some support in Matthew's Gospel: "His mother Mary was betrothed to Joseph; but before they came to live together she was found to be with child through the Holy Spirit. Her husband Joseph, being a man of honor and wanting to spare her publicity, decided to divorce her informally" (1:18-20).

Joseph's situation is even worse according to the apocryphal gospels, the Proto-gospel of John and the so-called Pseudo-gospel of Matthew. He wants to die when he learns that Mary is pregnant; he cannot believe her explanation. Women, friends of Mary who happened to witness the scene, confirm that she has not been unfaithful, that God worked through the angel. Poor Joseph, however, cannot bring himself to believe such farfetched explanations: "Why do ye mock and seek to make me believe that an angel of the Lord hath got her with child? Is it not that a man hath called himself an Angel of the Lord and deceived her?"[10]

After the rupture, the story continues, Mary married another man and had the other children by him. But this is all speculation. Jesus' first sermon did not contain any reference to his father, but by then Joseph had already been dead for a long time and no one remembered him. Such speculations exist only because of one premise, written into the Gospels of Matthew and Luke, propagated by the Church Fathers, and finally raised to a dogma: Jesus was not born naturally, but came into the world through a virgin birth. Craveri[11] declares,

> Rather than recognize the simple fact that the whole tradition of the birth of Jesus is legend and that no shadow of marital infidelity ever troubled the peaceful union of Joseph and Mary, they accept adultery on her part and they titillate themselves in a search for the guilty man, often to the accompaniment of vulgarly tendentious allegations, insults and slanderous nonsense.

It must be assumed that Jesus lived with his family up to early manhood. The family was certainly one of those extended families customary among Oriental Jews. As the oldest brother, he took over his father's carpentry shop (Mark 6:3), and may thus have substantially contributed to the family's support. At the same time, he probably made an intensive study of the Hebrew Bible. The family was disappointed when he gave up the trade he had learned in order to work as a healer (psychotherapist) and teacher; they would have been much more pleased had he stuck to his original trade. Nor did they think much of the smooth talk that he was wont to deliver, or the miracles he performed. There were spellbinders and miracle workers aplenty in Galilee and elsewhere.

The family must have also found it painful to see their son and brother mocked in his hometown. Jesus is said to have responded with a smile and the famous phrase, "A prophet is only despised in his own country, among his own relations and in his own house" (Mark 6:4).

But it becomes more than mere mockery; the situation grows serious. Herod Antipas, who has just ordered the arrest of John the Baptist because of his inflammatory speeches, pays attention to the Nazarene. In order to avoid an arrest (Mark 3:6), the relatives declare Jesus crazy and try to confine him: "He went home again, and once more such a crowd collected that they could not even have a meal. When his relatives heard of this, they set to take charge of him, convinced he was out of his mind" (Mark 3:20–21).

He gets out of his predicament, partly because even the scribes pronounce him mentally unfit and this is a legal judgment: "This was because they were saying: 'An unclean spirit is in him'" (Mark 3:30). Thenceforth Jesus will have nothing to do with his relatives—he leaves them. When his mother and siblings make an attempt at a reconciliation, they are not even received:

> His mother and brothers now arrived and, standing outside, sent in a message asking for him. A crowd was sitting around him at the time the message was passed to him. "Your mother and brothers and sisters are outside asking for you." He replied, "Who are my mother and my brothers?" And looking around at those sitting in a circle about him, he said, "Here are my mother and my brothers." (Mark 3:31–34)

Jesus' intransigence toward his family seems to have intensified later. He expected his disciples to share his radicalism on the subject. This is handed down by both Matthew and Luke: "Do not suppose that I have come to bring peace to the earth: it is not peace I have come to bring but a sword. For I have come to set a man against his father, a daughter against her mother, a daughter-in-law against her mother-in-law. A man's enemies will be those of his own household" (Matt. 10:34–36). Luke puts it even more crudely: "If any man comes to me without hating his father, mother, wife, children, brothers, sisters, yes and his own life too, he cannot be my disciple" (14:26–27). Only conflicts in his own family can explain such statements. They are the more difficult to understand in relation to the Fourth Commandment: "Honor your father and your mother so that you may have a long life in the land that Yahweh your God has given to you" (Exod. 20:12).

An ecclesiastical explanation of the passages cited above says that Jesus did not intend to sow family discord, but referred to the bond of faith that must be even stronger than blood ties. This strikes me as limp.

It must not be overlooked that Mary is seldom mentioned in the Gospels, even though she allegedly joined her son and his disciples (John 2:12). No textual passage testifies to any special mother love on Jesus' part. On the other hand, several passages reveal a cold and distant relationship between Jesus and his mother.

At the wedding at Cana, Jesus publicly humiliates his mother. According to the one Gospel account, John, it is a seemingly unimportant village wedding; it was probably that of one of Jesus' brothers or sisters. Jesus, who was still at the very beginning of his public activity, was expressly invited to this festive occasion with his disciples. The mother's presence is taken for granted. She seems to be the hostess and housewife; there is talk of the servants to whom she has given instructions. Her son Jesus orders them to see to it that wine is served, and an embarrassing clash takes place between mother and son. It is only thanks to the mother's submissiveness that an explosive incident is avoided: "When they ran out of wine, since the wine provided for the wedding was all finished, the mother of Jesus said to him; 'They have no wine.' Jesus said, 'Woman, why turn to me? My hour has not come yet'" (John 2:3–5). Ben-Chorin[12] notes, "If a word of Jesus is authentic, it is this harsh and obviously unjustified reproachful turn against his mother whom he publicly humiliated. For who could have invented such an invective?"

Jesus never gave his mother an affectionate or even respectful word.[13] The only form of address he used was *gynae*. For him she was merely the one who bore him, the "woman," as Luther translated it. Even on the cross, the tone of the son to his mother is reserved, at least according to the evangelist: "Woman, this is your son" (John 19:26).

Salcia Landmann writes, "How slight was the bond between Jesus and his mother, and how little the historical Jesus is suited to serve as a model for a religious Mother cult could not be clearer."[14] One further conclusion must be drawn in this connection: If Mary had conceived her son in a miraculous way the relationship between mother and son would surely have been different from that described in the Gospels.

Six

JESUS' STRANGENESS ENDURES

WE can assume that Jesus really existed, but we know virtually nothing about him. Both the traditional images and those of the contemporary Jesus cult are full of clichés: Jesus, the accessible God; the lovely child with curly hair; the son of a virgin; the ever present, only true friend; the Good Shepherd, energetic, resolute and yet infinitely mild; my sweet Lord; Jesus Christ Superstar.

The theological writer Adolph Holl sees Jesus as an outsider who keeps disreputable company, consorting with prisoners and other malcontents and avoiding those who are comfortable and complacent. By bestowing honors and titles on him, the Church made this sinister figure into a respectable citizen.[1] Hans Küng finds no objection to the provocative title of Holl's book *Jesus in Bad Company*, but distances himself from its content, though his own portrait of Jesus bears some resemblance to Holl's.

> Jesus was anything but a conventional type. His way of life was not what is usually described as a "career." His life-style in some respects resembled that of the hippies.

... Although he was the son of a carpenter and apparently himself also a carpenter he did not follow any occupation. Instead, he led an unsettled wandering life, ate, drank, prayed and slept quite frequently in the open air. He was a man who had left his native country and cut himself off from his family. . . . Jesus did nothing for his livelihood. According to the Gospel accounts, he was supported by friends and a group of women cared for him. . . . Was there not something unworldly, fanatical, almost clownish about him?[2]

The more one knows about the Nazarene, the more he defies judgment in the personal sphere. His figure is almost wholly enigmatic, like a statue, lofty, venerable, remote. Apart from Gethsemane where his fear and dejection bring him closer to us on a human level, his reserve dominates. It is difficult even to imagine Jesus breaking into a hearty laugh or telling a Jewish joke. Did he ever gossip, run wild, or, in Helmut Thielicke's words, "swing to the music at a wedding?" Of all that we know nothing.

Speculation on His Appearance

Nothing is known about the Nazarene's appearance.[3] He may have looked much older than he was: "You are not fifty yet, and you have seen Abraham!" (John 8:57). The various texts from the prophets or psalms that were later applied to Jesus make him out to have been everything from unprepossessing to a towering beauty: "See, my servant will prosper, he shall be lifted up, exalted, rise to great heights. As the crowds were appalled at seeing him— so disfigured did he look that he seemed no longer human. . . . Without beauty, without majesty" (Isa. 52:13–14; 53:2). But "Of all men you are the most handsome, your lips are moist with grace, for God has blessed you for ever" (Ps. 45:2).

In the Middle Ages, Jesus' height was assumed to have been 3 times the Palestinian measure of length, i.e., 1.66 m or 5 feet 5 inches. The fourteenth-century *Codex laurentianus* estimates 3 Florentine hands, which would be 1.75 m or 5 feet 7 inches.[4] Jews were strictly prohibited from making images, not only of God, but also of the human figure. Jesus was first portrayed by the European Christian communities. The earliest image to have been preserved is a fresco in the Domitilla catacomb in Rome, painted in the first half of the fourth century.⁵

In the Gospel accounts, John the Baptist appears as a country bumpkin, dressed in camel's hair, feeding on wild honey and locusts (Matt. 3:1–5). Jesus, by contrast, must have attached some importance to externals. Stauffer writes,

> His clothing was deliberately inconspicuous, neither plush nor poor (Luke 7:25; John 19:23). He wore a sleeveless undergarment with a belt (Mark 6:8; John 19:23), the customary cloak (Luke 8:45), sandals (Mark 6:9), and on his wanderings he carried a staff (Mark 6:8). The only detail we learn is that his tunic was seamless, woven throughout like a high priest's chiton. Jesus may have worn a white headdress as was customary in ancient Palestine, tied with a string and hanging down the shoulder in the back.⁶

This is sheer speculation but perhaps one or more details have some claim to probability.

No Ascetic

Anticonsumerists and ascetics would find it difficult to cite Jesus as a model. Mark 1:12–13, Matthew 4:1–2, and Luke 4:1–2 all agree that Jesus spent forty days fasting in the desert, but this must not be taken literally. The number forty is symbolic, and fasting is an old Semitic custom: Abstinence from certain foods (meat, for example) was thought to promote self-discipline. Honey and locusts were allowed—roasted locusts are even said to be a delicacy.⁷

The frequent mentions of drinking and eating in the Gospels are striking. Jesus himself reports that people called him a glutton and a drunkard (Matt. 11:19; Luke 7:34). The wine, incidentally, was resinated and highly sweetened, so headaches and hangovers must have been inevitable aftereffects. On one occasion he was reproached for his disciples' gluttony and reminded that the disciples of both John the Baptist and the Pharisees fasted. Jesus rejected the reproach with a parable: "Surely the bridegroom's attendants would never think of fasting while the bridegroom⁸ is still with them?" (Mark 2:19). Küng comments, "For the Baptist the baptism of penance was a typical sign in action; for Jesus and his message the sign took the form of feasts held in the atmosphere of joy, in which people celebrated their common membership of the future kingdom."[9]

Jesus seems not to have abstained even from contact with women. Luke describes the scene in the house of Simon the Pharisee where Jesus lets a woman serve him. Luke calls her a sinner, but Jesus condones her approaching him though it is too much for the otherwise tolerant host: "Then he turned to the woman. 'Simon,' he said, 'you see this woman? I came into your house, and you poured no water over my feet, but she has poured out her tears over my feet and wiped them away with her hair' " (Luke 7:44–45). This erotic scene can be seen in many remarkable paintings. The "beautiful sinner" is usually identified as Mary Magdalene, though Luke says nothing to support this.

Luke is apparently using his portrayal of Jesus to put down the petty moralists of his time and all times. Church teaching, always hostile to matters of the flesh, pays no joyous homage to the erotic in this incident but presents it as an example of repentant sin, although the woman whom Jesus allowed to anoint him is not a sinner according to Mark and Matthew. In John she is not Mary from Magdala, but the respected Mary of Bethany, the sister of Lazarus whom Jesus is said to have raised from the dead.[10] Jesus is equally tolerant in his conversation with the Samaritan woman (John 4:18) at Jacob's Well, though the woman had had five husbands, and was then living with a man not her lawful husband.

From the outset, the Church was based more on the Pauline idea of chastity than on Jesus' tolerance. A prime example of Jesus' attitude is his behavior toward the adulteress who was condemned to death and about to be stoned. "If there is one of you who has not sinned, let him be the first to throw a stone at her. . . . Neither do I condemn you, go away and don't sin any more" (John 8:7–11). Augustine saw fit to reprimand Jesus for this "excessive leniency."[11] Never has an adulteress escaped with so mild an admonition from the Church;[12] nor is there any indication that the woman followed his injunction.

Although ecclesiastical tradition declares Jesus' sexuality a taboo subject and represents him as a male virgin,[13] the question of Jesus' relations to the opposite sex was not always considered unseemly or un-Christian. Even some who preached the divinity of Christ in sacred Scriptures described Jesus as no different from other men in regard to sexuality. In the gospel of Philip we read, "The women always wandered with the Lord; Mary, his mother, her sister and Magdalene, who became her companions. The Savior loved Mary Magdalene more than all the disciples and he often kissed her on the mouth. The other disciples came to her and reproached her. To him they said: 'Why do you love her more than us all?' "[14]

Ben-Chorin is convinced that Jesus was married. In his parables he favors a bridegroom as protagonist, or he himself is the bridegroom (Matt. 9:15; Luke 5:34). This leads to the conclusion that "he himself had experienced a nuptial hour."

> Jesus was addressed as Rabbi by his disciples and the large community of his following. An unmarried rabbi is unthinkable. We must ask ourselves: if Jesus had been unmarried would not his disciples have questioned him about this omission? Would not his foes have charged that he had not fulfilled in his own life the first of the rabbinic catalogue of duties, "Be fruitful and multiply?" We must rid ourselves of the idea that a married Jesus would in any way have been shocking to those around him. The very opposite is true.[15]

I find these suggestions convincing, the more so as Jesus could hardly have expressed himself so favorably on the subject of marriage if he himself had remained a bachelor: "Have you not read that the creator from the beginning made them male and female and that he said: This is why a man must leave father and mother, and cling to his wife and the two become one body?" (Matt. 19:4–5). Ben-Chorin imaginatively suggests that Jesus' young bride remained at home with the children during the brief period of his public activity, whereas her widowed mother-in-law joined the band of disciples.

Neither do the Gospels mention the wives and children of the disciples, though a retinue composed mostly of male celibates would have been strange indeed. That the Gospels contain no reference to Jesus' marriage does not disprove its existence; on the contrary. A normal marital status would have been taken for granted and hence had no need to be mentioned. Voluntary celibacy, in the Jewish world of that time, would have ostracized a young man and disqualified him for the honorary title of Rabbi.

Martin Luther, who also assumed that Jesus was married "in

order to participate completely in human nature,"[16] guessed that his wife was Mary Magdalene. This conclusion is supported by the fact that Mary Magdalene plays an outstanding role in all four Gospels. Contrary to one current opinion, she is not presented as a prostitute, so it is safe to assume she was married. The idea of a single woman wandering around Palestine at that time, unaccompanied or as part of a rabbi's entourage, is inconceivable.

The high regard that Mary Magdalene enjoyed at the end of Jesus' ministry is firmly established. In the Gospels she is always the first woman mentioned. Whereas the disciples all fled the moment Jesus was arrested, Mary Magdalene accompanied him to Golgotha, and, according to John, even stood at the foot of the cross. It was Mary Magdalene who discovered the empty tomb (Matt. 28:1–2; John 20:1). According to Mark and John, the risen Jesus appeared first to her. All this could indicate that she was Jesus' wife, and that the woman Jesus kissed so often according to the Phillipus gospel was married to him. If so, the life she led before her marriage is immaterial, even if she had been a sinner!

That the Church invariably presents Jesus as single may perhaps be traced back to the apostle Paul—a strange character indeed—who praised his own bachelorhood and sought to make it a model for good Christians (1 Cor. 7:1–2). We have some clues as to his personality, but any idea as to Jesus' character is pure conjecture. All we know is that he is not on record as having said anything against the sensual aspects of marriage, sexuality in general, or female sexuality in particular.

A Champion of Social Justice?

Jesus' message was first and foremost a penitential homily proclaiming the approaching kingdom of God, modeled on that of John the Baptist. Like John, he evidently demanded repentance but ranked love equally highly. Deschner's image of Jesus corresponds on a deep emotional level to my own: "A tendency toward extreme radicalism seems to have marked him: a struggle against cultic worship and feigned piety, the self-righteous and the judgmental, oppression of the weak, exploitation of the poor, violence, revenge and murder."[17] But was all that really so? Do we know enough about the person of Jesus to accept such a picture unreservedly? Does he not in the end—as always, when we think we have succeeded in "knowing" him—elude our judgment?

Jesus' parables and actions show a certain consistency, conveying a message of God's unconditional mercy to all regardless of status or a previously sinful life. He is certainly no conformist: "I did not come to call the virtuous, but sinners" (Mark 2:17). He allegedly felt at home on the fringes of society; the very fact that he was generally sympathetic to women was unseemly at that time. Jesus even went a step beyond that by defending concubines and adulteresses. He promised more forgiveness to prostitutes than to the chaste: "For this reason I tell you that her sins, her many sins, must have been forgiven her, or she would not have shown such great love. It is the man who is forgiven little who shows little love" (Luke 7:47–48).

That Jesus befriended tax collectors,[18] who were despised as rogues and cheats and hated by the people, I doubt. This would have alienated him from the common people; and it would not have befitted him, a proud Israeli, to cultivate contacts with the collaborators of an occupying power. It is more likely that he recruited a tax collector, converted him, and made him a disciple (Luke 15:7). The reference to Jesus' friendly ties with the tax collectors probably came from the evangelists' efforts to impute to Jesus a pro-Roman attitude.

One group of parables highlights Jesus' criticism of the quest for wealth and worldly goods: "It is easier for a camel to pass through the eye of a needle than for a rich man to enter the kingdom of heaven" (Matt. 19:24); "Watch, and be on your guard against avarice of any kind. . . . But God said to him: 'Fool! This very night the demand will be made for your soul; and this hoard of yours, whose will it be then?' So it is when a man stores up treasure for himself in place of making himself rich in the sight of God" (Luke 12:15, 20–21).

Given all this, can we still call Jesus a champion of social equality? The answer must be no. Jesus does not threaten the rich or excoriate wealth; what he criticizes is "the foolishness of the corn grower who relies on his wealth. For when the kingdom of God arrives, the poor will no longer be poor and the rich no longer rich."[19] Even opponents of social justice could cite Jesus: "Which of you, with a servant plowing or minding sheep, would say to him when he returned from the fields, 'Come and have your meal immediately?' Would he not be more likely to say, 'Get my supper laid; make yourself tidy and wait on me while I eat and drink. You can eat and drink yourself afterward?' Must he be grateful to the servant for doing what he is told?" (Luke 17:7–9).

This injustice is even stronger in the parable of the laborers in the vineyard (Matt. 20:1–16). The proprietor pays all the day-laborers equally, whether they have worked from early morning or showed up at the workplace in the afternoon. In the parable of the entrusted talents Jesus seems the consummate capitalist: "So you knew that I reap where I have not sown and gather where I have not scattered?" (Matt. 25:26). The servants who increased the money by letting it earn interest are praised, while the one who has proven less sharp and enterprising is called wicked and lazy. Efficient entreprenurial types will be swamped with riches; the others are to remain poor:

> "Then why did you not put my money in the bank? On my return I could have drawn it out with interest." And he said to those standing by, "Take the pound from him and give it to the man who has ten pounds." And they said to him, "But, sir, he has ten pounds...." "I tell you, to everyone who has will be given more, but from the man who has not, even what he has will be taken away." (Luke 19:23–26)[20]

Pohlmann[21] writes as follows:

> Jesus' attitude toward the rich was not unequivocal. Thus he had no objections to his circle of disciples being supported by well-to-do women (Luke 8:2–3) or to his disciple Peter owning a house (Matt. 8:14). The same Jesus who exhorted his disciples to give their possessions to the poor allowed his head to be anointed... with costly pure nard ointment worth over three hundred denarii. The same Jesus who demanded of the rich young man that he sell everything he owned makes no such demands of the corrupt tax collector Zacchaeus, for whom it would have been much more to the point (Luke 19:8–10).

Given all these inconsistencies, we cannot possibly know how Jesus would have related to the social problems of our time. No political party, extraparliamentary opposition, or alternative action group can assume his support. The Sermon on the Mount, so often brought to bear on discussions of present-day problems, is utterly unsuitable as an answer to them.[22] No agenda for social or political reform can be derived from it. All too idyllic is the dream that with sufficient trust in God the problems of each one of us will be solved by themselves, and that God will attend to our needs as He attends to the flowers in the field and the birds in heaven. Jesus did not condemn the situation of slaves, of the "wretched and over-laden." But if we transposed the Sermon on the Mount to our own time, this would surely be the first step of a social program. Jesus, instead, enjoined slaves to put up with their lot: They were blessed, but they were not to rise up against their oppressors.

The beatitudes, imprecations, and threats in the Sermon on the Mount do no more than reflect the longings of the poor and oppressed, with whom Jesus could empathize and identify.[23] But he did not even begin to question the existing power structure. The fact that society was divided into masters and servants was no more shocking to Jesus than to his contemporaries. In many parables (e.g., Luke 12:42–46), the relation of the servant to his master is even used as a model for the relation of man to God.[24]

Part II

THE FACTS

Seven

THE PASSION STORY

THE story of the Passion is the central point of the Gospels. The aim here is to portray Jesus from the standpoint of the Easter faith, i.e., of resurrection and redemption. The narrative is suffused with Christological motifs, especially in the episodes dealing with the entry into Jerusalem, the Last Supper, and the hearing before the Supreme Council.[1]

Yet all researchers unanimously agree that the essentials of the Passion story are historical. This final phase of Jesus' life is set out comprehensively in all four Gospels. It is the oldest part of the synoptic tradition. Everything else was written later to expand this central idea: the synoptic Gospels are Passion stories preceded by lengthy introductions.

TO JERUSALEM

Tradition holds that Jesus taught mostly in Galilee, around Lake Gennesaret. His primary residence was Capernaum. From there he would take day trips on foot or cross the lake by boat, but he always returned after a short time. Jesus' audiences were Galileans. He could not effectively spread the word of the approaching kingdom of God; he was too much in the shadow of John, the popular Baptist and desert preacher. According to the evangelist John, Jesus' reception was lukewarm and vacillated between approval and rejection. His ministry was marred by disagreement with those around him: "The world cannot hate you, but it does hate me because I give evidence that its ways are evil" (John 7:7–8).

The whole account smacks of resignation and desolation, saying that even his closest associates withdrew their support: ". . . many of his followers said, 'This is intolerable language. How could anyone accept it?' " (John 6:60).[2] Followers and friends left in droves: "After this, many of his disciples left him and stopped going with him" (John 6:66). Jesus became discouraged, fearing that even the twelve closest disciples would turn from him: "Then Jesus said to the Twelve, 'What about you, do you want to go away too?' " (John 6:67). All this shows that there was no "Galilean spring" before the Jerusalem disaster.[3]

Jesus' failure in his homeland may have been one reason why he decided to leave this idyllic country. Inwardly he must have been deeply hurt. Only this would explain why he directed the drastic imprecations described in Matthew and Luke at Galilean towns. They stand in frightening contrast to the Sermon on the Mount:

> Then he began to reproach the towns in which most of his miracles had been worked, because they refused to repent. "Alas for you, Chorazin! Alas for you, Bethsaida! For if the miracles done in you had been done in Tyre and Sidon, they would have repented long ago in sackcloth and ashes. And still, I tell you that it will not go as hard on Judgment day with Tyre and Sidon as with you. And as for you, Capernaum, did you want to be exalted as high as heaven? You shall be thrown down into hell. For if the miracles done in you had been done in Sodom, it would have been standing yet. And still, I tell you that it will not go as hard with the land of Sodom on Judgment day as with you." (Matt. 11:20–24)

On the other hand, it is doubtful whether such curses were actually articulated. To wish ruin and destruction on entire towns and their inhabitants because of a personal disappointment would have been reacting out of all proportion; even angered, Jesus would not have gone that far. It is more probable that the evangelist placed these words in Jesus' mouth, that the authors merely projected onto Jesus their own problems with the proclamation of the new faith in Palestine.[4]

But there may have been a more important reason behind the decision to leave Galilee and set out for Jerusalem. If Jesus wanted to reach a larger and more significant constituency, if his message was to effect a real breakthrough, he had to bring it into the Jewish heartland, and that meant Jerusalem. Only in Jerusalem, with its sanctuary the Temple, could he reach an entire people and challenge them to make a decision. The disciples probably urged their master to go to Jerusalem with his message. In their opinion (Luke 19:11), preaching in Jerusalem would usher in the kingdom of God more quickly.

Jesus certainly did not go to Jerusalem to seek martyrdom.[5] Nevertheless, he must have been realistic enough to see the trip as an extremely risky venture, not so much because of any threat of crucifixion by the Romans as because he might be beheaded or stoned by Jewish authorities. Schillebeeckx[6] writes, "One would have to say that Jesus was naive if it is claimed that he left Galilee and set out for Jerusalem without any awareness of the life-threatening opposition that he would encounter."

Already in Galilee, Jesus is said to have clashed with some especially orthodox Pharisees who saw his behavior as a capital crime (Mark 3:6); but their threats were abstract. The Pharisees were not a homogeneous caste; some were sympathetic to Jesus and some were even his friends. At the time of Jesus, the Pharisees were divided into two main schools of thought: one strictly conservative, headed by Rabbi Schammai, the other essentially liberal, led by Rabbi Hillel. Between these two there was a wide spectrum of opinion.[7]

But Jesus' entry into Jerusalem would inevitably constitute a real challenge to the priestly establishment. He would no longer be dealing with essentially harmless scribes whom he could vanquish in free discussions even though he lacked any theological or legal learning (Mark 6:2; John 7:15). In Jerusalem, the center of power, any discussions would be mainly with the Sadducees, members of the Temple party who by virtue of their authority could easily rid themselves of anyone they deemed undesirable.[8]

98   THE COURT-MARTIAL OF JESUS

John the Baptist had been viewed as a security risk in the province; he had been executed by Herod Antipas in the Machaerus Fortress only a short time before.[9] Jesus must have kept the fate of his teacher in mind, the more so as he must have known that people were whispering that he was a "John . . . risen from the dead" (Mark 6:14). Herodians were a powerful faction in the Jerusalem establishment. The challenge Jesus represented would increase if he gained approval and could win the masses over to his cause. From time immemorial, potentates have known how to trump up charges in order to crush such trends. Resolution and personal courage, as well as a conviction of his mission that dispelled all doubt, must have been the decisive factors in Jesus' decision to incur these risks.

Entry into the City

Jesus' entry into Jerusalem clearly had to coincide with one of the high Jewish feast days, when great crowds of pilgrims would be streaming to the city. Which of the Jewish holidays Jesus chose is still being debated.

As John 5:1 indicates, Jesus had probably been in Jerusalem many times as a pilgrim. Moses had enjoined all Jewish males to make pilgrimages to Jerusalem three times a year (Deut. 16:16). He specified the Passover feast in the spring, which commemorates the exodus from Egypt; the so-called Feast of the Weeks (Shavuoth) seven weeks later, dedicated to the reception of the Law; and the Feast of Tabernacles in the early autumn, following the fruit and grape harvests. In practice, this precept was not strictly observed, but it must have played some part in the life of a Jew as pious as Jesus. He must at least have visited the Holy City at appointed times to pray in the Temple and bring offerings. Luke 2:41 reports that Jesus' family regularly made a pilgrimage to Jerusalem for the Passover feast.

According to the Synoptic Gospels the entry is closely connected to the Passover, when Jesus' ordained death is accomplished. The Church teaches that Jesus entered Jerusalem as an unknown, five days before Passover, on so-called Palm Sunday. But there is no mention of palms in the Gospels in this connection, only of "branches" that the crowd cut in fields or chopped off trees (Matt. 21:8) to strew along his way in greeting. The Greek word used by Mark and Matthew is *stibas,* meaning "straw" or "a bundle of straw." But straw is found only in the autumn. In the old translations *stibas* is rendered as "greenery"; but this is a deliberate mistake to support the story that Jesus entered Jerusalem in the spring:

> Many people spread their cloaks on the road, others greenery which they had cut in the fields. And those who went in front and those who followed were all shouting, "Hosanna! Blessings on him who comes in the name of the Lord! Blessings on the coming kingdom of our father David! Hosanna in the highest heavens!" (Mark 11:8–11)

Matthew's text agrees almost verbatim with this passage, whereas Luke 19:37–40 mentions only the good and festive mood of the disciples. Some authors (Ben-Chorin and Craveri, for example) have conjectured that Jesus entered Jerusalem not just before the fateful Passover feast but on the Feast of Tabernacles the preceding autumn. Matthew's and Mark's descriptions reflect the rituals prescribed for the Feast of Tabernacles: "On the first day you shall take choice fruits, palm branches, boughs of leafy trees and willows from the riverbank, and for seven days you shall rejoice in the presence of Yahweh your God" (Lev. 23:40–41).

The branches are bound in a bouquet, which is wound around the altar during the procession. A verse from Psalm 118 is recited, "Please, Yahweh, please save us. Please, Yahweh, please give us prosperity." This "save us" in Hebrew reads *hoschia na!,* which in the colloquial form becomes "Hosanna."

The words of greeting addressed to Jesus were not spoken exclusively to him. They were a formal welcome, likewise taken from Psalm 118, with which every pilgrim arriving in Jerusalem was greeted: "Blessings on him who comes in the name of Yahweh!" This formula was used for all pilgrimages to the Temple, but only on the Feast of Tabernacles was it related to branches.[10]

The assumption that Jesus had already attended the Feast of Tabernacles in Jerusalem the year before his death is supported by John 7:2–5:

> As the Jewish Feast of Tabernacles drew near, his brothers said to him, "Why not leave this place and go to Judea, and let your disciples see the works you are doing; if a

man wants to be known he does not do things in secret; since you are doing all this, you should let the whole world see."

The evangelist John assumes that Jesus was active in Jerusalem for several months and incurred the hostility first of the ruling Jewish circles and eventually of all the Jews. On the feast of the dedication of the Temple in winter, Jesus walks up and down in the Portico of Solomon talking to the people, and is almost stoned by the excited crowd (John 10:22–31). In between he undertakes some short trips but does not lose contact with Jerusalem. Seven days before Passover he returns to the Holy City.

There is an altogether different reason to assume that autumn was the entry date. Mark 11:12–14 and Matthew 21:18–19 both report one episode of no great significance in itself: Jesus passed by a fig tree. He was hungry and wanted to pluck a few figs, but the tree bore no fruit. This so angered the Master that he cursed the tree. This episode makes sense only if Jesus could have expected the tree to bear fruit, but this could happen only in the autumn, not in the spring.[11]

Ben-Chorin[12] concludes that Jesus' entry into Jerusalem occurred in the autumn but that the decisive events took place the following spring, and that the synoptists thought it more important to highlight the inner connection between the entry and the denouement than to specify the time span between the two events. Matthew 23:37 and Luke 13:34 also point to a longer sojourn, if multiple appearances are ruled out.

Like so much about Jesus, the question as to whether only a week elapsed between the entry and the crucifixion (as claimed by the synoptists and Church doctrine), or whether he spent the several months between the Feast of Tabernacles and Passover in Jerusalem (as borne out by John and other indications), must be left unresolved.

Fulfilled Prophesies?

The Protestant theologian Bornkamm[13] points out that the detailed account of the Passion of Jesus in the Gospels does not result primarily from the fact that the authors had better source materials at their disposal. Rather, they intended to reveal the hand of God in the event and to portray Jesus as the one who realized God's decrees and suffered in their fulfillment. In this way the shock felt by Jesus' followers at their Master's inglorious end could be somewhat softened. "The 'great stumbling block,' to use Paul's expression . . . was the execution of the alleged Messiah as a common criminal. Therefore the Passion stories, more than any other gospel text, refer to and lean on the Old Testament."[14]

The Old Testament is replete with fulfillment legends. For example, the entry into Jerusalem is a fulfillment of Zechariah 9:9, "Rejoice heart and soul, daughter of Zion! Shout with gladness, daughter of Jerusalem! See now, your king comes to you; he is victorious, he is triumphant, humble and riding on a donkey." Jesus' words at the Passover supper (Mark 14:18–19), "One of you is about to betray me, one of you eating with me," correspond to Psalm 41:9, "Even my closest and most trusted friend, who shared my table, rebels against me."

The allegedly base motive of Judas, avarice, as reported in Matthew 26:15 is reminiscent of Zechariah 11:12–13, "And they weighed out my wages; thirty shekels of silver. . . . Taking the thirty shekels of silver, I threw them into the Temple of Yahweh, into the treasury."

The cleansing of the Temple fulfills the word of Isaiah 56:7, ". . . for my house will be called a house of prayer for all the peoples."

Anyone who reads the account of the Sanhedrin's death sentence should recall Psalm 31: line 13, "As they combine against me, plotting to take my life." Mark 14:61–63 has Jesus reply to the High Priest's question as to whether he is the Son of God, "I am . . . and you will see the Son of Man seated at the right hand of the Power and coming with the clouds of heaven." This reply mixes Daniel 7:13 and Psalm 110:1, "And I saw, coming on the clouds of heaven, one like a Son of Man," and "Sit at my right hand." Jesus' silence before the Sanhedrin and Pilate echoes Isaiah 53:7, "He never opened his mouth, like a lamb that is led to the slaughterhouse, like a sheep that is dumb before its shearers never opening its mouth." The shout "Crucify him!" relates to Psalm 31:13, "I hear their endless slanders, threats from every quarter, as they combine against me, plotting to take my life." The scourging of Jesus finds its parallel in Isaiah 50:6, "I offered my back to those who struck me, my cheeks to those who tore at my beard; I did not cover my face against insult and spittle."

Psalm 69:21 corresponds to Matthew 27:34, 48: "They gave me poison to eat instead, when I was thirsty they gave me vinegar to drink."

Pilate's washing of his hands corresponds to Psalm 26:6, "I wash my hands in innocence and join the procession around your altar." The darkness that is said to have come over the whole land from the sixth to the ninth hour corresponds to Amos 8:9, "That day—it is the Lord Yahweh who speaks—I will make the sun go down at noon, and darken the earth in broad daylight."

The prayer of Psalm 22:1, "My God, my God, why have you deserted me?", according to Mark 15:34 and Matthew 27:47, is Jesus' last utterance on the cross. And Luke, who does not place this cry of despair in the mouth of Jesus, has him quote Psalm 31:5, "Into your hands I commit my spirit."

Many other examples could be added. If one does not accept that, from his entry into Jerusalem, Jesus deliberately spoke and behaved so as to let the predictions of the Old Testament be fulfilled,[15] then one must acknowledge that the evangelists had almost no biographical information, no more about this final portion of Jesus' life than about any preceding part. Clearly, they were concerned that the predictions of the Old Testament should be seen to have been fulfilled.[16]

Uncertain Date of Death

The evangelists are at odds over the date of death; the synoptics do not agree with John. They concur only on one point: Jesus was crucified on Friday of the week in which Passover began (Mark 15:42; John 19:31), having been arrested the preceding evening.

The Jewish lunar calendar year consists of 360 days and is divided into 12 months. The seventh month, Nisan, coincides with our April; the last month is Adar. At the discretion of the Sanhedrin, an extra month was added after several years; it followed Adar and was called the "second Adar." This was done to make the year conform to the solar calendar and the seasons' natural cycle.[17]

The Passover begins on the 14th of Nisan—which each year falls on the first full moon of the month[18]—and lasts seven days: "The fourteenth day of the first month, between the two evenings, is the Passover of Yahweh; and the fifteenth day of the same month is the feast of Unleavened Bread for Yahweh." The night of the 14th of Nisan is a time of celebration (Seder night), commemorating the happy exodus of the children of Israel, guided by Moses, from bondage in Egypt. The Passover meal is consumed after ritual readings; the lambs that have been slaughtered about eight hours before are eaten. Unleavened bread (matzo) is passed around and four ritual cups of wine are drunk.

The Synoptic Gospels describe Jesus partaking of a Passover meal with his disciples. But some authors have questioned whether a Passover meal was really meant. Bornkamm[19] points out that Jesus is not recorded to have uttered one word of the text customarily spoken by the Seder host on the meaning of the Passover feast. Others base their doubts on the fact that Jesus celebrated the meal only with his disciples, not with the wives of his followers, as would have been usual for Passover.[20] In view of the paschal lamb mentioned in the synoptics (Mark 14:12; Matt. 26:19; Luke 22:7) and the mention of the "first day of Unleavened Bread" (Matt. 26:17), I am of the opinion that the synoptists wanted Jesus' last supper to be understood as a Passover meal.[21] The external course of the meal was exactly in keeping with the Seder ritual as it is celebrated to this day.

According to the synoptic accounts, the time between the meal and Jesus' arrest could only have been a matter of hours. At the end of the meal those present sang the customary Passover hymn and then decided to take a long walk. The group wandered in the direction of the Mount of Olives and paused to rest in the so-called garden of Gethsemane. This may have been a country estate or a kind of olive mill, within the city limits of Jerusalem. There the disciples aroused Jesus' indignation. Tired after the sumptuous meal, the heavy wine, and the walk, they immediately fell asleep instead of remaining awake and praying with him as he had enjoined them. His persecutors took him into custody as Jesus was still reprimanding the disciples:

> After psalms had been sung they left for the Mount of Olives. . . . They came to a small estate called Gethsemane, and Jesus said to his disciples, "Stay here while I pray." . . . And once more he came back and found them

sleeping, their eyes were so heavy; and they could find no answer for him. He came back a third time and said to them, "You can sleep on now and take your rest. It is all over. The hour has come. Now the Son of Man is to be betrayed into the hands of sinners. Get up! Let us go! My betrayer is close at hand already." (Mark 14:26, 32, 40–42)

This would mean that Jesus was arrested and interrogated on the night of the 14th of Nisan and executed the following morning.

According to John, the crucifixion took place not on the 14th but on the 13th of Nisan; but the earlier date is seldom cited in scholarly literature. Instead, a distinction is drawn between the 14th of Nisan as the presumed Johannine death date and the 15th of Nisan as the presumed date of death recorded in the synoptics.[22] That reasoning overlooks the fact that, according to the Jewish calendar, a new day does not begin at midnight but after sundown. If Jesus was executed not on Passover but on the Preparation Day for Passover (to which John attaches a great importance), it must have been on the 13th of Nisan. It is expressly stated that the Passover feast, which is ushered in by the Passover meal, was still in the offing when Jesus was delivered up to Pilate: "They then led Jesus from the house of Caiaphas to the Praetorium. It was now morning. They did not go into the Praetorium themselves or they would be defiled and unable to eat the passover" (John 18:28–29).

John 19:31 notes that in the year of Jesus' death the 14th of Nisan fell on a Sabbath day ("a great Sabbath day," in Luther's translation). Since all the Gospels agree that Friday was the day of execution, Jesus must have died on the 13th of Nisan, the Preparation Day for the Passover feast.

From the outset the Church subscribed to the date given by John. It cites as kerygmatic evidence the fact that Jesus' death would then have occurred exactly as the Passover lambs were being slaughtered in Jerusalem. Paul also describes the Christ allegorically as the paschal lamb (1 Cor. 5:7).

Several factual reasons also point to the Johannine death date. First, it is inconceivable that the Jewish authorities would have collaborated in doing away with Jesus on a high religious holiday. Anything that was forbidden on the Sabbath would most certainly have been prohibited on Passover. In the Gospels there is no mention of the holiday's having been profaned, as it would have been by a condemnation and execution. Mark 14:2 and Matthew 26:5

expressly state, "It must not be during the festivities, or there will be a disturbance among the people."

Then, in contradiction to their own statements that Jesus' arrest occurred on the Seder night (with the inescapable conclusion that the trial would have followed on the Passover), both Mark 15:42 and Luke 23:54 state that it was still Preparation Day when Jesus' body was taken down from the cross and buried.

All the synoptics mention a peasant, Simon of Cyrene (African Cyrenaica), who had just come in from working in the fields and was forced by the Romans to help Jesus carry the cross (more exactly the crossbeam, since the stakes were always firmly stuck in the ground at the execution site). But no Jewish peasant would have gone to work on the Sabbath, let alone on a holiday like Passover.[23]

Many attempts have been made to reconcile the contradictions surrounding the date of Jesus' death. The easiest explanation says that the meal mentioned in Mark, Matthew, and Luke was not really a Passover feast, but just a farewell repast after Jesus had had a presentiment of death. John is not describing a ritual meal; his reference in Chapter 13 is to an evening before Passover. The meal and the washing of feet were the occasion of the discussion between Jesus and his disciples that the synoptics transferred to the Seder night.

Another opinion is that Jesus partook of the Passover meal before the 14th of Nisan and that this was attributable to his association with the Essenes.[24] The Essenes did not use the lunar calendar, as was official at that time, but the solar calendar, which placed the 14th of Nisan and thus the Passover one, even several, days before the lunar calendar date.[25]

In short, the day of Jesus' death is still controversial.[26] Astronomical reckonings—to the extent that these are reliable—have revealed two Passover nights from Thursday to Friday (the synoptics' date) when there was a Passover full moon within Pilate's term of office (A.D. 26–36): April 11, 27, and April 23, 34. Within that time there was only one Passover night from Friday to Saturday (the Johannine date), with a full moon, April 7, 30; and this Friday was the Preparation Day for Passover. Accordingly, this is the most probable date of Jesus' death.

How old was Jesus when he died? If we accept both the Lucan birth year (A.D. 6 or 7) and the earlier of the synoptics' death dates (April 11, 27), Jesus was dead at twenty. If we take A.D. 7 as the year of birth (the year of Herod's "slaughter of the innocents" and the "star of Bethlehem"), and the later of the synoptics death dates (April 23, 34), Jesus was forty-one when he died. Following the two dates I consider most likely—7 B.C. as the year of his birth and April 7, 30, as the date of death—Jesus' earthly life lasted thirty-seven years.

Missing Witnesses

Except for the crucifixion, we do not know what happened to Jesus in Jerusalem, we can only guess.[27] No one reported on the trial before the Sanhedrin, if one actually took place. The same applies to the proceeding before the Roman tribunal. All the potential witnesses, the disciples, had fled as Jesus was arrested.[28] To spare themselves his fate, they only returned to Jerusalem after the terrible events of Golgotha, when the city had resumed its daily routine. The Passover feast was over, the pilgrims had departed, and the Romans had retired to the Antonia Fortress.

At most, there was the possibility that Joseph of Arimathea would bear witness to the events of the trial. He was said to be "a prominent member of the Council," one of the Sanhedrin. In John he is called a "secret disciple" of Jesus. But Joseph of Arimathea is mentioned only in connection with Jesus' burial. He is never cited as a reporter on the trial (which would have been a key role), and has no significant part in the Gospels. Apparently he was not a member of the early Christian community.

Blinzler[29] offers the following explanation: The members of the early community could easily have found out the essentials about the session before the Sanhedrin, since Joseph of Arimathea was well disposed toward Jesus. Moreover, according to Acts 6:7 and 15:5, a considerable number of priests and Pharisees had already joined the Christian community.[30]

According to Mark 14:52, one of the disciples actually fled naked. This must really have happened: It is explicitly stated by Mark and Matthew and can be inferred from Luke. Such an embarrassing episode would hardly have been handed down if it had not been based on truth. John's Gospel likewise clearly implies that the disciples deserted the master but, typically, presents the facts with a different emphasis. The disciples did not flee, but beat an orderly retreat following an imperious command from Jesus to his captors:

"If I am the one you are looking for, let these others go" (John 18:8–9).

Even at the crucifixion, according to the synoptics, none of those close to Jesus was present except Mary Magdalene. John indicates that Jesus' mother stood at the foot of the cross;[31] but something that important would also have been chronicled by the other evangelists if it were based on historical truth. John 19:25 also mentions Mary Magdalene and another Mary who is presented as Jesus' mother's sister. Thus three women, all named Mary, stood under the cross, among them two sisters with the same first names.

John's unreliability in the depiction of concrete events (in contrast to his relatively exact grasp of historical interconnections) is proved by the fact that he calls himself an eyewitness to all the events described in his Gospel (21:24). He falsely claims identity with the so-called beloved disciple John. In many crucifixion scenes the beloved disciple is presented alongside the three Marys as an example of touching loyalty in contrast to the shameful betrayal of Judas and the cowardly denial of Peter.[32]

According to the synoptics, only some Galilean women were present. Aside from Mary Magdalene—only Luke does not refer directly to her presence[33]—they are unknown and insignificant in Jesus' life and work. The fact that these women are mentioned by name in Mark 15:40 and Matthew 27:56 speaks for the historicity of this account. But even the women mentioned did not stand directly under the cross; they were "watching from a distance," as Mark and Matthew report, because the execution sites were screened off by the Roman guards, perhaps only to prevent acts of sabotage.

The evangelists' statements that the high priests and the scribes filed by the cross to heap abuse and mockery on the crucified are also legend. "The passersby jeered at him; they shook their heads and said, 'Aha! So you would destroy the Temple and rebuild it in three days! Then save yourself; come down from the cross!'" (Mark 15:29–31).

Here, too, a prophesy was ostensibly being fulfilled: "All who see me jeer at me, they toss their heads and sneer, 'He relied on Yahweh, let Yahweh save him! If Yahweh is his friend, let Him rescue him!'" (Ps. 22:7–8).

Peter's Denial

It is written that Peter kept on Jesus' trail and secretly followed him into the palace of the high priest. He did not overhear the interrogation but waited below in the courtyard with the servants and warmed himself by a fire (Mark 14:67). The story of Peter's denial appears to have a historical basis; the assumption is that he himself confessed his failure to the later community. But of course, there is no definitive indication that Peter denied his master three times in succession; the number three was used because of its symbolic significance. That the cock crowed at his denial is probably also a legend, since it would fulfill Jesus' own prophesy: "I tell you solemnly, this very night, before the cock crows, you will have disowned me three times" (Matt. 26:34).

Peter did not curse himself, as Luther wrongly translated ("He, however, began to curse himself"). He got out of his dilemma by cursing—more exactly, by execrating—his rabbi Jesus.[34] This is an especially crass case of cowardice and betrayal, by a disciple who a short time before (Mark 14:31) had emotionally sworn fidelity unto death. He failed Jesus not before "an authoritative magistrate's court of first instance but before a very unauthoritative tribunal of servant girls."[35]

According to Gospel accounts, Judas committed suicide after his betrayal; Peter only weeps bitterly, and soon thereafter assumes a leading position in the Jerusalem Christian community. But the historicity of Peter's denial has been questioned. Goguel[36] doubts that Peter could have assumed a leading role in the community if it were true. He believes the evangelists described the denial to justify Jesus' reproach of Peter and his fear that Peter might abandon him. For Conzelmann the denial story is a typical dramatization of Christological teaching, as is also the scene of Peter's confession.[37] This conception deviates from the Gospel account in holding that Peter behaved just like the other disciples when Jesus was arrested. He fled, and returned to Jerusalem later.

Eight

THE ROMANS, NOT THE JEWS

ONE fact that can be established with absolute certainty is that Jesus was killed not by the Jews but by the Romans. Despite all the efforts to make the Jews primarily responsible and to cast the Roman procurator in the role of an unwitting instrument of Jesus' death, the biblical accounts make it quite clear that Pontius Pilate pronounced the death sentence. The sentence was then carried out by his legionnaires,[1] probably Syrians working for the Romans.

THE CRUCIFIXION DEATH PENALTY

Jewish law recognized four death penalties: stoning, burning (i.e., choking the condemned by sticking a burning torch in his mouth), decapitation, and strangulation. Crucifixion is a Roman method of execution.[2] Even scourging a criminal to be crucified, as was done to Jesus, corresponded to the procedure prescribed by Roman law. The verdict reads *Condemno. Ibis in crucem, lictor conliga manus Verberetur* ("I sentence thee: thou shalt go on the cross. Lictor, Bind his hands. Let him be flogged").[3] Another question remains: Would the sentence have been so formally pronounced in a summary court-martial? It was probably a curt order of execution: *Abi in Crucem!* ("Off to the Cross!"). Scourging followed as a matter of course.

Four soldiers were assigned to each execution. John 19:23[4] alludes to this custom: "When the soldiers had finished crucifying Jesus they took his clothing and divided it into four shares, one for each soldier." The methods of crucifixion varied. As a rule the condemned were tied to the cross with cords; this method was probably used for Jesus. Cases have been described in which people tied to the cross lived for at least five days. But the Romans also nailed their victims to the cross; in such cases death occurred sooner due to heart failure.[5]

Whether Jesus was tied or nailed is an unanswerable question. "The view that Jesus was 'nailed' on the cross was in no way the prevalent one in early Christianity. Ambrose, for example, speaks only of the 'cords of the cross' and the 'shackles of the Passion.' Consequently he knew nothing of the nails that supposedly were used."[6] Nor does Luke mention nail marks; he refers only to wounds, which would also have been present if Jesus had been bound with cords. There is only one reference to nailing, John 20:25, which says the disciple Thomas could not believe for a long time that the one standing before him was Jesus risen from the dead, until he saw "the holes that the nails made in his hands."

In a rock tomb in Jerusalem, in 1968, archaeologists came upon the bones of a man 5 feet 7 inches in height, between twenty-four and twenty-eight years old, who had been crucified in A.D. 50.[7] Nails had been used on this young man. The right heel had been placed over the left one and a nail about 15 centimeters long had been driven through the bones. The wristbones showed no injury of any kind, the iron pegs had presumably been hammered between the forearm and the radius onto the crossbeam. The wood was olive. A wooden peg *(sedile)* served to support the body, so the man died in a crouched position.[8] All pictures of the crucifixion of Jesus, without exception, show him hanging on the cross, never in a crouching position. This could indicate that he was not nailed but tied to the cross.

Generally death was precipitated by breaking the victim's legs (the so-called *crurifragium*) before nightfall to prevent flight. If the body was not supported by a *sedile* it sagged completely. The two who were crucified with Jesus had their legs broken, the evangelist reports, but Jesus was spared this cruelty because he was already dead. His death must have been especially swift, probably because he had already been greatly weakened by loss of blood from the scourging. This is borne out by the report that Simon of Cyrene was made to carry the cross (more exactly, the crossbeam) to the execution site. John, intent on drawing a parallel to the Passover lamb whose bones it is forbidden to break (Exod. 12:47), depicts the course of events with a horrible clarity (19:31–35):

> It was Preparation Day, and to prevent the bodies remaining on the cross during the sabbath—since the sabbath was a day of special solemnity—the Jews asked Pilate to have the legs broken and the bodies taken away. Consequently the soldiers came and broke the legs of the first man who had been crucified with him and then of the other. When they came to Jesus, they found he was already dead, and so instead of breaking his legs one of the soldiers pierced his side with a lance; and immediately there came out blood and water.[9]

Crucifixion exemplifies the inhumanity of which humankind has been capable in all times. Just who invented this punishment is not exactly known. Before the Romans it was practiced by the Persians, then by the Greeks and the Carthaginians. Josephus, an eyewitness, reported that during the siege of Jerusalem Titus, the Roman commander, had at least five hundred Jewish refugees crucified daily:

> . . . and when they were going to be taken, they were forced to defend themselves for fear of being punished; as after they had fought, they thought it was too late to make any supplication for mercy; so they were first whipped, and then tormented with all sorts of tortures, before they died and were then crucified before the wall of the city. (*The Jewish War*, Book v, xi:1)

Not only rulers who have gone down in history as tyrants condoned this agonizing method of execution. Cicero describes it as "the most cruel and the most hideous form of the death penalty," but under Julius Caesar, for example, it was taken for granted as it had been centuries before by Alexander the Great.[10] In the fourth century Emperor Constantine replaced crucifixion with a more humane death penalty, the gallows.[11]

The "Execution Legend"

It cannot be claimed that the Romans pronounced and carried out the death penalty against Jesus of Nazareth only because of the technicality that they had exclusive jurisdiction.[12] Even if it were basically true that the Romans reserved for themselves the right to hand down all death penalties, it is known that the Jewish authorities of that time did pronounce and carry out death sentences;[13] John the Baptist and Stephen are perhaps the most prominent of their victims.

John the Baptist was eliminated by the monarch Herod Antipas on political grounds (danger of unrest), after being interned for several months in the Machaerus Fortress. The assumption is that Antipas had his prisoner beheaded, but he was more probably strangled. As for Stephen, the description in Acts 7:55–60 says he was condemned to death by the Sanhedrin and "duly" executed, with Saul-Paul an especially active participant.[14]

A further example of the competence of the Jewish courts over executions (assuming the story's historicity) would be the woman caught in adultery, who would have been stoned after a judicial procedure if Jesus had not saved her with his famous utterance: "If there is one of you who has not sinned, let him be the first to throw a stone at her" (John 8:7).[15] Jesus himself was allegedly threatened with execution from the Jewish side: "The Jews answered him, 'We are not stoning you for doing a good work but for blasphemy; you are only a man and you claim to be God'" (John 10:33).

Josephus Flavius also highlights the competence of the Sanhedrin to pronounce and execute death sentences: ". . . our law, which hath forbidden to slay any man, even though he were a wicked man, unless he had been first condemned to suffer death by the Sanhedrin" (*Antiquities of the Jews*, Book xlv, ix:3).

Jews had a limited jurisdiction, including the right to mete out the death penalty, even over Roman citizens. A marble block[16] has been found with the following inscription in Greek: "Foreigners are forbidden to enter the sanctuary; violators will be punished by death." This warning was placed in front of the Temple in Jerusalem. Josephus Flavius cites the words of Titus, the Roman commander, to the besieged Jews: "Have you not been allowed to put up the pillars thereto belonging ... and on it to engrave in Greek, and in your letters, this prohibition—That no foreigner should go beyond that wall? Have not we given you leave to kill such as go beyond it, though he were a Roman?" (*The Jewish War*, Book vi, 2:4).

The execution of a priest's daughter was handed down in the Talmud of Rabbi Eleazar ben Zadok, an eyewitness. Around A.D. 40 she was sentenced to death by the Sanhedrin on a fornication charge. Finally, Jesus' brother James was condemned to death by the Sanhedrin presided over by Ananias, and stoned in A.D. 64. This despite the fact that the verdict was technically illegal because the composition of the court was not correct.[17] Eighteen years earlier James's namesake the son of Zebedee was executed by the Jewish King Agrippa.[18]

The theological riposte to the plentiful evidence of the Sanhedrin's power to pronounce and enact death sentences has been mostly to deny that the Jews had this authority at the time of Jesus' death. There are obvious grounds for this assertion: Only thus can the fact of Jesus' crucifixion by the Romans be incorporated into the thesis that the Jews bear the actual guilt for his violent death. The Sanhedrin pronounced sentence, but Jewish authorities lacked the competence to carry it out.[19]

John's Gospel serves as a spurious source for the assumption that the Sanhedrin had to concede blood-jurisdiction to the Romans: " 'Take him yourselves, and try him by your own Law.' The Jews answered, 'We are not allowed to put a man to death' " (18:31–32). According to this passage, the Roman procurator believed the Sanhedrin had the right to pronounce the death penalty. Should he, of all people, have required instruction by the Jews on how competences were divided in occupied Judea? Goguel[20] writes, "That the Jews were forced to remind Pilate that the Roman Government had taken from them the right to try cases in which the extreme penalty could be pronounced is extremely improbable. The only point of this idea is to stress the fact that Pilate was forced to take up the case against his will." John's tendentiousness comes through again when he goes so far as to suggest that Pilate invited the Jews to practice the Roman method of execution: "Take him yourselves and crucify him" (19:6).

The Acts provide a far more historically reliable explanation of this point. There the Sanhedrin's competence in matters of the death penalty and its execution is, at least indirectly, affirmed. Thirty years after Jesus' death, the apostle Paul was a prisoner of the procurator Festus. The question arose as to whether he should be turned over to the jurisdiction of the Sanhedrin as a Jew or to the jurisdiction of the emperor as a Roman. Paul insisted on being brought before an imperial court. His plea is based on the assumption that if a verdict of guilty were pronounced by the Sanhedrin he could be sentenced to death and executed: "I have done the Jews no wrong, as you very well know. If I am guilty of committing any capital crime, I do not ask to be spared the death penalty. But if there is no substance in the accusations these persons bring against me, no one has a right to surrender me to them. I appeal to Caesar" (Acts 25:10–12).

The assertion that Pontius Pilate merely had to "confirm" the death sentence handed down by the Sanhedrin is just as misleading as the Johannine account, though it is often advanced. This theory, developed by the Jena theologian and jurist Johannes Stelter in 1674,[21] might have been a late flowering of the thesis of Jewish guilt. But this does not mean that all who later espoused the theory wanted to demonstrate the collective guilt of the Jews.[22] There may even have been a requirement to the effect that any death sentence pronounced by the Sanhedrin had to be confirmed by the procurator before it could be carried out; obviously, the occupying power could not allow the Sanhedrin to execute people who could be useful to Rome or who had earned Roman benevolence. The death verdict pronounced and carried out on Stephen had probably been approved by the procurator. In Jesus' case, however, the sanction theory is irrelevant. Had the procurator approved a Jewish punishment for the offense of blasphemy, Jesus would have died by stoning as prescribed in Leviticus 24:16, not on the Roman cross.

Nonintervention in civil and criminal proceedings was part and parcel of the general Roman policy of nonintervention in the internal affairs of occupied territories. The Roman governor's official residence was not in the Holy City, but in the seaport of Caesarea. The procurator came to Jerusalem as a visitor for a few days or weeks. Compared to other Roman provinces, Palestine enjoyed very special privileges. To cite two examples, Josephus Flavius says that Jews were exempt from military service and were not required to worship the emperor. In the context of this *privelegia judaica* the Romans behaved with a certain respect and consideration toward Jewish religious affairs—they were respectful about religious matters in general, and nobody was questioned about faith. Each individual could live according to his or her religious conviction. The police intervened against "alien superstitions" *(superstitio externa)* only when it was felt that they directly endangered the state religion.[23]

There is no doubt that the governor had a despot's authority to pursue, judge, and execute whomever he wished. Gibbon[24] writes, "His power was not limited by any court or legal trial proceedings and the execution immediately followed his judgment without further appeal." But no law, legal convention, or practical case is known where a Roman military governor in Judea approved or carried out death sentences that had been handed down against a Jew by a Jewish court. On the contrary, it is well known that the Romans did not want to interfere in conflicts among Jews, much less in their religious controversies.

An Alleged Rebel

The Romans applied the punishment of crucifixion mainly to rebels in occupied Palestine, hoping that this form of execution would be an especially potent deterrent. So a high Jewish holiday, when great crowds of pilgrims flocked to Jerusalem, would have been a logical choice for an execution decreed by Romans. If one prefers the assumption that it was the Jewish authorities who were primarily interested in eliminating Jesus, then there is no obvious reason why everything had to be done so quickly. If the reason was the imminence of the Passover, why was Jesus not simply arrested and held in custody until after the feast, to be tried at leisure? An imprisoned Jesus, after all, would not have been any greater a security risk than a dead Jesus.

The Gospels chronicle a race against time: Jesus is arrested late in the evening of Maundy Thursday. In the middle of the night he is brought to the house of the high priest. The latter in turn must summon the rest of the seventy members[25] of the Sanhedrin, most of whom must have been in an especially deep sleep because of the wine they had consumed at the Seder.[26] The trial follows. Then comes the delivery to the Romans; the formal trial before Pontius Pilate; and the shouting crowds (who would have had to be rudely awakened and mobilized). The trial before Pontius Pilate is interrupted by Jesus' removal to the royal palace of the Hasmoneans, in the northwestern part of the upper city, where an intermediate trial is held before Herod Antipas. He is returned to the Praetorium, and the trial before Pilate resumes, proceeding to the entrance of Barabbas. Then the trial is again interrupted: The accused is led to the inner court of the Praetorium. The guard detail orders all Roman soldiers stationed in Jerusalem, the entire cohort, to gather around Jesus. The *soldatesca* mocks him cruelly[27] and Jesus is flogged. Afterwards he is brought back to the Praetorium. Pilate continues the trial, makes further attempts to release him, and finally pronounces judgment. And after all this it is only around eight o'clock in the morning!

After the ensuing death sentence, the cross and the people must be at the gates of Golgotha before nine o'clock, for according to Mark the crucifixion took place at that hour.[28] Jesus dies at three o'clock in the afternoon, and by six o'clock the corpse must be taken down from the cross and buried, since the Passover festivities begin then.

> It was the third hour when they crucified him. . . . When the sixth hour came there was darkness over the whole land until the ninth hour. And at the ninth hour Jesus cried out in a loud voice, "Eloi, Eloi, lama sabacthani?" which means, "My God, my God, why have you deserted me?" . . . But Jesus gave a loud cry and breathed his last. (Mark 15:25, 33–34, 37)

And if he had not expired on the ninth hour, what would have happened then? Of course, the soldiers could have still broken his legs, so that death would come sooner because of the weight of the hanging body. But even that would have been no guarantee that the schedule could be met. Thus, if the Gospel account is to be believed, Jesus died so opportunely, purely by chance, that he literally could be taken down from the cross and buried at the last minute, just before the onset of the Passover.[29]

A three-day Passion has occasionally been postulated to make the time frame more credible. This thesis, polished and elaborated with impressive arguments, was espoused by the French researcher Jaubert.[30] After initial approval it gave way again in scholarly circles to the one-day chronology, which is now the prevailing version.[31]

Since events could not possibly have unfolded as smoothly as the Gospels describe, they are plausible only with the following proviso: The Romans had been alerted to Jesus after his entry into Jerusalem had caused a stir, possibly a considerable one. As a zealot in matters of faith, he would have been viewed as a potential rebel. It was for this reason that he was arrested by the military authorities and that final judgment was passed on him in a summary court-martial proceeding. Goguel writes, "Thus Jesus was not arrested as a blasphemer but as an agitator, or as a person who might furnish a pretext for, or become, the occasion of a riot."[32]

Such an assumption is not only warranted by the Johannine Gospel but also confirmed—albeit indirectly—in the synoptic reports. Jesus himself allegedly protested against arrest with the remark that after all he was not a "brigand": "Am I a brigand ... that you had to set out to capture me with swords and clubs?" (Mark 14:48–49).[33]

"Brigand" and "thief" are the usual translations. But the evangelists use the Greek word *lestes*. This word—even in the secular writing of that time—is applied not only to highwaymen but also to gang leaders, bandits, and insurgents of all sorts. Josephus Flavius, in the Roman service, writes as follows about the fanatical resistance groups based in the mountains of Judea:

> And now Judea was full of robberies and, as the several companies of the seditions light upon anyone to head them, he was created a king immediately, in order to do mischief to the public. They were in some small measure indeed, and in small matters, hurtful to the Romans but the murders they committed upon their own people lasted a long while. (*Antiquities of the Jews*, Book xviii, 10:8)

Barabbas, the partisan fighter who acquires a certain importance in the proceedings before Pilate, is likewise called *lestes* (John 18:40). In Mark 15:7–8 we read, "Now a man called Barabbas was then in prison with the rioters who had committed murder during the uprising." The two men crucified with Jesus who are called "robbers" (Mark 15:27; Matt. 27:38) were fanatical resistance fighters.[34] No one can say whether Jesus knew them before, whether they were connected with Barabbas, or possibly even followers of Jesus; but they were condemned on the same charges as Jesus. Thus on one Friday Pilate had at least three Jews executed because he had found them guilty of rioting against the occupation power and viewed them as enemies of Rome.

I would go so far as to say that these persons were condemned in the one and same summary court-martial proceeding. The principle of the so-called economy trial has consistently played a special role in military penal law. There is no reason to assume that parallel trials were held independently of each other, since from the court's point of view the culprits would have been considered accomplices: "Now with him they were also leading out two other criminals to be executed" (Luke 23:32).

Depending on the translation, Jesus' companions on the cross are called variously murderers, criminals, brigands, or hucksters. Clearly these epithets were intended to show that the prophesy of Isaiah 53:9 was being fulfilled: "And the text of scripture was fulfilled that says: He was taken for a criminal" (Mark 15:28). According to Luke 23:40–41, one of the other victims mocked Jesus from the cross and was rebuked by the other:[35] " 'Have you no fear of God at all?' he said. 'You got the same sentence as he did, but in our case we deserved it: we are paying for what we did. But this man has done nothing wrong.' "

This rebel was seemingly resigned to his fate. His lot was that of a partisan fallen into enemy hands, and tried according to martial law. Nevertheless he saw Jesus' execution as a scandalous injustice. A Zealot himself, he knew that Jesus had neither been involved in acts of revolutionary violence nor incited others to commit them. He recognized that Jesus was the victim of a devastating miscarriage of justice.[36]

According to all four Gospels, Pilate's first question to Jesus was, "Are you the King of the Jews?" From the outset the Roman's investigation was concerned with political and military security.[37] The question was altogether logical if Pilate had heard that Jesus was passing himself off as the Messiah or was being viewed as such, since the title "Messiah" implied kingship. Moreover, as Josephus Flavius reports, "king" is the designation for the leader of a band of insurgents, so there were many Jewish kings.[38]

A board that Pilate allegedly had fixed to Jesus' cross bore the reason for his conviction: "King of the Jews," a purely political crime. The evangelist John adds the twist that the high priests had asked Pilate to write not "King of the Jews" but "This man said, I am King of the Jews," and that Pilate rejected this demand. Here is a further indication that the procurator cared not a whit about the opinion of the Jewish authorities; he had formed his own opinion, which became the basis for the condemnation and the execution. If Jesus had been executed for blasphemy because he had represented himself as a divine being (the "Son of God" in the sense of the later Christian proclamation), the inscription on the board would have read not *I.N.R.I.* but *I.N.F.D.* (*Jesus Nazarene Filius Dei,* "Jesus of Nazareth, Son of God"). But the Romans did not trouble themselves with the God of the Jews; it was all the same to them whether this God was blasphemed or not. Their sole concern was to carry out the *lex Julia maiestatis:*[39]

> Gallio[40] said to the Jews, "Listen, you Jews. If this were a misdemeanor or a crime, I would not hesitate to attend to you; but if it is only quibbles about words and names, and about your own Law, then you must deal with it yourselves—I have no intention of making legal decisions about things like that." (Acts 18:14–15)

I cannot think that Jesus told Pilate he was "King of the Jews," or that he did not answer the question with a firm negative. The Gospels never say that he appropriated such a pretentious title, even among his disciples. Nor did he claim to be a Messiah (which both Jews and Romans would have interpreted as "the Anointed one from the royal House of David"). Why then should he have passed himself off before Pilate as a rebel chief, a militant Messiah from the House of David who had come for the final battle against the foreign Roman occupation?

If there actually was a board on the cross with the inscription "King of the Jews,"[41] its purpose was obviously to proclaim that the crucified man was an insurgent. But the inscription *I.N.R.I.* is more likely an invention of the evangelists. Their underlying intention was to bear witness to Jesus as Christ and king, not as a rebel leader: He is the Christ-King of the post-Easter community. According to Luke and John, it was proclaimed in three languages: Hebrew (Aramaic), Greek, and Latin—"a teaching *urbi et orbi.**"[42]

It was customary or even prescribed to place an inscription *(titulus)* over the head[43] of the crucified, giving the reason for the death sentence. But the *titulus* for Jesus is not known. The most likely possibility is that only the word "rebel" was inscribed.

At all events Jesus' trial was no more sensational than those of

*To the city and the world.

hundreds and thousands of his companions in misfortune who were likewise executed under the crucifixion-happy Pontius Pilate. Jesus would have been treated in exactly the same way as any other rebel (or anyone viewed as such): a summary court-martial, and "Off to the Cross!"

Reason and Warrant for Arrest

The Gospels describe Jesus' triumphal entry into Jerusalem. Virtually the entire population and crowds of pilgrims greeted him with shouts of joy and prepared a Messianic reception. But Jesus applied himself first—to the satisfaction of all people (Mark 11:18) and hailed by the children (Matt. 21:15)—to stirring up a real tumult. He had reportedly been offended by the scene that he discovered in the Temple precincts. Sacrificial animals, which the pilgrims had not been able to bring with them on their long trek, were being sold on the Temple square. Roman and Greek coins were being exchanged for special Temple money, the old Tyrian currency, because it was forbidden to pay Temple taxes in pagan coin.[44]

Ignoring Temple authorities and the Temple police,[45] Jesus is said to have overthrown the tables and begun to lash out with a whip at merchants, brokers, and pilgrims. These were gathered in the so-called forecourt of the pagans, and going about their business. Jesus drove them outside the Temple precincts, thus fulfilling the prophesy of Jeremiah (7:11): "And he taught them and said, 'Does not scripture say: My house will be called a house of prayer for all the peoples? But you have turned it into a robbers' den'" (Mark 11:17–18).

The story of the cleansing of the Temple is definitely not historical. Incidentally, it is much toned down in Luke 19:45–46, which says that Jesus was only concerned with persuading the traders to leave the Temple precincts. The historical circumstance cannot have existed, if only because "one individual could not have carried out the cleansing on a square of such magnitude" (Lohse)—something to which Mark, Matthew, and John paid no attention. After all, according to the Swiss theologian Haenchen, the area was as large "as the old town of Chur."[46] "One forgets in all this that the evangelist (along with his tradition) is not giving an objective description but presents only that which is of theological interest, regardless of practical impossibilities."[47]

The story takes on a quixotic dimension in the context of security and public order. It reads as though Jesus went berserk on the Temple square, yet did not provoke the intervention of the Temple police or the occupation troops stationed nearby in the Antonia Fortress.[48]

After so turbulent a day, Jesus allegedly withdrew peacefully with his disciples to the city gates (Mark 11:19). Anyone who wanted to follow him could have done so, but seemingly the authorities did not consider this necessary; no measures were taken against him. Whether the money changers and merchants then resumed their trade is not mentioned by the evangelist, but common sense would indicate that this is precisely what happened.

In any case, no objection seems to have been raised to Jesus' preaching for three days in the forecourt of the Temple before a great crowd of people, after his tempestuous arrival. The high priests, scribes, and elders gathered around him and engaged with him in learned debates (Mark 11:27–33; 12:1–4), in which Jesus proved to be a particularly ingenious disputant.[49]

Strikingly, there is no reference to Jesus himself viewing the situation as dangerous in any way. He praised the scribes when they sided with him (Mark 12:34) and violently attacked them when they did not (Mark 12:38–40). He is said to have "silenced the Sadducees" (Matt. 22:34). Obviously neither he nor his entourage thought it necessary to take any kind of security precautions. True, he was overcome by the fear of death in the night just before his arrest, but the disciples remain utterly unworried to the end: They fall asleep.

In the course of further events, the Temple authorities must have undergone a change of mind, at least according to the Gospels. Suddenly Jesus was to be arrested. And now the reports become even more curious; there were some difficulties in tracking down the delinquent. Instead of waiting to arrest him until his return the following day—when he could have been led quietly away under any appropriate pretext without causing a stir—the Temple police issued an absolutely senseless search warrant: "Anyone who knew where he was must inform them so that they could arrest him" (John 11:57). Yet huge crowds of people and above all the authorities and the police must have known where Jesus was staying. John reports that he was in Bethany,[50] a village on the outskirts of Jerusalem, where he had reportedly raised Lazarus from the dead. There his feet were anointed with costly nard by Lazarus's sister Mary. "A large number of Jews" came there to see him and Lazarus, but no one complied with the warrant by aiding his arrest. Nor were any steps taken against him when he returned to Jerusalem, obviously unaware that a warrant for his arrest had been issued. The authorities seemed resigned: "Then the Pharisees said to one another, 'You see, there is nothing you can do; look, the whole world is running after him!' " (John 12:19).

When Jesus was finally arrested on Maundy Thursday and led to the former high priest Annas, he rightfully pointed to the contradictory behavior of the authorities: "I have spoken openly for all the world to hear; I have always taught in the synagogue and in the Temple where all the Jews meet together: I have said nothing in secret" (John 18:20–21).

Betrayal by Judas?

The figure of Judas has assumed a disproportionate importance in Christian consciousness. To be called a "Judas" is particularly ignominious. According to a poll taken in 1967,[51] "91 percent of those who believe almost nothing believe that Judas betrayed Jesus to his enemies." The reported deep remorse that seizes Judas and drives him to suicide when he sees his master condemned to death (a development that he had obviously not intended) does nothing to redeem him in the eyes of posterity. On the contrary, the suicide adds to his burden of sin.[52]

Even the following fundamental concept does little to lessen general horror over the deed, much less lend it acceptance: Judas, too, was merely an instrument in God's plan of salvation. Limbeck writes, "In the delivery through Judas came to pass the giving away of Jesus by God, in which Jesus by his self-sacrifice also participated."[53]

God predestined this disciple to be a traitor, according to Mark and Matthew; but the choice could have fallen on any one of the Twelve. When Jesus announces the imminent betrayal at the Last Supper all the disciples react "disconcertedly." Actually, only Judas would have felt "disconcerted," unless each of the Twelve had to reckon that the lot could fall to him. All, one after the other, ask the Master, " 'Not I, Lord, surely?' . . . Judas, who was to betray him, asked in his turn, 'Not I, Rabbi, surely?' 'They are your own words,' answered Jesus" (Matt. 26:22, 25).

The announcement of Judas' betrayal at the Last Supper cannot be verified historically, yet surely a real uproar would have broken out among the disciples after so dramatic a revelation. Kolping writes, "The nonhistoricity of the announcement of the betrayal is also proved by the fact that nobody in Jesus' circle waxes indignant at Judas."[54] It is unthinkable that the disciples would have remained unruffled and enjoyed the ritual meal normally, and then set out on foot for Gethsemane as though nothing had happened, lain down to rest, and fallen into a deep, carefree sleep.

It is altogether questionable whether the betrayal as such is historical fact, or whether the pious chroniclers merely sought to show fulfillment of David's psalm of lamentation: "Even my closest and most trusted friend, / who shared my table, rebels against me" (Ps. 41:9). Paul makes no mention of Judas' betrayal, but reports that on Easter Sunday the risen Christ appeared before the Twelve.[55] Matthew 27:5, which says that the grief-stricken Judas hanged himself, is especially suspect in this regard. A similar episode is described in 2 Samuel 17:23, where the chronicler reports the suicide of Ahithophel, King David's counsel, who had planned to betray his king. Matthew adds that the words of the prophet Jeremiah were fulfilled by Judas' death. Furthermore, Matthew's report cannot be brought into line with the account in Acts 1:18–20, which says that, far from suffering remorse, Judas purchased a little piece of land with the reward for his betrayal and later died as the result of an accident.

It is striking that Judas did not appear as a witness in the trial before the Sanhedrin that followed immediately after the betrayal and arrest. This is all the more surprising given that the synoptics cite a dearth of evidence for the court because of conflicting and unreliable witnesses. Judas would have been a classic witness for the prosecution; after all, he had accurate inside information about the rabbi and his opinions.

Simonis[56] views Judas' betrayal as fictitious:

> After Easter the group of the Twelve to which, among others, Simon and Judas belonged, found itself in Jerusalem. These Twelve, among whom Simon unquestionably was the leading man, formed a special circle within a larger group. Judas had again deserted this circle. A substitute was picked by lot in the circle initiated by Simon. Judas' departure was viewed as a defection, indeed as a betrayal of the common cause for the sake of which the

Twelve and their followers were in Jerusalem. Thereby Judas became a "negative figure," a "non-person".... Anyone branded as a traitor is deemed capable of anything. As soon as one began to relate the story of the end of Jesus, the "traitor" Judas also found his place and the role appropriate to him in it.

In contrast, even so critical a scholar as Ben-Chorin considers that the historicity of the person of Judas and his betrayal of Jesus are not to be doubted, if only because Judas posed such an embarrassment to the early community that he could not have been invented.[57] Accordingly Ben-Chorin restates the prevailing opinion among scholars, which was similarly formulated fifty years earlier: "For early Christianity the story of Judas was the scandal of scandals. It could be told only because there were very strong reasons at hand for holding it to be true."[58]

Then again, the evangelists could well have found it very expedient to cloak the betrayal from within as fulfillment of a prophesy. Thus they could introduce a traitor with the name Judas, so that a particularly shameful deed would be associated with the name of Judaism: Judas, the Eternal Jew, the prototype of the traitorous Jew! Eleven apostles go into the Church; one goes into the synagogue.[59]

The Catholic theologian Trilling also suggests such a thought without, of course, explicitly drawing this conclusion: "Christians belong wholly in the light of the faith, Jews in the darkness of unbelief.... Characteristically Judas from the outset was on the side of 'darkness,' so strongly that it has been suggested that he was possessed by Satan."[60]

Parallels between Judas and the Jews are also drawn by the evangelist John, albeit covertly. Despite the fact that the Johannine Jesus directly ordered Judas to carry out his deed ("What you are going to do, do quickly" [13:27]), the evangelist asserts that Judas is possessed by the devil: Satan entered him (13:27); Judas himself is a devil (6:70). This reasoning is a specialty of John's, and he further applies it to the Jews in general: "The devil is your father, and you prefer to do what your father wants. He was a murderer from the start" (8:44).

To John not only is Judas a devil, but all Jews are the devil's offspring. Whenever Christians expressed their anti-Semitism and chose Judas as the chief focus of their hatred, they could cite John's

Gospel in their defense: "When Easter began in medieval times, which are still not times past, the houses of Jews were closed and barricaded. For not only Jesus, Judas also was a Jew. Suddenly the joy in Jesus turned—and turns—into anger toward Judas, into anger toward Jews to boot and, literally, into murderous anger."[61]

What a contrast and contradiction this is, to the unshakable love that Jesus bore his disciple Judas to the bitter end. Although the Gospel accounts tell us that Jesus knew he would be betrayed by Judas, he placed him in an apostolic capacity, on exactly the same level as the rest of the disciples. In the seating arrangement for the Last Supper, he assigned Judas the place of honor at his side (John 13:26). Luke emphasizes that the betrayal by Judas was planned, stating (6:12) that Jesus spent the entire night before he selected the disciples in prayer to God. In other words, the selection of Judas was based on divine inspiration as was that of the others.

The cordial bond between Jesus and Judas is expressed even in the Gethsemane scene: "So he went straight up to Jesus and said, 'Greetings, Rabbi,' and kissed him. Jesus said to him, 'My friend, do what you are here for' " (Matt. 26:49-50). Jesus responds to the defector disciple with the forgiving love of the teacher. Ben-Chorin writes, "Now he calls the enemy friend. No longer only disciple, no longer the distanced relationship of Master and pupil: my friend! Precisely at this hour."[62] But was an act of forgiveness at all necessary? And if so, who was to forgive whom?

According to the Gospels, three interpretations of Judas' betrayal are possible:

1. This so-called betrayal was a component of God's plan for salvation. Judas was God's instrument; he had neither the opportunity nor the right to rebel against God's will. Consequently, he is beyond reproach.
2. Judas did not carry out God's will, but acted from base motives. He abused Jesus' trust; he was the wolf in sheep's clothing and betrayed him cruelly. Nevertheless Jesus was not angry with him, but meets him with forgiving love. This interpretation is widespread. But to what conclusion does it lead? Jesus erred; he was an erring human being. But more than that, he had a poor understanding of human nature. He let himself be deceived; a sly fellow like Judas could take him in; the devil could dupe him.[63] God neither protected him nor listened to his constant petitions for correct counsel in the selection of the disciples.

3. Nobody could deceive Jesus. He had seen through Judas from the start, and had always known that he would be shamefully betrayed by him. He knew that Judas would implicate himself and that Satan would carry him off to eternal damnation. Those who believe this interpretation—which is no less widespread than the preceding two—must ask themselves why Jesus did not prevent Judas from sinning against him. The end the disciple suffered because of his action is so terrible that Jesus must have spoken cynically when he called him "my friend" at their last meeting (and must really have been thinking to himself, "Judas, drop dead!"). All that Luke writes about Judas in Acts, citing Psalm 109, happened with Jesus' approval:

> He fell headlong and burst open, and all his entrails poured out. . . .[64] "Give him a venal judge, find someone to frame the charge; let him be tried and found guilty, let his prayer be construed as a crime! . . . May his children be orphaned and his wife widowed! May his children be homeless vagabonds, beggared and hounded from their hovels; may the creditor seize his possessions and foreigners swallow his profits! May no one be left to show him kindness, may no one look after his orphans. . . ." (Acts 1:18; Ps. 109:6–12)

Jesus could have prevented all this, but he never once tried to dissuade Judas from his plan. Instead he let him rush to his ruin; indeed, he even pushed him toward the accomplishment of his act.

How, one might ask, does that fit in with the precept of love as expressed in the Sermon on the Mount; how does it mesh with the prayer "and lead us not into temptation" that Jesus taught his disciples? That which he asks God not to do for His own sake, he, the teacher, does with one of his own pupils. It is not Jesus who ought to forgive Judas, but Judas who should have to forgive him. A terrible thought! And it would be no less so if the interpretation were slightly varied to assert that, after all, Judas had to take responsibility for this act committed of his own free will. The fact remains that Jesus, who was privy to the act of volition, could at least have prevented its execution so as not to expose himself to the charge of complicity.[65]

In a fictional narrative, a German Franciscan in 1960—with the approval of his order—set a lengthy trial in motion through the Latin Patriarch of Jerusalem. The proposal was that Judas be beatified, on the following grounds:

> I ask the Holy See to declare that this Judas attained heavenly glory and merits public veneration. For he and no other is to be thanked for the fact that what is written about the Son of Man in the Law and in the Prophets has been fulfilled. . . . Without Judas, no cross; without the cross, no fulfillment of the plan for salvation. No Church without this man, no tradition without its transmitter.[66]

Much has been conjectured and written on the reason for the alleged betrayal. Some think Judas was a Zealot who wanted to force Jesus to a decision and spark a revolt against the Romans. Others argue that Judas staged a mock betrayal, so that Jesus might prove himself "lord of the world."[67] The idea that Judas acted only out of greed, for thirty pieces of silver—the average purchase price of a young male slave—is hardly taken seriously any more. As the group's treasurer, which he was, Judas would have done much better by simply taking off with the money bag.

Moreover, according to the synoptics the betrayal was absolutely unnecessary. For one thing, it would only have been possible if Jesus had carried out his activity clandestinely, not in public. For another, the synoptics' description of Judas' role reduces Jesus to the level of a petty and insignificant itinerant Galilean preacher, a troublemaker who cannot even be identified for purposes of arrest without assistance.

Arrest in Gethsemane

The many inconsistencies in connection with the arrest warrant and Judas' role suggest that even the arrest was carried out not by the Jewish authorities but by the Romans. When the arresting party arrived in Gethsemane where Jesus was lingering with the small circle of his disciples, they did not even know what their quarry looked like. If Judas had not identified him, another might have been arrested in his stead.[68] Only the idea that the arrest involved a military unit of the occupation force can explain why difficulties arose in identifying Jesus; a Roman officer could not be expected to know what he looked like. Thus it might, to some extent, be plausible that the officer would have let someone who knew him finger the prospective prisoner.

Mark and Matthew recount that, besides the Roman soldiers armed with swords, only low-level officials of the Sanhedrin ("servants") were present.[69] Only the Romans were allowed to carry swords; the officials of the Sanhedrin had to content themselves with clubs and staves.

The famous story of Judas' identification of Jesus does not appear in John, where even the arrest is described from the perspective of the risen Christ: The arrest detail organizes a procession "with lanterns and torches and weapons" (18:3); and its members move back and fall to the ground when they see in front of them Jesus incarnate (18:6). John would not saddle Jesus with anonymity; it would not fit his image of Jesus, the Son of God.

On the other hand, it is precisely in John's Gospel that the theory of Jesus having been arrested by the Romans finds its support. In 18:3 and 18:12 mention is made of a *speira* and a *chiliarchos*, which Luther translates as "band" (and occasionally as "band of troopers" under the command of a "chief captain"). A *speira*, Latin for cohort (a tenth of a legion), consisted of six hundred men. That would have meant all the Roman troops stationed in the Antonia Fortress, as Mark 15:16, Matthew 27:27, and Luke, in Acts 21:31, also interpret it. *Chiliarchos* is the title of the commander in chief of this cohort.[70]

A natural objection would be that the evangelist John inflated the number of soldiers called up.[71] Was it necessary to order the entire garrison to apprehend one man surrounded by eleven (mostly unarmed) followers? As far as I know, Stauffer seems to be the only one who asserts such a necessity and indeed raises the number of troops engaged to a thousand in a fantastic description:

> It is a large and motley detachment that on this night marches through the Kidron valley to occupy the Mount of Olives, to cordon off the terrain and to search every hiding place with lanterns and torches. . . . First of all there are the Roman commandant of Jerusalem and his occupation troops, a cohort. The troop is in battle alert. Obviously the Romans are expecting armed resistance and prepared for a mass disturbance despite all their precautions. The huge number of troops is striking, yet

not at all unprecedented or inconceivable.... Jesus' disciples have two swords, not very much against a force of a thousand men, but enough to summon God's help for the final messianic conflict on this apocalyptic night in which all angels and devils are on the alert.[72]

I salute Stauffer's imagination: The decisive fact is that the arrest detail was a unit of the occupation force, commanded by a Roman officer. Goguel writes,

> It is impossible to suppose that the cohort and the centurion have been introduced into the narrative by John. Thus we must admit that he is here following a source that referred to a collaboration between the Jews and the Romans, or mentioned the Romans only.... Whether that be so or not, if the Romans did proceed to arrest Jesus, or if they merely collaborated, the initiative, or at least part of the initiative, must be attributed to them.[73]

According to John, the Romans were involved from the outset, which clearly does suit those who want to burden the Jews with guilt for the drama of Golgotha. This is how Blinzler,[74] for example, closes the circle: Because the Jews put Jesus on trial and accordingly bear the actual guilt for his violent death, he must accordingly have been in Jewish custody from the start of the Passion and thus could not have been arrested by the Roman soldiers. John is arbitrarily reinterpreted: The evangelist expressed himself inaccurately, made a slip of the tongue, so to speak. By "cohort" he means the Jewish Temple police, and by *chiliarchos*, the Temple colonel.[75] This is untenable from the outset because the evangelist speaks explicitly of the cohort with its chief captain on the one hand, and of the servants of the Jews on the other. Moreover, Blinzler's assertion that his reinterpretation theory is gaining acceptance is erroneous. In new editions of the Bible, the Herder edition among others, the persons described in the Johannine Gospel as making the arrest are called "soldiers" or specifically "Roman soldiers."

Those who cling to the notion that Jesus was not seized by an arrest detail of the Roman occupying power but by the officials of the Jewish Sanhedrin must admit the discrepancies between their account and the reportage in John's Gospel. Nor can they ignore the synoptics. They, too, assume at least the participation of the Roman military, and none of them—except perhaps Luke—excludes the possibility that it was a Roman force that made the arrest. Their lack of any specific reference to a Roman commanding officer may give the impression that Jesus was arrested by the Temple police on orders of the Sanhedrin; but that does not outweigh the detailed description in John, especially because, as has already been mentioned, only the Johannine presentation can account convincingly for Judas' "betrayal."

John's statement (18:3) that the Roman military unit had called in Jewish bailiffs is of minor importance. A language barrier might have necessitated some legal assistance on the part of the Jewish authorities. This might even explain why Peter, who grabbed a sword to cut off the ear[76] of the high priest's servant, was not prosecuted by the state on charges of grievous bodily injury, perhaps even attempted manslaughter. It might also explain why the whole group was not arrested and taken away at once, after one of them had put up armed resistance. The Roman soldiers had orders to arrest only Jesus, the alleged partisan leader, and they accordingly did not trouble themselves over the injured ear of a Jewish servant. Or such may have been the narrator's intention.[77]

The "Brief" Hearing in John's Gospel

John's version says that only the Roman authorities ever officially concerned themselves with Jesus: He was arrested by a Roman officer, condemned by a Roman court, and crucified by Roman soldiers. On the other hand John takes special pains to attribute the guilt for Jesus' death to the Jews alone. The Johannine Jesus is constantly exposed to the Jews' hostility during his ministry. The mob is alleged to have made it their mission literally to hound the Galilean prophet to death. The Jewish people in its totality is portrayed as initiating the trial before the Roman tribunal, and appears before Pilate in the role of accuser.

But John never reports that Jesus was found guilty by a Jewish court. He omits the story found in the synoptics of the trial before the Jewish Supreme Council. This is all the more remarkable since that trial is no trivial incident but, according to both the synoptics and later ecclesiastical presentations, an event of central importance. At the climax of the Sanhedrin trial Jesus is supposed to have been asked whether he was the Messiah, the Son of God, and allegedly replied affirmatively, or at least failed to deny it outright. Haenchen[78] writes, "Since Christians perceive the actual guilt of the Jews to be that they did not recognize Jesus as the Messiah, they must assume that the Messiah question was the decisive point in the trial."

Doctrinaire theologians like Stauffer and Blinzler find it difficult to reinterpret the Johannine version of events to fit their opinions. They contend[79] that John omitted the story of the trial before the Sanhedrin because he assumed that it was already well known and that pagan Christian readers would have little interest in the Jewish proceedings.

John tells things differently. The Roman commander of the fortress led the bound Nazarene first to the house of the former high priest Annas. Annas no longer had any competence in such matters, a historical fact of which the evangelist was clearly unaware.[80] Annas had been deposed in A.D. 15, five years before, by the Roman prefect. The new high priest was Caiaphas, Annas' son-in-law. The designation "high priest" is applied to Annas and Caiaphas alike—rightly so, since the former high priest retained his title. He also had a seat and vote in the Sanhedrin.[81]

After Jesus had been brought before Annas, he was led in chains to the officiating high priest, Caiaphas. Neither of these made any disposition, so the prisoner was taken to the Roman Praetorium.

> The cohort and its captain and the Jewish guards seized Jesus and bound him. They took him first to Annas, because Annas was the father-in-law of Caiaphas, who was high priest that year.... The high priest questioned Jesus about his disciples and his teaching. Jesus answered: "I have spoken openly for all the world to hear; I have always taught in the synagogue and in the Temple where all the Jews meet together; I have said nothing in secret. But why ask me? Ask my hearers what I taught...." Then Annas sent him, still bound, to Caiaphas the high priest. (John 18:12–14, 19–21, 24)

Obviously John's implication is that Jesus had been a prisoner of the Roman military unit throughout this time. He was brought to Annas by the fortress commander; after a superficial interrogation, Annas ordered that the prisoner be taken to Caiaphas before being handed over to his Roman jailers. According to John's Gospel, this is where the participation of the Jewish authorities ends. He implicitly refutes the idea that there was any formal contribution of Jewish authorities, any charge or trial.

Indeed, according to John, the Romans never requested the Jewish authorities to provide legal assistance. To this extent the trial of Jesus differed from Paul's. In Acts 22:30 it is reported that Paul, who had been arrested by the Romans, was brought before the Sanhedrin so that a preliminary investigation might be conducted by order of the Roman authorities.

This leads one to wonder whether the few minor details that John gives as to the activities of the Jewish rulers are anything more than the embellishments that are typical of precisely this evangelist. One must ask why a Roman officer should have behaved in so curious a fashion[82] with a Jew arrested on suspicion of being a rebel. The Roman occupying power was certainly not a mere flunkey of the Sanhedrin, particularly in the case of an itinerant preacher from the provinces. Whenever the Roman authorities intervened, they did so by legal right or by exploiting their position as an occupation power.[83]

The Johannine description of Jesus' brief appearance before Annas and the latter's few and essentially trivial questions is so meaningless in relation to the whole course of events that it says nothing whatsoever to support the idea of Jewish participation in Jesus' condemnation. In substance, in the Johannine description, the arrest and sentencing remain an exclusively Roman affair.

Cooperation of the Jewish Establishment?

Whether the Jewish authorities could have prevented so straightforward an arrest and protected Jesus from the Romans is, of course, a wholly different question. If the Temple authorities had seen this prophet from Galilee as the man entrusted with Israel's liberation, Jewish leaders would probably have been carried away by the general enthusiasm, and would have revered him as they did the freedom fighter Bar Kochba one hundred years later. But in the eyes of the Jewish authorities, unfortunately, it was not in the national interest to protect Jesus.

The evangelist Luke restates the thinking of the so-called Emmaus disciples as they assessed the Golgotha catastrophe. Typically, he is anxious to spare the Romans:

> "All about Jesus of Nazareth," they answered, "who proved he was a great prophet by the things he said and did in the sight of God and of the whole people; and how our chief priests and our leaders handed him over to be sentenced to death, and had him crucified. Our own hope had been that he would be the one to set Israel free." (Luke 24:19-21)

The disciples were disappointed with their rabbi who had met such a sudden and inglorious end without having fulfilled the promises. But they were also disappointed and indignant that the Jewish authorities had not recognized Jesus' importance for the liberation of Israel and had allowed this prophet to be condemned and crucified by the Romans. The pericope expresses a further thought: Here, unlike the rest of the Gospels and Acts, the reproach is not leveled at the Jews, but at the chief priests and leaders. Only they, not the simple people, had the opportunity to intercede with the Romans and prevent the crucifixion.

It was primarily the party of the Sadducees who exercised sovereign power over the Jews, within the limits laid down by the Romans. The ruling Jewish stratum was always at pains to maintain good relations with the occupation power. The Sadducees were pragmatic politicians; they went so far as to pray for the Roman Caesar in the Temple. This was tantamount to a quid pro quo for a series of privileges that the Roman state had permitted the Jews: exemption from military service, sanctification of the Sabbath, and the general freedom to live according to Jewish law and ritual.

The possibility cannot be ignored that the Sadducees, notably the clique around Caiaphas, were quite content to rid themselves so simply of this heretic prophet from Galilee who was stirring up confusion among the people, this "demagogue of a cabinetmaker." They may themselves have arrested him and handed him over to the Romans; they may have maligned him and thus provoked the Romans' intervention; or they may just have remained passive in the face of the arrest being initiated by the Romans, and just let things take their course. In any case these people, who were "members of the high-priestly families" (Acts 4:6), are also alleged to have persecuted members of the early Christian communities. In so doing they had to be careful not to arouse the people's anger (Acts 5:26). It was the Pharisees, above all the esteemed Rabbi Gamaliel, who protected the Christians against such persecution and who arranged through the Sanhedrin that they be released with unrestricted freedom of preachment (Acts 5:34–42). This is further proof that the Pharisees were not enemies of Jesus, and that their people were even ready to rise up against the authorities to the extent that they took actions against Christians. To the Pharisees, the Christians were harmless and defenseless.

Like all ruling circles, Israel's were conservative, mistrustful of evolutionary or revolutionary tendencies of any kind. Socially privileged, accustomed to the modern Hellenistic life-style, they were concerned not to arouse any doubt about their loyalty to Rome. "Modern historical studies have shown that the chief responsibility for the crucifixion [of Jesus] lay with the Romans, that the Jewish 'leaders' who were involved in it, in truth were not the representatives of their people but Roman puppets who conducted a Roman rather than a Jewish policy."[84]

Ben-Chorin sees the problem from a different aspect leading to the same conclusion.

> If we consider carefully the situation in which the Jewish people suffered in their occupied country, we will see plainly that it was imperative for responsible circles to render harmless agitators like Jesus of Nazareth, to whom the people flocked, and also political activists of the likes of Judas Iscariot.[85]

The following argument, set forth by Stauffer, also has a plausible ring.

> Since the overthrow of Sejanus in October A.D. 31, Caiaphas was also threatened, and the police raids of the imperial regime in search of conspirators continued. If at that time any news of messianic movements in Palestine had reached Rome, Caiaphas' ecclesiastical governance would have been finished. For this reason Jesus had to be eliminated before it was too late.[86]

One problem with this theory must be pointed out. In citing the overthrow of Sejanus in October 31, Stauffer dates Jesus' death as Passover of 32. But this does not agree either with the synoptic dating (April 11, 27, or April 23, 34) or with the Johannine (April 7, 30). Moreover, Stauffer should have accompanied his theory with a reference that becomes necessary once Sejanus is mentioned. This notorious Jew-hater, who in A.D. 23–31 acted more or less as prime minister, running all government affairs while Tiberius retired to Capri, was a great patron and close personal friend of Pontius Pilate. Pilate owed his position as military governor in Palestine to him.[87] After Sejanus was overthrown, the fear of jeopardizing his own position that Stauffer imputes to Caiaphas would have applied even more strongly to Pilate.

How the "Jesus problem" was viewed in the Sanhedrin is described in John's Gospel in such a way as to give an especially striking picture (though it cannot claim historicity):

> Then the chief priests and Pharisees called a meeting. "Here is this man working all these signs," they said, "and what action are we taking? If we let him go on in this way everybody will believe in him, and the Romans will come and destroy the Holy Place and our nation." One of them, Caiaphas, the high priest that year, said, "You don't seem to have grasped the situation at all; you fail to see that it is better for one man to die for the people, than for the whole nation to be destroyed."[88] (John 11:47–51)

It is of course unthinkable that the content of a discussion among the Supreme Council would have been communicated to a Jesus-follower. Yet some members of that authoritative body may have sympathized with Jesus (John 12:42–43), perhaps Nicodemus and Joseph of Arimathea.

More important than the question of whether a discussion in the Sanhedrin of the kind that John describes has been documented is the fact that the report in itself is consistent. From it can be inferred that this was not a court session of the Sanhedrin, but a gathering of Council members. It further establishes that the assembly had no primary interest in Jesus' death: The Council members were undecided about what they should do with this rabbi from Galilee. Caiaphas got the idea of sacrificing him in order to avert the threat of disaster that the Roman occupation force posed to the entire people.

The Jewish authorities might have had a similar reaction to the one that had haunted Herod Antipas in Galilee in regard to John the Baptist: If they did not intervene in time but forced the Romans to act first, they would be held accountable for this incompetence. At all events the Supreme Council was responsible for maintaining peace between the Jewish population and the army of occupation. Lapide[89] writes as follows:

> We may assume that Caiaphas was anxious to maintain the freedom which was part of the bargain in exchange for political subordination to Rome, when he advised the sacrifice of Jesus. That he was ready to accept that Jesus himself was innocent is proved by the fact that he spoke of him as "one man" (John 11:50), not defaming him as "brigand" or "rebel" or a "false prophet."

Caiaphas comes off as a real politician, in today's terms.

On the other hand, such considerations as expressed in John 11:47–50, especially with the political justification in verse 48, always seem to be interpreted by Christians as an actual death sentence pronounced on Jesus by the Supreme Council. Yet even the most anti-Jewish and pro-Roman depictions of Jesus' trial in the Gospels do not ignore the fact that without Pilate's order and its execution by Roman soldiers Jesus could never have been crucified, even if the entire people of Israel had wished it.[90]

Perhaps the Supreme Council was even glad to have in its custody a man about whom it could later be said that he set himself up as Messiah. They could then hand him over to the Romans as a gesture of their willingness to collaborate. There was a very great concern about possible clashes with the occupation force on the holidays; Pilate's hypersensitivity and ruthlessness were well known. Now it was necessary for the Jewish authorities to be as circumspect as possible in order to avoid a bloodbath among the population such as had already happened many times before. It was bound to have a soothing effect on the governor's disposition if, immediately upon his arrival, a prisoner could be handed over to him with the comment that here was someone who that very day had exhibited agitational behavior and made inflammatory speeches. The Supreme Council would thereby have shown its goodwill and the resolution of the problem would have been up to the Romans.

Bultmann writes as follows:

> Jesus was crucified by the Roman procurator Pontius Pilate. What role the Jewish authorities, on whom the

Christian tradition puts the chief blame, actually played is no longer discernible. It is probable that they, as in other cases, worked hand in hand with the Romans in the interest of political tranquillity. At least there can be no doubt that Jesus, like other agitators, died on the cross as a Messianic prophet.[91]

The greater probability is that, as presented above, the entire event was a Roman affair, from the arrest to the execution (though presumably with the participation of some Jewish bailiffs). It is also conceivable that there was a small official Jewish contribution to the trial proceedings. But Jesus was killed by the Romans, not by the Jews.[92]

THE UNKNOWN GRAVE OF A PATRIOT

Even after his death Jesus was still under Roman jurisdiction, as the Gospels all confirm. Joseph of Arimathea, a respected member of the Sanhedrin, presented himself to Pilate in the late afternoon of the day of the execution to ask him for the release of the corpse so that he could bury it according to Jewish rites. The permission of the Roman military authorities was evidently required before the body could be taken down from the cross and interred.[93]

> It was now evening and since it was Preparation Day (that is, the vigil of the sabbath), there came Joseph of Arimathea, a prominent member of the Council, who himself lived in the hope of seeing the kingdom of God, and he boldly went to Pilate and asked him for the body of Jesus. Pilate, astonished that he should have died so soon, summoned the centurion and inquired if he was already dead. Having been assured of this by the centurion, he granted the corpse to Joseph. (Mark 15:42–45)

As far as the Romans were concerned the delinquent could just as well have hung on the cross for a few more days as an added deterrent, but the Jewish authorities—according to the Gospel—attached importance to a dignified interment. This meant that Jesus had to be taken down and buried before sundown, or to be exact, before the appearance of the first evening star, since this marked the beginning of the Sabbath[94]—as prescribed in Deuteronomy 21:22–23.

The evangelist John reports in great detail that Jesus received an honorable burial for that time: "Nicodemus came as well—the same one who had first come to Jesus at nighttime—and he brought a mixture of myrrh and aloes, weighing about a hundred pounds. They took the body of Jesus and wrapped it with the spices in linen cloths, following the Jewish burial custom" (John 19:39–41). So two high Jewish officials buried a Jew who had died on the Roman cross as a patriot and martyr. (Nicodemus had allegedly participated in the sentencing!) Had the Jewish Supreme Council condemned Jesus for blasphemy, two of its members would never have taken pains to ensure that the hanged man was immediately rehabilitated and buried with special honors. To do so would have been a grave, if not punishable, offense. Josephus Flavius cites the following prescription from the Mishna: "He that blasphemes God, let him be stoned, and let him hang upon a tree all that day, and then let him be buried in an ignominious and obscure manner" (*Antiquities of the Jews*, Book iv, chapter 9).

In describing a ritual burial, the evangelists unwittingly bear out what the Gospels overall are not disposed to concede: Influential Jews, even those who sat on the committee that allegedly sentenced him to death, demonstrated a great affection for Jesus. Luke emphasizes in his Gospel, as do Mark and Matthew, that it was Joseph of Arimathea who had arranged for the removal of the body from the cross; but he gives another version in Acts 13:27–30. Here not merely one prominent member of the Council is involved in the burial procedure but the entire population of Jerusalem together with the magistrate.

Whether the Gospel account is itself credible is another question. It could arise from, say, the fulfillment legend of Isaiah 53:9, which says that God's servant will find his grave "with the rich." Thus it is probably not by chance that Matthew 27:57 introduces Joseph of Arimathea as "a rich man of Arimathea."

According to Roman common law, only relatives and friends could request the corpse of a crucified person. But Joseph of Arimathea was not in this category. Alas, the most likely assumption is that the Roman legionnaires simply buried Jesus as they normally buried crucified bodies. Jesus was probably thrown into a common grave along with the two men crucified with him; later it was not possible to identify the grave.[95]

If Jesus was buried in the individual grave described in the Gospels, it is inconceivable that the Jerusalem Christian community never made the grave an object of worship. Jewish ritual has always been marked by a strong interest in the graves of relatives or venerable figures such as martyrs and prophets. This would have been even more true of an "empty tomb" that had come about through the word of God.

In Luke 24:5 the angels say to the women, "Why look among the dead for someone who is alive?" This expresses the conviction of the early Christian community and the early Church that the actual site of Jesus' tomb is of scant importance compared to the true faith that Jesus is not a deceased person to be memorialized, but the living Lord present among his own.[96]

After Christians and the Roman Empire made peace with each other, hasty efforts were made to rectify past omissions. Eusebius[97] reports that Emperor Constantine agreed to make the site of the Savior's resurrection accessible to visitors and worshipers, but the site had to be found first. Bishop Macarius, to whom the emperor entrusted the search operation, became greatly confused. He invited his followers to pray with him and received a revelation that prompted him to dig on the site of the temple of Aphrodite. Goguel: "The most holy place in Jerusalem had been covered up by the most abominable thing in the city, whence comes the idea of looking for a site of Calvary and the Holy Sepulchre under the temple of Venus."[98]

Constantine had a basilica erected on the ruins of this formerly "sinful" structure after his mother, Helena, inspected the site and reported that she had found Jesus' cross there—after three hundred years! Since then Christendom has believed that Jesus' execution and interment took place on that site, that Golgotha was located where the Church of the Holy Sepulchre stands. Since Constantine, the Holy Sepulchre has been the site most venerated by Christians. Crusaders swarmed from Europe in order to free it from the hands of the infidels. The blood of hundreds of thousands was shed for the sake of this site, to the battle cry "God wills it!" The alleged cross of Jesus found by the emperor's mother, Helena, has long since been broken into small pieces that have been shipped all over the world as relics. What remained was "The Cross," and that transformed the pious warriors into killers.

Publicists Under Political Pressure

According to "detheologized" findings, the evangelists may have invented the entire story of the Jewish authorities' complicity in Jesus' violent death, or at least the participation of the Jewish Supreme Council, the Sanhedrin, in which the influential and patriotic Pharisees were also represented. It must be remembered that the Gospels were written at a time when the Christian sect, whose first generation had been purely Jewish, had cut itself off from Judaism and come into conflict with the mother religion.

The need to distance Jesus as much as possible from any kind of Jewish insurgency movement was perceived very early. It was the only way that Paul, who preached not in the Jewish homeland but to Jews and pagans outside Palestine in the Roman Empire, could hope to achieve success. The collapse of the Jewish revolt against the Romans in A.D. 70 reinforced the need. Nowadays it is often claimed in theological circles that the crushing defeat of the state of Israel was reason enough for the Gospels to saddle the Jews with responsibility for Jesus' death (suffice it to cite the Protestant theologian Schmithals). But this is going too far. Schmithals sees this attribution of guilt as a product neither of anti-Semitism nor of consideration for the Romans. He puts it down exclusively to the fact that after the Jewish catastrophe of 70 Christians were driven out of the reconstituted synagogue, thereby losing the protection accorded to permitted religions in the Roman Empire. The animosity came ostensibly from the synagogue, not the Church. This is used to explain the Gospels' attribution of guilt as a defense against the slanders of Christians[99] concocted by the synagogue.

The fact is that the Romans did not distinguish between permitted and forbidden faiths.[100] (They were tolerant of all religions, and never persecuted Christians because of their faith.)[101] This argument can be dismissed on other grounds also: The transfer of the guilt to the Jews did not happen after A.D. 70, when the Gospels were first compiled, but much earlier. The fateful idea of the Jews' guilt for the death of Jesus clearly goes back to Paul; it emerged in the quarter-century before the outbreak of the Jewish-Roman war. According to Pauline teaching, the Jews (meaning the Jewish religious community) killed the Lord as they had murdered the prophets in the past: "The people who put the Lord Jesus to death, and the prophets too. And now they have been persecuting us, and acting in a way that cannot please God and makes them the enemies of the whole human race" (1 Thess. 2:15).

The Pauline thesis that the religious authority of "apostate Israel" had "always" killed the prophets and finally, through the killing of the great Messianic prophet, brought judgment upon itself, also dominates the Gospel accounts. It is notable that the parable of the wicked husbandmen appears in all the Synoptic Gospels.[102] A vineyard owner (God) hands over his vineyard (Israel) to tenants (the Jews). The owner occasionally sends his servants (the prophets) to collect the produce. But the unfaithful tenants kill all the servants one after the other. At last the owner sends his son, assuming that the tenants will not lay violent hands on him. But the tenants also kill the son, thinking the vineyard will then become their property. But what will the owner of the vineyard do now? He will come and kill the tenants and give the vineyard to other tenants.

All the Gospels—indeed, all the New Testament writings—evince a strong overall anti-Jewish attitude. Jesus becomes the "true Israel." Only believers in Christ are children of Abraham, Isaac, and Jacob; they are the "Israel of God." To them now belongs the Hebrew Bible, to be used as a weapon against the Jews of the old covenant. It is not the Christians who have fallen from the faith, but the Jews. The Jewish teachers are thieves who sneak in to the flock of sheep through the wrong gate (false exegesis). The people of the Covenant of Sinai are doomed to destruction through God's wrath. A small number, however, who have arrived at faith in Christ, can be saved. For this reason alone, God has not rejected his people in the sense of Romans 11:2.[103]

I am not convinced by the explanation, often given of late, that this is an intra-Judaic controversy and that anti-Judaism can be excluded for that very reason. This is an anti-Jewish apology, joyfully seized upon now that it is unseemly to express anti-Jewish sentiments overtly. Church Fathers, Church teachers and popes, and theologians of all shadings thought altogether differently about the matter. They were glad to be able to cite the New Testament to buttress their anti-Semitism. If Luke writes, for example, that practicing Jews are "loathsome in the sight of God" (Luke 16:15), and Paul teaches that the Jews of the old covenant "cannot please God" whose "retribution is overtaking them at last" (1 Thess. 2:16), they must reckon with being judged according to their stated words, following the acknowledged rules of legal and social custom.

When the Gospels were composed, the Hellenistic (Pauline) trend within the group of Jesus-followers had definitively prevailed over the Hebraic tendency.[104] As a result of the tragic outcome of the Jewish war, the Nazarites, founders of the early Jerusalem community, had essentially lost their influence. The Christians in the Diaspora, whether Jews or non-Jews, sided with the victorious Romans. "Hence an important task of the Gospels was to show a direction to the pagan Christians and, after the 70s, to make it possible for them to say, 'We are not Jews, Jesus himself actually was not a Jew, he was born as such only by chance. Jesus stood loyal to Rome as we also do.' "[105] The destruction of the Temple was interpreted as the rejection of Judaism because of its refusal to believe in Christ (Matt. 24:15; Luke 21:22).

The most important Christian community outside Palestine was that founded by Paul in Rome. The members of this community were naturally swept up in the whirlwind of the Roman victory over Israel. Moreover, Paul had instructed the community to remain absolutely loyal to the emperor: "You must all obey the governing authorities. Since all government comes from God" (Rom. 13:1). Specifically it is in Nero's state that Paul writes his admonitory letter: "the State of a political clown, of a fratricide, a matricide. . . . While Roman intellectuals sharply attacked the unjust Roman system, Paul and his pupils closed their eyes before the injustice."[106]

Most of the disagreements and controversies for the young Church arose with the Pharisees (Matt. 23:29–35). The Zealots and the Essenes had been stamped out in the wars; the Sadducee nobility lost its possessions and influence; the Herodians had dissolved or become assimilated into the Romans. The only Jewish sect to have survived the catastrophe of 70 was of the Pharisees.[107] These men, loyal to the Mosaic law and perforce anti-Roman, put up the greatest intellectual resistance to Christian missionary activity, with a characteristic pedantry.[108] It follows that this group was thought of especially negatively, as being in a permanent state of hostility to Jesus. The authors and revisers of the Gospels presented them thus, notwithstanding that their mentor Paul himself had been a Pharisee (Phil. 3:6; Acts 23:6) and that it was the highly respected Pharisee leader in Israel Rabbi Gamaliel whom Peter had to thank for being released following his arrest two years after Jesus' death on orders of the high priest (Acts 5:34). Overall, the

Pharisees were the first to have been sympathetic toward the new Jewish Christian sect, as demonstrated by their massive protest against the condemnation of the Jerusalem bishop James, the brother of Jesus. James was himself an observant Pharisee (in contrast to Paul, who only alluded to his Pharisaism if it was to his advantage).

The situation changed after A.D. 70, when the Church had largely detached itself from Pharisaic Judaism and become friendly to the Romans. A confrontation ensued between Christians (including Jewish Christians) and Pharisees. There is no doubt that the evangelists, above all Matthew, reflected in the Gospel accounts their arguments with and aversions to the Pharisees. Nor did they have any scruples in profiting from the Jews' dissatisfactions, as they were expressed in the traditional rabbinical self-criticism. "Beware of the sourdough of the Pharisees!" read the warning of the early Church. Ruth Kastning-Olmesdahl[109] writes, "They believed that the Pharisees encompassed the whole of Judaism; criticism of the Pharisees was viewed as a criticism of Judaism altogether."

This is a crude distortion of historical fact. For Christianity leaned more on the Pharisees than on any other spiritual branch of Judaism. On this point Kolping writes as follows:

> Personal immortality and judgment after death, Resurrection (at least of the just), existence of angels, freedom of man and the action of Providence are the creeds professed by this religious party. Their ethics of love of neighbor also included non-Israelites. Moral guilt was conceivable only in reference to the divine will; one's own piety did not cancel the necessity of divine grace. In comparison to the conservative Sadducees, the Pharisees constituted the theologically progressive trend. They won great influence through their scribes in the Sanhedrin, despite their relatively small number. Their understanding of the Law did not cling so closely to the letter as did that of the Sadducees. From A.D. 70 on, the newly formed Sanhedrin was completely under their control. The Pharisees should not be viewed only according to the model of the hypocritical Pharisees in the Gospel, and certainly not according to their negative portrayal in the New Testament.[110]

In a broader sense Jesus himself may be counted a Pharisee, which some may find shocking. Like a highly educated Pharisee, one of the so-called scribes,[111] Jesus answers to the honorary title of Master.[112] Though Jesus criticized the title Rabbi, an exclusive Pharisaic designation reserved for eminent people, he taught chiefly in parables, the typical pedagogical method of the rabbis. As regards the religious question that most concerns people, of what happens after death, Jesus believed like the Pharisees in the resurrection of the dead at the end of time. The rabbis declared, "Whoever denies the resurrection of the dead has no share in the world to come."[113] Rabbi Hillel formulated the Golden Rule of the Pharisees: "Do not do what you hate to others." The evangelist Matthew has Jesus say, "Do unto others as you would have them do unto you."

The patriotic and Israelite sentiments expressed in Jesus' sayings and deeds also correspond to the Pharisaic mentality, as opposed to that of the Sadducee priest caste or that of the lords and their followers (the Herodians), who exhibited a great readiness to collaborate with the Roman occupying power. The Pharisees were Jesus' real constituency; his activities were directed at them, and he sought chiefly their company. As Küng writes, "It should not be forgotten that the Pharisee whom Jesus took as an example was not a hypocrite. He was a sincere, devout man and spoke the simple truth. He had done all he said. The Pharisees were of exemplary morality and consequently enjoyed the respect of those who could reach their standards."[114]

Jesus gladly shared meals with Pharisees (Luke 7:36), and Pharisees warned him betimes to flee (Luke 13:31) when Herod Antipas had sent out a search party for him. They likewise warned him that Roman informers might be listening when the disciples hailed his entry into Jerusalem all too joyfully (Luke 19:39).

In Jesus' time there were about six thousand Pharisees. They themselves called their party a "fellowship" and each other "comrade."[115] Because of Jesus' closeness to the Pharisees, it was natural for him to engage in most of his discussions with them. This must often have led to violent arguments, especially with those who in Jesus' view abided too strictly by the letter of the Law and did not inquire into the deeper meaning of a precept. Probably Jesus also had personal enemies among them, who would sooner have seen him dead than alive. Many of his interpretations—for example, those of the Sabbath observance and purity regulations—must have been a real challenge to the orthodox Pharisees. But it is inconceivable that Jesus flatly insulted the Pharisees with expressions such as "hypocrites [who] will receive the greater damnation" (Matt. 23:13) or "brood of vipers" (Matt. 12:34).

Heated exchanges, moreover, are altogether typical of Jewish debate; they do not come anywhere near the level of personal enmity depicted in the Gospel accounts.

> For the understanding of Jesus and of the New Testament it is most imperative not to interpret Jesus' verbal battles with the Pharisees as in principle anti-Pharisaic, but as ongoing and customary inter-Jewish contentiousness going back to Old Testament times, whose sharpness is all too easily understood in the context of the approaching kingdom of God.[116]

The political aim of creating antagonism between the Pharisees and Jesus is all too apparent in the Gospels. From 70 on, this meant removing Jesus as far as possible from Judaism and placing him in the world of pagan Christendom that was friendly toward Rome. Viewed thus, the effort evident throughout the New Testament to play down Roman guilt for Jesus' violent death can be seen as prerequisite for proclaiming the Gospels in the Roman Empire, where they stood the most chance of success.

In the apocryphal gospel of Peter, the Roman procurator is exonerated to such an extent that the Jewish tetrarch Herod Antipas, not Pilate, condemns Jesus to death on the cross. The Jews see to Jesus' execution, while Pilate professes Jesus' divine sonship:

> They [the Jewish people], however, seized the Lord and rudely and hurriedly bundled him off and said: "Let us drag off the Son of God, since we have received power over him." And they placed a purple robe over him and sat him on the judgment seat, saying: "Judge justly, o King of Israel!" And one of them brought a crown of thorns and placed it on the head of the Lord. And others who were standing there spat in his face, and others slapped him on the cheeks, others struck him with a cane and some scourged him saying: "This is the honor with which we wish to honor the Son of God." . . . They became angry over him and ordered that his legs not be broken so that he would die amid torments . . . Pilate spoke: "I am pure of the blood of the Son of God, you have decided thus." (Verse fragments 6–9, 14:46)

Peter's gospel corresponds not only to the spirit of the emerging Church, but also to later Church teaching. Origen: "The Jews nailed Jesus to the cross." Thomas Aquinas: "The Jews sinned as crucifiers not only of the man Jesus, but also of the Christ of God."[117]

Of the canonical Gospels, the political apologist theme is most pronounced in Luke. His version reads as though Pilate did not hand down the death sentence, but instead delivered Jesus to the Jews, who then brought him to the cross: "and handed Jesus over to them to deal with him as they pleased.... As they were leading him away . . ." (Luke 23, 25–26).

Luke (or a reviser) even places in Peter's mouth words that would surely have taken the latter's breath away had he read them. Shortly after Golgotha, Luke has Peter say, "For this reason the whole House of Israel can be certain that God has made this Jesus whom you crucified both Lord and Christ" (Acts 2:36).[118]

According to John, the Jews explicitly demanded that Jesus be crucified not as a political dissident but as a blasphemer (19:7), and thus the Jews themselves carried out the deed: "So in the end Pilate handed him over to them to be crucified" (19:16).

The Roman occupation force recedes completely into the background of the Gospels. It is mentioned only in a few passages, and then only indirectly; yet the Romans were perceived by the people as an oppressive yoke and a constant provocation.[119] But only the Roman legionnaires are negatively portrayed. They are the ones who mocked Jesus as soldiers would and played rough and cruel tricks on him. But from the centurion on up, the occupiers come off rather well.

Of course the synoptics do not go as far as the apocryphal gospel of Peter, which has even Pilate confess of faith in Jesus' divine sonship. But they do place such a confession in the mouth of the Roman centurion (Luke 23:47–48; Mark 15:39), as though he were in a sense the first member of the Christian community in formation after Jesus' death. This passage is undoubtedly a variation on a handy literary theme: the conversion of the executioner. But a political consideration must be added. Haenchen puts it thus:

> It is the Christian community that makes the centurion speak thus, that places its own profession of faith in his mouth. . . . Since none of his followers was present to make his profession of faith in the hour of Jesus' death,

the community had to pronounce this profession through the Roman captain. In this act Rome itself recognized the divine sonship of the executed Jesus.[120]

It was considered best not to portray Jesus merely as a man who died a rebel's death. Even an author such as Blinzler, who otherwise never ceases to burden the Jews with complete responsibility for Jesus' death, concedes that it did not seem advisable "to present the founder of Christianity too conspicuously as one legally sentenced to death by a Roman tribunal and executed."[121] Consequently the Jews, not the Romans, were presented as the actual enemies of Jesus. Peter Fiedler writes as follows:

> Let us for once make ourselves clear about the incriminatory burden that weighed upon the early Christian missionaries in the Roman Empire! The proclaimed Lord and founder of the new religious community had been sentenced by the official representatives of the sovereign state power as a rebel and executed in the customary ignominious way. Nothing could lessen such a burden more effectively than the assertion that the relevant functionary had recognized and established Jesus' innocence but that at the sentencing he gave ground under Jewish pressure.[122]

Turning to the Christian faith was not to be viewed as siding with a rebel. So the event was described as if Jesus had been found guilty by the Jews on religious grounds and hence condemned to death. Lutz writes, "Israel, which was already despised, shunned, and rejected after the Zealot uprisings, became a scapegoat to be highlighted so that the palpable conflicts of the Christians with the Roman supreme power could be attenuated."[123]

The aim was to convince the Roman imperial authorities that the Empire had nothing to fear from the founder of the new religion; that such had also been Pilate's view; and that that was why he had handed down the death sentence only after much hesitation and under pressure from the Jews. Only through a fictionalized account of the trial and a reversal of the attribution of guilt could there be any hope of a tolerant response from Rome. This was important to the survival of the fledgling Church. Lapide writes, "It was a vital question for the evangelists to reduce the responsibility for the death of their Savior to a minimum, employing all possible stylistic and editorial skills to make the guilt of the Jews, already taboo as rebels, appear as grievous as possible."[124]

Roman records reveal not the slightest interest in denying Roman responsibility. There is absolutely no awareness of any responsibility in the real meaning of the word; from the Roman point of view, the case was too unimportant. For Romans of the first century, Christianity was only a contemptible Oriental superstition.[125] Tacitus' *Annals*, Book xv:44 reported only briefly on the Christ from whom the *Christiani* derived their name. He saw the founder of the sect simply as an executed criminal, no matter what he may have been called (Tacitus did not know the name of Jesus of Nazareth). Whereas Tacitus states that the man was executed *per* ("through") Pontius Pilate, the Apostles' Creed asserts that it was *sub* ("under") Pontius Pilate. In the intervening time, it had become shocking and offensive to make the Romans responsible for the crucifixion.

These circumstances and the fact that John's Gospel stresses the participation of the Romans even at the time of the arrest, make it clear that it was exclusively the Romans who staged the trial of Jesus of Nazareth, from his arrest to the carrying out of the death sentence.

An exquisitely ironic reaction to the tendentious Gospel reports surfaced in July 1972, when a motion (the second one)[126] was presented by Christian theologians to the Israeli Supreme Court recommending the nullification of the judgment pronounced against Jesus of Nazareth. The Chief Justice politely explained that, regrettably, he could not consider the motion because of a lack of jurisdiction, and referred the petitioners to an Italian court.[127]

Nine

THE ALLEGED TRIAL BEFORE THE SANHEDRIN

THE trial before the Sanhedrin is at the heart of the Passion story in the Synoptic Gospels. It is the basis for the later break between Christians and Jews and as such it precipitated a tragic progression that burdens the Christian-Jewish dialogue to this very day.[1]

Committed theologians of both Christian confessions such as Küng, Kolping, Bornkamm, and Holtz have called into question the historicity of a trial before the Sanhedrin. Kolping writes, "Those investigators who contend that a juridically proper trial before the Sanhedrin is completely unhistorical may be right."[2] Dibelius considers the trial simply a myth.[3] This critical attitude of a minority of Catholic and Protestant theologians, not surprisingly, is still overshadowed by the prevailing attitude: At a trial by the Sanhedrin on charges of blasphemy, Jesus was found guilty and condemned to death. To cast any doubt on this version of events has always been frowned upon.[4]

The Court and the Presiding Judge

The Sanhedrin consisted of the high priest as president and seventy councilors.[5] A quorum—empowered to pronounce a death sentence—consisted of the high priest and twenty-three judges present at his invitation.[6] The Gospels do not say how many judges decided on the death sentence for Jesus. It would have been illegal for the high priest to summon only judges whom he assumed would side with him. In A.D. 62, the behavior of the high priest Ananias gave rise to a real judicial scandal (at the time Jesus' brother James was sentenced to death and executed). He was removed from office and replaced by a man called Jesus, the son of Damnaus, according to Josephus Flavius.[7]

Jerusalem's upper stratum (priests and influential families) was represented in the Sanhedrin; they comprised the party of the Sadducees.[8] Pharisees also belonged to the Sanhedrin; in Jesus' time they constituted the strongest faction.[9] The members of the Sanhedrin were nominated by the high priest who was awarded his office by the Roman procurator. (Its official title was, confusingly, Messiah.) This naturally obliged him to be loyal to Rome.

In earlier times the high priest was the head of the Jewish royal dynasty (1 Macc. 16:23–24). The Jewish vassal King Herod the Great nominated and deposed the high priests at will. In Jesus' time the office, awarded by the Romans, was envisaged as a lifetime appointment, but the Romans frequently deposed and replaced their high priests, whom they themselves had appointed.

It is historically confirmed that at the time under discussion a certain Joseph, surnamed Caiaphas,[10] was high priest and president of the court. Caiaphas, son-in-law of Annas[11] (who had been deposed in A.D. 15), was appointed in A.D. 16 or 18 by the procurator Valerius Gratus. In 36 he was removed from office by Vitellius, the governor of Syria—who deposed the procurator Pilate the same year.

There was only one high priest (or grand priest); the Gospels' frequent mentions of "high priests" are misleading and refer to Caiaphas and his priestly clan. Caiaphas' unusually long term of office—most high priests (except for Annas) were in office only one year, or at the most six—attests to his skill as a politician and ability to maintain tolerably good relations with the Roman occupation force. No judicial scandal comparable to the one that was triggered three decades later by his brother-in-law Ananias ever took place under Caiaphas. He was not a dishonest judge, though Jewish chroniclers were not on the whole sympathetic to him. This can probably be ascribed to his pro-Roman policy.

The Sanhedrin was not only the Supreme Court of the Jews, but also their foremost ecclesiastical and secular authority. Criminal proceedings were nothing but inquisitions but the judges were enjoined to unearth every conceivable argument in favor of the accused.[12] There was no way to lodge an appeal. The sentence was pronounced in the name of God:

> He said to these judges, "Give due thought to your duties, since you are not judging in the name of men but in the name of Yahweh, who is with you whenever you pronounce sentence. May the fear of Yahweh now be on you. Keep the Law, apply it, for Yahweh our God has no part in fraud or partiality or the taking of bribes." (2 Chron. 19:6–7)

The professional ethics expected of a Sanhedrin judge were thus not at all inferior to those required of a judge in our own time and place.

INCONSISTENCIES IN THE TRIAL ACCOUNT

The Gospel accounts of the trial before the Sanhedrin are no more than a testimony of faith by the community.[13] It would be a mistake to take these accounts as a court record. The very structure of the description in Mark 14:55–65 (which corresponds to Matthew 26:59–68) gives reason to question its veracity. The account of the trial is apparently a later interpolation into the story of Peter's denial. The denial story begins with Mark 14:54. One verse later it is interrupted by an account of the trial proceedings, to be continued in Mark 14:72 with no transition.

Furthermore, the Pharisees have up to this point been portrayed as Jesus' main enemies (especially by the synoptics). Suddenly they no longer appear. The scribes are mentioned alongside the high priests and elders.[14] Whereas before they had always been shown in close association with the Pharisees,[15] in the Passion story they are placed on the side of the Saduccees.¹⁶ Only in John's Gospel are the Pharisees occasionally mentioned within the framework of the Passion event. But even there they are no longer designated as Jesus' enemies or advocates of the death penalty for him; they appear either as government officials (John 18:3) or as undecided on how to deal with "the Jesus problem" (John 11:47-48). It would be inconceivable that the Pharisees, who had a seat, a vote, and influence in the Sanhedrin, would not have been mentioned in connection with so decisive an event as a death sentence, had such a death sentence actually been handed down by a Jewish court.

Nowhere outside the Gospels is there any record of a trial of Jesus of Nazareth. Such a trial, if only because it was held both before the Sanhedrin and the Roman procurator's court, would inevitably have caused a considerable stir, and would definitely have found its way into historical chronicles as an exceptional case. In addition, it was extremely unusual for a death sentence to be pronounced by the Sanhedrin, which was known for its great leniency. This is manifest in numerous decisions of the rabbis.¹⁷ Josephus Flavius, who chronicles practically every event worth mentioning in the first century of our era up to the outbreak of the Jewish War in Jerusalem, would certainly have mentioned this sensational double trial around A.D. 30 if it had taken place. The trial would also have interested him personally; Josephus Flavius came from a distinguished Jerusalem family. He himself was initially a Pharisee. At the time that the death sentence is supposed to have been pronounced on Jesus, his father was an officiating priest, which permits the assumption that he was also a member of the Sanhedrin and had participated in the sentencing.

Furthermore, the evangelists' reports themselves give rise to doubt. The oldest tradition, Mark, associates only the name Pilate, not Caiaphas, with the Passion story; Mark had obviously known nothing about a trial before Caiaphas. The name Caiaphas is mentioned, but outside the Passion story itself. According to Acts 4:6, Annas, not Caiaphas, was the officiating high priest and he was still in that post at the time of Peter's trial, several years after Jesus' death. And the fourth evangelist, John, completely excludes any trial before the Sanhedrin.

Jesus was condemned by Pontius Pilate and crucified by Roman soldiers. Later, in order to exculpate the Romans and blame only the Jews for Jesus' violent death, it proved absolutely essential to fabricate a trial before the Jewish Supreme Council, with a guilty verdict and a death sentence.

Finally, directly and necessarily linked to this discussion, there is the thesis (refutable, of course) that the Sanhedrin might indeed have conducted capital trials but could not carry out death sentences because the so-called blood jurisdiction lay exclusively with the Romans. This seems implausible and fundamentally nonsensical from a judicial point of view. Why should the Sanhedrin have gone to the trouble of holding a trial if it was established from the outset that no consequences would result from it, and specifically that a death sentence would not be carried out? The court had to assume that the Roman tribunal could not draw on any facts established at its hearing but would have to conduct a new trial from scratch and along entirely different lines. The obvious course for the Sanhedrin would have been to limit itself to police measures, to order the culprit's arrest and hand him over to the Romans, who were vested with full authority to act on their own verdict.

Massive Violations of Established Law

If we now consider the trial of Jesus before the Sanhedrin as described in the Gospels, especially Mark and Matthew, we are confronted with a whole series of serious violations of the law.[18] They were more overt than any we know of, even, for example, the abuses in the court of Roland Freisler,* which was at pains to give at least the appearance of legality:

> It was forbidden to hold trials on the Sabbath, holidays, or Preparation Days (Sanh. iv:1a). Yet the proceedings against Jesus allegedly took place on the Seder night, of all times. Trials could be held only during the day (Sanh. iv:1a); the trial against Jesus is said to have taken place at night.
>
> Trial proceedings had to be conducted in open session, and indeed in the Temple courtyard, the *Beth Din* (Sanh. xi:2b). But the proceedings against Jesus are said to have taken place in the private residence of the high priest.[19]
>
> Only acquittals could be announced immediately following trial proceedings; a sentence had to be

*A ruthless judge of the Nazi People's Court who cruelly sentenced thousands to death—Tr.

postponed until the following day.[20] This regulation would also have been grossly violated.

The facts on which a sentence is based must be contained either in the deposition of the injured party (Deut. 21:18–21) or in the evidence of at least two informers (Deut. 19:15). The evidence against Jesus was introduced by the presiding official of the court during the session.

For capital crimes a sentence could only be issued if the deed had been attested to unimpeachably by at least two witnesses (Deut. 17:6). In contrast to Roman criminal procedure, the confession of the accused was not sufficient. But Jesus was allegedly sentenced on the basis of a confession alone, not as a result of testimony of two or more witnesses.

Arguably, Jesus committed the offense of blasphemy, for which he was allegedly condemned, for the first time in the courtroom; and Caiaphas called his fellow judges as witnesses. In that case there could be no question of a confession. Although witnesses were prohibited from participating in the final verdict (Sanh. v:4b), in Jesus' case all the members of the Council, hence all witnesses, supposedly participated in the verdict.

It goes without saying that the participants in a trial, particularly a chief judge and his colleagues, were required to be in a state of mental sobriety and clarity. This court supposedly sat in judgment on Jesus not only after having been rudely awakened from sleep, but only a few hours after all of its members had drunk quantities of wine at a Seder. A minimum of four cups was prescribed, and many of the judges must have consumed even more. Certainly anyone who had drunk four cups or more of wine, according to the Pharisaic tradition, would have been barred from sitting in judgment.[21]

Thus the trial before the Sanhedrin depicted in the Gospels is rife with deficiencies of so grave a character that its illegality could be irrefutably established by any critic. This very fact classifies it as nonhistorical.[22]

Assuming that the trial before the Sanhedrin did take place, everything recorded about its course is wholly suspect. Not a single disciple was there to bear witness, and the depiction in the Gospels is so contradictory that it can immediately be dismissed as a basis for a historical interpretation.

Only Mark (thirteen verses) and Matthew (twelve verses) cover the trial in any detail. The inference from their reports is that there must have been two separate trials: one before the Jewish court, which took place at night in Caiaphas' private residence, the other before the Roman court on the following morning.

> The men who had arrested Jesus led him off to Caiaphas, the high priest, where the scribes and the elders were assembled.... When morning came, all the chief priests and the elders of the people met in council to bring about the death of Jesus. They had him bound, and led him away to hand him over to Pilate the governor. (Matt. 26:57–58; 27:1–2)

In Mark and Matthew the charge of blasphemy does not constitute the basis of the trial but turns up only at the end of the session. In the eight verses of Luke, a Greek writing for a Greek public, the Sanhedrin's reproach is limited to one single issue, Jesus' alleged claim that he was the Son of God.[23] Nor does Luke record a nocturnal trial. After the arrest Jesus is led to the house of the high priest; during the night he is harassed and mocked by those who arrested him (Luke 22:63–65). The trial begins on the following morning, in the court of the Sanhedrin: "When day broke there was a meeting of the elders of the people, attended by the chief priests and scribes. He was brought before their council" (22:66–67).

Luke depicts not two separate trials but one trial divided into two parts: a hearing before the Supreme Council (without evidence of witnesses) and a trial before Pilate. He does not discuss Jesus' interrogation by the high priest, but says the entire Sanhedrin asked Jesus whether he was the Messiah and the Son of God. After Jesus replied affirmatively (or perhaps failed to give an unequivocal denial), the Sanhedrin considered the trial closed so that Jesus could be delivered to the jurisdiction of the occupying power: " 'What need of witnesses have we now?' they said. 'We have heard it for ourselves from his own lips' " (22:71). Thereupon "the whole assembly" rose and brought the culprit to Pilate.

Luke does not see fit to mention any alleged blasphemy charge of the Sanhedrin against Jesus, nor a death sentence based on it.[24] His report contains a singular feature: He says that the decision against Jesus was not unanimous. "Then a member of the council arrived, an upright and virtuous man named Joseph. He had not consented to what the others had planned and carried out. He came from Arimathea, a Jewish town, and he lived in the hope of seeing the kingdom of God" (23:50–52).

Whereas Mark 14:64 and Matthew 27:1 say that Jesus' sentence was decided without a nay vote, Luke does cite this one dissenting voice. This plainly has a deeper significance: According to Jewish law of that time, an accused person had to be acquitted if he had been unanimously found guilty. The assumption was that in such a case the court must be prejudiced.[25] Luke's description seeks in general to play down the violations of proper procedure, omitting the nocturnal hearing in the house of the high priest. He evinces the same circumspection in citing the one negative voice in the verdict of guilty.

To Pilate, Luke continues, the councilors voiced charges against Jesus of inciting rebellion, tax evasion, and unauthorized exercise of a public office or insulting the emperor—exclusively political offenses. He quotes the charges exactly: "They began their accusation by saying, 'We found this man inciting our people to revolt, opposing payment of the tribute to Caesar, and claiming to be Christ, a king' " (23:2–3).

The description is different again in the fourth Gospel. According to John 18:12–40 and 19:1–16, an interrogation takes place at night in the house of the former high priest Annas and on the following day a trial is held before Pilate. To be sure, the interrogation before Annas is crude: His unintimidated answer earns Jesus a slap in the face, which he protests. But the Jewish authorities press no charges; he is merely questioned about his disciples and teachings. After his evasive answer on this matter, the prisoner is handed over to Pilate.[26] Only then, under massive Jewish pressure, is the trial conducted on the following grounds: " 'We have a Law,' the Jews replied, 'and according to that Law he ought to die, because he has claimed to be the Son of God' " (John 19:7).

Untrue, then, is the assertion made by many theologians—Blinzler must again be singled out—that the Jews shrewdly dropped their original charges (violations of religious law) before the Roman governor, and replaced them with a political accusation to ensure a hearing before Pilate. Luke's Gospel is the only basis for such an assertion. Mark and Matthew do not specify the charges in the trial before the procurator. But in John, precisely the religious charge is dominant. The evangelist John obviously took no note of the fact that such a charge was bound to strike the Roman procurator as irrelevant.

Almost an Acquittal

If the charges that could have been brought against Jesus are compared with the actual charges as recorded by Mark and Matthew, the indictment turns out to be strikingly meager. No Sabbath violations are cited, the offense that could most easily have secured a conviction. Jesus is not even accused of riotous behavior in the precinct of the Temple.[27] According to both Gospels, there should have been a whole series of charges. But they must have been so slim and so groundless that the evangelists never enumerate them individually. "The chief priests and the whole Sanhedrin were looking for evidence against Jesus on which they might pass the death sentence. But they could not find any. Several, indeed, brought false evidence against him, but their evidence was conflicting" (Mark 14:55–56).

Here the charge of false prophesy comes to mind, a punishable offense cited in Deuteronomy 18:20. In fact, the broad authority that Jesus had claimed for himself might have been questioned based on Jewish understanding of the Law. But the essence of what he proclaimed, the Good News, the approaching Kingdom of God coupled with the exhortation to repent, could not be contested legally. The same ideas had been proclaimed earlier by John the Baptist and no one had accused him of false prophesy.

Not infrequently, the idea is voiced that Jesus was cited on the charge of enticement as it is spelled out in Deuteronomy 13:2–12.[28] But this cannot be accepted. Jesus had never enjoined anyone to commit anything that could be even remotely regarded as "idolatry"; but that charge alone—turning someone away from the binding obligation to believe in the one and only God—would be an enticement under the terms of the penal code. The reproach of being an "enticer" of Israel was raised against him only very much later, more than sixty years after his death when, influenced by the Pauline teaching among Christians, there had been a certain dilution of Jewish monotheism.

Only one incident from the Gospel accounts remains to be examined, namely Jesus' demand that the Temple be torn down and a more worthy one built in its place, and his statement that he could do this in three days. In Mark several false witnesses are summoned in connection with this charge whose evidence was conflicting:[29]

> Some stood up and submitted this false evidence against him. "We heard him say, 'I am going to destroy this Temple made by human hands, and in three days build another, not made by human hands.'" But even on this point their evidence was conflicting. The high priest then stood up before the whole assembly and put this question to Jesus. "Have you no answer to that? What is this evidence these men are bringing against you?" But he was silent and made no answer at all. (14:57–61)

In Matthew 26:61[30] this pericope appears much attenuated. The question of tearing down the Temple did not come up. Mark and Matthew obviously thought Jesus did not consider it necessary to counter these absurd allegations. Why should an observant Jew like himself, faithful to the Law, want to tear down the Temple that he considered a sanctuary, "my Father's house of prayer?" The people who brought these charges had fundamentally misunderstood him. In Mark the pericope relating to the destruction of the Temple reads:

> As he was leaving the Temple one of his disciples said to him, "Look at the size of those stones, Master! Look at the size of those buildings!" And Jesus said to him, "You see these great buildings?[31] Not a single stone will be left on another: everything will be destroyed." (13:1–2)

The destruction of the Temple[32] is announced in the passive voice and equated with the threatening catastrophe of the imminent end of the world. But such a prophesy would not have amounted to a punishable offense. Indeed there was a historical precedent: the trial of the prophet Jeremiah (Jer. 26:1–19).[33] Jeremiah's prophesy of the destruction of Jerusalem had initially aroused great resentment and resulted in a capital charge against him. But Jeremiah was acquitted and fully rehabilitated once he had proved that his prophesy was motivated by deep concern for Israel.[34]

True, Jesus himself ostensibly said, "Destroy this sanctuary, and in three days I will raise it up" (John 2:19); but that was meant allegorically, not literally. Jesus was obviously referring to the Temple cult, not the edifice; and to criticize that was not only permissible but typical of the exaggerated utterances that marked intra-Jewish controversies.[35]

Since it is said that contradictory depositions were presented about the destruction of the Temple, we must assume that a number of witnesses for the defense denied hearing anything about it. This is significant because the evidence of witnesses played an especially vital role in Jewish criminal proceedings. The exact instructions that judges were required to convey to witnesses are informative:

> Perhaps you do not know that we will thoroughly check your affidavits in a cross-examination. You must understand that there is a fundamental difference between crimes for which a death sentence can be pronounced and all other cases. The latter cases can be settled through a fine, but in the former cases the witness is responsible for the blood of a man unjustly condemned and his descendants (who now will not be begotten) until the end of the world. Adam was created in order to teach that when a man causes the fall of a single soul, the Law will treat him as though he had annihilated a whole world, and when a man merely saves the life of a single soul, the Law will treat him as though he had saved the life of the whole world.[36]

Investigating a charge of encouraging destruction of the Temple was obviously a difficult job for a judge. Mark and Matthew report that he did not think the statements of the witnesses were sufficient to warrant a conviction. Thereby the charge would have collapsed. But the high priest then supposedly asked Jesus whether he had anything to say—a breach of legal procedure that would not even have yielded admissible evidence. He received no answer, so an acquittal was in prospect.[37]

The imagination and the storytelling skill of a theologian such as Stauffer presents the course of the trial thus far, as described by the evangelists, quite differently:

> The president walked right up to the accused in the middle of the hall. Trial procedure requires the examining

judge to "intimidate" the accused; obviously this is the intention of the experienced Grand Inquisitor here. He wants to unsettle Jesus. . . . But Jesus doesn't let himself be taken by surprise or scared. He knows that . . . the depositions presented by the witnesses have already definitively collapsed. According to Jewish Law the Sanhedrin must now acquit the accused and condemn the false witnesses. Caiaphas wants to gloss over proper procedure using his highly effective intimidation tactics, and lure Jesus into a trap. Jesus sees through this and maintains his composure. He remains silent. The show trial has reached a deadlock.[38]

Compared to the theologian Stauffer, what the theologian von Schlotheim[39] has objected to in Caiaphas' conduct of the trial sounds more or less harmless: "The president . . . left his seat and went over to the table of the members sitting in the courtroom (Mark 14, 60). But one who 'sits' in judgment must indeed remain seated to demonstrate his exalted position over those summoned before the court. Only thus can he properly dispense justice."

Leaving aside these contributions, if we do not read more into the trial than is there, the upshot is that Caiaphas, in examining the charge of intent to destroy the Temple, adhered fully to the required judicial procedure: "It is your duty to look into the matter, examine it, and inquire most carefully" (Deut. 13:15). Otherwise we can think whatever we please about Caiaphas: He has gone down in Jewish history also as an opportunist and a biased judge.[40] But in the judgment of the chroniclers he comes off far better than Pilate; specifically, no one has attributed any acts of outright cruelty to him.

Disregarding the grotesque procedural violations that would overshadow the trial if it had actually taken place, the Gospel reports do tell us something about Caiaphas himself: This ancient Jewish judge conducted a hearing that contained essential elements of a constitutional, fair trial (which, of course, it was not the evangelists' intention to point out). Caiaphas did not bow to pressure from any quarter. He weighed one deposition against another. Where contradictions cropped up, he decided according to the maxim *in dubio pro reo*.* He did not hold the silence of the accused against him, a precept that took almost two millennia to

*When in doubt, favor the accused.

find its way into court rules. There can thus be no question of the show trial that Matthew 27:1 is meant to imply.

ARE YOU THE CHRIST, THE SON OF GOD?

After the original charges are dropped, a completely new charge is brought: Jesus has claimed Messiahship. Conzelmann writes, "At the climax it is impressively shown—to the Christian reader!—how Jesus expressly refers to himself as the Messiah for the first time before the supreme authorities of his people, and thereby seals his fate. At the same time, Israel's unbelief is exposed."[41]

The question of Messiahship is multifaceted and exceptionally problematic, more so than any other aspect of the entire trial as described by the synoptics. Jesus' followers saw him primarily as a prophet, not the Messiah:

> On the way he put this question to his disciples, "Who do people say I am?" And they told him. "John the Baptist," they said, "others Elijah; others again, one of the prophets." "But you," he asked, "who do you say I am?" Peter spoke up and said to him, "You are the Christ." And he gave them strict orders not to tell anyone about him. (Mark 8:27–30)

Jesus himself supposedly once indirectly confirmed the view that he could be a prophet: "But for today and tomorrow and the next day I must go on, since it would not be right for a prophet to die outside Jerusalem" (Luke 13:33).

In the newer theology—Catholic and Protestant alike—the prevailing view is clearly that Jesus never said he was the Messiah. Its proponents include Blank, Zahrnt, Conzelmann, Bultmann, Braun, and Kolping, who states, "We do not know of the historical Jesus that he believed himself to be the Messiah."[42] Bornkamm thinks likewise: "Actually there is not a shred of certain proof that Jesus ever claimed one of the Messianic titles that tradition attributed to him."[43]

Jesus did not pass himself off as the Messiah even within the circle of his closest disciples. And conversely, in Jesus' lifetime, at any rate, only one of the disciples, on one occasion, was prepared to identify him as such.[44] The disciple is Simon Peter; the scene takes place in Caesarea Philippi. It is the famous passage (Matt. 16:13–20; Luke 9:18–21) on which the concept of the so-called Messiah secret is based because of Jesus' subsequent strict orders to the disciples not to talk to anybody about Peter's confession of Messianic faith: "Peter spoke up and said to him, 'You are the Christ.' And he gave them strict orders not to tell anyone about him" (Mark 8:29–30).

The historicity of this scene can be questioned on various grounds.[45] Scholars have highlighted the fact that Jesus reprimanded his disciple Peter especially severely in the conversation at Caesarea Philippi. This reprimand follows the statement "You are the Christ," and is taken to mean that Jesus firmly rejected the title. Bultmann opines that Peter's utterance is a part of the Easter story that Mark inserted into the life of Jesus.

The evangelist Matthew (24:5) also has Jesus himself establish a connection between his person and the Messiah: "Many will come using my name and saying, 'I am the Christ,' and they will deceive many." But even this pericope, which stands in complete isolation in the Gospels, surely says nothing to suggest that Jesus was alluding to himself as Messiah. He was warning the disciples against future bogus Messiahs who, at the same time, would claim to speak in his, Jesus', name.[46]

A further pericope, likewise isolated, this time in Luke 19:39–40, merits mention here. As Jesus enters Jerusalem with his little group it is not—as in Mark and Matthew—a multitude that greets him, some hailing him as Messiah, but the disciples who shout, "Blessings on the King who comes, in the name of the Lord!" Thereupon the Pharisees in the crowd ask Jesus to silence his disciples. Jesus rejects this unreasonable demand and thereby implicitly raises a Messianic claim. "Some Pharisees among the crowd said to him, 'Master, check your disciples,' but he answered, 'I tell you, if these keep silence the stones will cry out!'" (Luke 19:39–40).

This scene, as is generally accepted,[47] is an ecclesiastical interpolation after the event, a *vaticinio ex eventu* (prophesy after the fact). The utterance "the stones will cry out" is inspired by the prophet Habbakuk: The stones of the city soon to be destroyed will bear witness to Jesus' royalty if the disciples (at the Passion) remain silent.[48]

The only title—insofar as it is one—that Jesus is ever said to have applied to himself is "Son of Man." This designation is used more than seventy times in the Gospels, but, strikingly, not even once in Paul. The notion crops up only in Jesus' own words, a solid proof of its authenticity. Although in the final analysis it may be that all the talk of the Son of Man is part of community theology, most researchers assume that Jesus appropriated this title (seldom used in the late Jewish linguistic orbit) and gave it a distinct stamp as a designation of his own being.[49]

Insofar as Son of Man betokens sovereignty, which must be questioned based on Daniel 7:13, Jesus never applied it to his own person. This becomes very clear in Matthew 10:23 (and in Mark 8:38 and Luke 12:9), where he prophesies the coming of the Messiah with the words "before the Son of Man comes," and is not at all referring to himself. There are numerous passages in which Jesus applies the title Son of Man to himself, but clearly not in the sense of sovereignty: "Jesus replied, 'Foxes have holes and the birds of the air have nests, but the Son of Man has nowhere to lay his head'" (Matt. 8:20).

Ben-Chorin[50] points out that in common usage Son of Man is equivalent to *Barnasch*, meaning "every man" or "anyone." This interpretation is convincing given the following passage, for example: "The Son of Man is master even of the sabbath" (Mark 2:28); i.e., the Sabbath has been created for the enjoyment of everyone.

The early Greek-speaking Christian communities apparently could not cope with this difficult expression; at all events, it disappeared from Church liturgy. Ernst Bloch writes, "How simple this word would be, if nothing was behind it but a somewhat superfluous description of an entity that is not at all mysterious but simply, in Aramaic, walks on two legs."[51]

The Gospels, even John 16:15, concede that Jesus was very reserved in regard to titles that could touch on the religious sphere. For him the worship of his own person was unthinkable. Nor did he ever say that he was a scion of the House of David. He let himself be addressed as Master (Rabbi), but found even "Good Master" an exaggeration and promptly reprimanded anyone who addressed him thus: "Why do you call me good? No one is good but God alone" (Mark 10:18). Given such modesty, it appears virtually impossible that Jesus should suddenly have asserted that he was the Messiah before the Sanhedrin.

A Decisive Question and Answer

No charge of appropriating Messiahship was contained in the indictment before the Sanhedrin court. (It is mentioned, by the way, only in Mark and Matthew.) On what pretext, then, could the high priest suddenly charge that Jesus had claimed to be the Messiah? The only explanation would be that Jesus had cast suspicion on himself in this respect in the course of the hearing, and that is never alleged.[52] For immediately after witnesses brought their charges, which did not suffice for a sentencing, Caiaphas allegedly himself questioned Jesus about Messiahship, out of the blue, without any connection to the previous line of questioning: "The high priest then stood up and said to him, 'Have you no answer to that? What is this evidence these men are bringing against you?' But Jesus was silent. And the high priest said to him, 'I put you on oath by the living God to tell us if you are the Christ, the Son of God'" (Matt. 26:62–63). Still harder to substantiate than the high priest's question is the answer he allegedly received: " 'The words are your own,' answered Jesus. 'Moreover, I tell you that from this time onward you will see the Son of Man seated at the right hand of the Power and coming on the clouds of heaven'" (Matt. 26:64–65).

As a believing Jew, Jesus of course could not think that the Jewish Messiah would be raised to heaven by God to sit at His right hand and rule jointly with Him. As for the text relating to his return "coming on the clouds of heaven," this is the completion of "seated at the right hand of the Power."[53] Altogether, the pronouncement is a combination of Old Testament quotes (Dan. 7:13 and Ps. 110:1), which Mark and Matthew use to prove that Jesus fulfilled a prophesy.

Matthew then continues (26:65–66): "At this the high priest tore his clothes and said, 'He has blasphemed. What need of witnesses have we now? There! You have just heard the blasphemy.'" It was prescribed that a judge was to tear his robe when he heard blasphemy,[54] but Caiaphas had heard no blasphemy from Jesus' mouth. The angry gesture described was obviously mere legend. Ben-Chorin writes, "The narrative technique is to make the tearing of the high priest's robe prefigure the tearing of the veil in the Temple at the hour of the crucifixion (Matt. 27:51)."[55]

No explanation is ever given as to why Jesus—here, for the first time—passed himself off as a Messiah. Kolping writes as follows:

> Had he perhaps . . . lifted the visor that till now had covered his true being? Many who see the Marcan account of the trial before the Sanhedrin . . . as historical respond affirmatively to this question. But they overlook the fact that this depiction is an artificial structure and that, especially in Jesus' reply, many different Christological elements are combined, a sign that the text cannot directly refer to Jesus.[56]

Why Jesus, in court, of all places, should have gone against his own precepts and virtually lied and fabricated remains a mystery. Such conduct would have been extremely foolish. If he himself did not believe he was the Messiah, why should he have deliberately provoked the wrath of the high priest by such arrogant utterances? Jesus had, after all, advocated totally different behavior and applied his rule to his own life: "Be cunning as serpents and yet as harmless as doves" (Matt. 10:16). He abhorred foolish behavior as much as lying. Kolping writes further:

> Jesus' reply in Mark 14:62 does not describe a real event in the proceedings before the Sanhedrin; it is not a historical pronouncement that expresses Jesus' view of his own identity. Rather, it reflects the faith of the later community. It expresses how Jesus' confrontation with the Sanhedrin unfolded according to the view of this community.[57]

Moreover, Mark is the only one who reports that Jesus replied with a clear "I am" to the high priest's question as to whether he was the Christ, the Son of the Blessed One. Matthew puts an evasive answer in Jesus' mouth; there (as well as later before Pilate) he replies, "The words are your own," which permits the interpretation, "That is what you are saying, not I." The reply recorded in Luke, "It is you who say I am," permits the same interpretation.

It is often assumed that Mark's "I am" is the result of an oversight, that according to the original Marcan text as in Matthew and Luke, Jesus evaded the question and answered ambiguously with the words, "You say it, not I!"[58] One could thus speculate that none of the three synoptics was willing to put a clear affirmative in Jesus' mouth. Instead, they resorted to the famous rabbinical formula that was at the same time a subtle play on words, *atha amartha*, "You say it." At that time this expression was used to parry an interlocutor.[59]

Thus Jesus never unambiguously claimed Messiahship (or consistently kept the so-called Messiah secret when anyone sought to impute that he viewed himself as such). Caiaphas and his Council allegedly found him guilty nevertheless and sentenced him, apparently on the grounds that the accused had replied unequivocally to the Messiahship question.

What would have happened if it had occurred to Jesus—in an effort to put up a meaningful defense or even for tactical reasons—to answer the high priest's question negatively or with silence? Can there be any doubt that the result would have been acquittal? After all, Caiaphas had maintained that Jesus' silence on the original charge—advocating destruction of the Temple—was insufficient to warrant a sentencing. He thus would have been less inclined to sentence Jesus had he truly denied the incriminatory proposition that he was the Messiah![60]

According to the Synoptic Gospels, Jesus had it in his power to determine the upshot of the trial before the Sanhedrin. But then what remains of the commonly accepted thesis, based on Mark 14:55 and Matthew 26:59, that the Sanhedrin was determined to sentence Jesus to death one way or another, that it was a show trial, that the verdict was a foregone conclusion? Denial of Messiahship, or even silence on the subject, would have given the Passion story a quite different trial result. Matthew, Mark, and Luke would have had to write their accounts differently; they might, for instance, have been more like John's, or even an outright imitation thereof. Caiaphas, at any rate, could not have been cast as the archvillain.

Messiah and Son of God

Most people reading the Gospel passages relating to the central question of the trial assume erroneously that the high priest's question was two-fold, concerning Messiahship on the one hand and divine sonship on the other. They believe Caiaphas was seeking to determine whether Jesus was the Messiah of the House of David, long yearned for by the population, or whether he considered himself not only a human but also a divine being.[61]

According to the Jewish view it would of course have been a monstrous blasphemy for anyone to claim that he was a divine being, comparable to God. It would have been a sacrilegious violation of the First Commandment even to admit a possibility that another god could exist beside the one true God. Caiaphas would have committed blasphemy by even asking his question; it would have created an uproar in the Sanhedrin. Thus the incriminating question, as it is generally understood by Christian readers (and the Church, as is well known, supports this interpretation), would be viable only if both Caiaphas and Jesus were Christians, not Jews, and knew about the resurrection. In the dialogue between the Jew Caiaphas and the Jew Jesus, the question could never have referred to a personal son of God. That would have been unthinkable as much for the presiding judge as for the accused.

Nor could the Jew Paul or the synoptics have thought otherwise. The divine sonship, as preached by Paul, does not refer to the earthly Jesus. It first became relevant in the context of the resurrection, "Who . . . was proclaimed Son of God in all his power through his resurrection from the dead" (Rom. 1:4–5).[62] In other words, the question concerning a divine personality, attributed to Caiaphas, could not possibly have been posed, and an affirmative answer by Jesus could not have constituted blasphemy.

Against this backdrop, it can be seen that Caiaphas' question, allegedly so decisive, could only have been concerned with Messianic claims. The question concerning divine sonship must be understood as in apposition to the Messiahship question. Even apart from this, all the Gospel passages that use the construct "Son of God" come under suspicion of having been formulated by the early Christian community.[63]

Messiah is the Hebrew word for the Greek *Christos*, which was latinized to *Christus*. In Church tradition, as reflected in the so-called Apostles' Creed, Christus signifies the risen Redeemer, the believed in and proclaimed Son of God. "Jesus," on the other hand, is associated with the historical man from Galilee. Thus the dogma of Jesus' dual nature as "true man and true God" is expressed in the name Jesus Christ. The Christ about whom Caiaphas inquired has nothing to do with the Christ of the Christians.[64]

Over the millennia, the concept of Messiah or Christ has become so fundamental to Christian thought that hardly anyone thinks of its original meaning.[65] Handel's magnificent work *Messiah* is supposed to make one think of Christ Jesus of Nazareth, not the Messiah of the Jews. The aria derived from Isaiah 40 ("O thou that tellest good tidings to Zion, get thee up into the high mountain. Lift up thy voice with strength; be not afraid. Say unto the cities of Judah: Behold your God.") is not meant to refer to Isaiah's prophesy; it is the Savior of the Christians who is being proclaimed. Yet the Christ Messiah who is the object of Caiaphas' question is a wholly Jewish national figure.

The Messiah who will free Israel from foreign domination and usher in the kingdom of God is mentioned more often in the Old Testament than any other figure except God. This prophesied Messiah is not vested with divine powers, nor is he a corporeal relative of God, but a fully human being. To be exact, he is a member of the royal House of David: a prince, to stretch a point.

In Jesus' time more than previously, there was a strong current of thought among the people of Israel holding that the Messiah promised in so many histories, textbooks, and books of prophesy was finally about to appear. The Jews had not been a free people since the Babylonian captivity roughly five hundred years before (except for a brief period after the Maccabee uprising in 160 B.C.). Now they were under Roman rule; their land resounded with exhortations to convert and repent. John the Baptist was perhaps the most prominent preacher of repentance. For many the time seemed to have come; they lived in the conviction of an imminent advent of God's rule. Bultmann has this to say:

> Because of the close connection between obedience and hope, one particular expectation especially filled many minds: the hope that God would destroy the rule of the heathen, that He would again make Palestine a completely holy land in which only the law of their fathers would prevail. It is true that the official class of the Jewish people welcomed the Roman rule which gave peace to the land and, in the very act of depriving the race of its national existence, allowed the religious man to work in peace and live faithful to the Law. In the Temple at Jerusalem, too, sacrifices and prayers were offered regularly for the Caesar, and Jewish leaders were satisfied so long as the Romans showed a certain consideration for the holiness of Jerusalem. But among the people themselves, and especially in the strictly legal [observant] groups, the Pharisees, there grew out of the Messianic hope a flaming activity which itself undertook to end the rule of the heathen.[66]

Nor did Jesus as he proclaimed his message have any doubt that the beginning of a new era was imminent: "I tell you solemnly, there are some standing here who will not taste death before they see the kingdom of God come with power" (Mark 9:1). Only the promised Messiah would be able to free the people of Israel from Roman domination and reconcile them with their angry God. Lapide writes, "The role of the Messiah kings was political; all the Messianic prophesies of the end of time had a political coloration. Israel's predicament, from which the people of God were to be saved, was above all, political. An unpolitical Messiah at the time of the Romans would have been a contradiction in terms."[67] The consciousness of being God's chosen people was overlaid with an immense religious guilt complex. Israel had to learn again to obey the words of the Law. Israel must desire to do only God's will and the kingdom of heaven would appear to it.[68]

But this meant first of all that Israel had to be liberated from its enemies; the Romans had to be driven from the land. That was the general expectation tied up with the personal readiness to repent—and both were linked to the Messiah of the House of David. David epitomized the ideal king.[69] The Messiah would be an unknown descendant of David who, with God's miraculous help, would restore the old dynasty and establish a "heavenly Jerusalem" as the capital of a divine kingdom where (according to Isaiah's vision) swords would be changed into ploughshares, the wolf would live with the lamb, and a child could play before a nest of vipers:[70] "I have sworn on my holiness, once for all, and cannot turn liar to David. His dynasty shall last forever, I see his throne like the sun, enduring for ever like the moon, that faithful witness in the sky" (Ps. 89:35–37). The same expression, with an out-and-out martial tone announcing the national hero and final peacemaker, is found in Isaiah 9:1–7:

> The people that walked in darkness has seen a great light; on those who live in a land of deep shadow a light has shone. You have made their gladness greater, you have made their joy increase. . . . For all the footgear of battle, every cloak rolled in blood, is burned, and consumed by fire. For there is a child born for us, a son given to us and dominion is laid on his shoulders; and this is the name they give him; Wonder Counselor, Mighty God, Eternal Father, Prince of Peace. Wide is his dominion in a peace that has no end, for the throne of David and for his royal power, which he establishes and makes secure in justice

and integrity. From this time onward and for ever, the jealous love of Yahweh Sabaoth will do this.

In the Synoptic Gospels Jesus appears as this promised Messiah of the House of David, despite the prevailing opinion of his own followers and disciples that he was only a prophet. All the evangelists, of course, take pains to present Jesus as an "unpolitical" Messiah. They swallow the inherent contradiction, in order to avoid a conflict with Rome as much as possible.[71] Despite these efforts the militant aspect of the Messiah occasionally shines through, especially in Luke. In the annunciation to Mary there is mention of the one who "will rule over the House of Jacob" (Luke 1:33). Mary herself in her Magnificat rejoices not because she is expecting a child but because she will bear the one who will come "to the help of Israel"; and the two Emmaus disciples make no secret of their disappointment that Israel's liberation has not taken place (Luke 24:21).

Jesus' Davidic descent is also mentioned by Paul (Rom. 1:4) and there is even a passage from a letter in which the apostle dares to proclaim his believed in and again expected Christ as Israel's avenger: "After that will come the end, when he hands over the kingdom to God the Father, having done away with every sovereignty, authority and power. For he must be king until he has put all his enemies under his feet" (1 Cor. 15:24–25). On the other hand, it was Paul who first questioned Jesus' merely human identity and surrounded him with an aura of divinity. According to Pauline teaching, because Jesus in his personal identity was called to new life, death was made more or less a non-event: "Death is swallowed up in victory. Death, where is your victory? Death, where is your sting?" (1 Cor. 15:55–56).

Paul's probable motives are obvious. He was proselytizing in the Hellenistic-Roman orbit, competing with the pagan religion's cult of gods. He would stand little chance of success if he had only a martyr killed in Jerusalem to talk about.

Paul's statements about Christ's divinity (of course, there was not yet a doctrine of the Trinity) are so discreet and ambiguous that in the final analysis one is not sure just what he believed in on the matter. He speaks of Jesus Christ as "the one man" (Rom. 5:15), and stresses the "human nature" of Jesus (Rom. 1:3). In Romans 8:14 he writes that everyone who lets himself be moved by the Spirit "is a Son of God." It would be difficult to authenticate the apostle's belief in divine sonship in the Christian sense based on his letters. What can be established as the quintessence of Pauline thought is that God always stands above Jesus, and that Jesus was not with God before his birth but that he "was proclaimed Son of God . . . through his resurrection from the dead" (Rom. 1:5). Hence the Church teaching that Jesus' divine status existed from the beginning of the world goes far beyond Paul's.

The evangelists are at pains to proclaim their Pauline mission[72] and ascribe to Jesus supernatural powers that enable him to work miracles.[73] They share the ambivalent attitude of their mentor Paul. In the synoptics Jesus' earthly existence is in the foreground;[74] in John, whose Gospel is suffused with the Hellenistic spirit, there is almost no trace of an earthly Jesus. The divine status clearly dominates, "that you might believe that Jesus is the Christ, the Son of God."

Nevertheless John had difficulty, as his many circuitous notions show, in making Jesus' "otherness" clear to his reading public. He did not yet have at his disposal the more manageable formulas that were devised a few centuries later by the various Church Councils. His first chapter presents Jesus as the "word" or the "voice" of God, to express Jesus' divine will and powers. Throughout, there appear passages where God clearly ranks above Jesus (10:34–36; 14:21). The dialogue with Pilate, in which Jesus tells the procurator that he would have no power over him if this had not been given by God (19:11), seems to portray him as a human, not a divine, being.

Some Church Fathers, Tertullian, for example, taught that Jesus was begotten at the time of the creation of the world, at the moment that God had pronounced the *fiat lux* ("Let there be light") of Genesis. Others, such as Origen or Theodotus of Byzantium and his pupils, viewed Jesus' lineage from God as purely symbolic; they thought that Jesus was fully human, but was adopted by God as a son through his baptism (the theory of adoptionism). The presbyter Arius, who was undoubtedly the most important of the Church teachers, also placed Jesus closer to God. The Arian Jesus, however, was not God Himself but only a creature of God: "We profess a God who alone is unbegotten, alone eternal, alone without beginning, alone immortal, alone wise, alone good, alone Lord, alone the Judge of all." The Arian concept may approach the Pauline concept in its true sense, as when the apostle writes in 1 Timothy 2:5–6, "There is only one God, and there is only one mediator between God and mankind, himself a man, Christ Jesus."[75] Lehmann[76] writes, "He [Arius] arrives at the humanity of Christ because he started out from the notion that only a man can be a model for man, not an abstract God; it is not God who leads to God, but the man graced by God who lives in one world and divines the other."

To end the quarrel between Arius and his opponents, Emperor Constantine (himself not yet baptized, but still of the pagan faith)[77] called the Council of Nicaea in A.D. 325. There the Arian teaching was rejected in favor of the Gnostic-derived doctrine of Athanasius, the Bishop of Alexandria. According to his teaching, God and Jesus are "consubstantial" *(homousios)*; the Arian teaching held that they were "analogous" *(homo-i-ousios)*. More than three hundred years after Jesus' death, and 1,665 years ago, great minds parted ways over this one small letter "i." It gave rise to the profession of faith that is the cornerstone of the so-called Apostolic or Nicene Creed: "Jesus Christ, the Son of God, light from light, real God from real God, begotten not created, consubstantial [*homousios*] with the Father." The Nicene Creed was elevated to official doctrine by imperial decree, i.e., by layman and pagan. The theological basis was supplied subsequently: A man did not become God, but God became man. The formula is still retained. Despite the dogma of consubstantiality proclaimed at Nicaea, Arius' teachings continued to exert an influence in Church circles. They do so—if I have correctly understood Hans Küng who can also cite Karl Rahner, Karl Barth, and Dietrich Bonhoeffer—up to our own day. This is regardless of the fact that "Arian" became a term of abuse and insult in the language of the Church.

Paul, undoubtedly without the approval of the original Jerusalem community,[78] introduced the development of Christian theology from which emerged the dogma of the dual nature of Jesus as true man and true God, in A.D. 451 at the Council of Chalcedon. This dogma is the last link of a whole series of polemical discussions among the Church Fathers. One can judge the violence of the controversies at this Council from the extremely wide spectrum of views expressed there. Some councils degenerated into real brawls, leaving people dead and wounded; the Council of Ephesus in A.D. 449 was dubbed the "Council of Thieves" because of such disorders.

The Messiah Question in Jesus' Time

In the pre-Pauline period, at that time when Jesus was asked by Caiaphas whether he was the Christ, the Son of the Blessed One, the question could have meant only one thing: Did Jesus claim to be the promised Messiah of the House of David? The expression "Son of the Blessed One" or "Son of the Most High" is an allusion to a royal psalm in which God speaks to the king[79] at his coronation: "You are my son, today I have become your father" (Ps. 2:7).

If Jesus did, as the Gospels report, present himself at the trial as the Messiah of the House of David and thus "King of the Jews," it would have been logical for him also to designate himself as the Son of God.[80] But in this sense the "Son of God" is always a human being, *Ben-Adam*, a Son of Man, having nothing to do with the later Christian dogma of the "only begotten Son."[81]

The Jewish interpretation of divine sonship was still accepted unconditionally by the faith directly after Jesus' death. After abandoning Jesus to his fate, the disciples reassembled a little later in Jerusalem. No one has been able to determine the time span between the flight and their reunion. It could have been a few weeks,[82] or several months, perhaps even a year or more. Probably most of the disciples had first returned to their homeland in Galilee. Galilee can be viewed as the birthplace of the Easter faith.

There is a gap between the last verses of the Gospels and the first chapter of Acts, a sort of grey zone of the faith. It has been established that after the disciples reunited in Jerusalem, their faith went on from where it had left off at the time of the arrest and execution of their master. They "waited there for what the Father had promised," as recorded in Acts 1:4, for the prophesied inauguration of the kingdom of God. The members of the original community (only Peter, the twin brothers James and John, and Jesus' brother James are mentioned by name) were deeply convinced that Jesus was not just a prophet but the Messiah. From this conviction was born the idea that their executed rabbi would soon reappear (Acts 3:20), in another form perhaps, but in Messianic splendor. Their expectation was akin to Jesus' idea (Matt. 17:12–13) that John the Baptist was a reembodiment of the prophet Elijah.[83] The Messiah would come—no matter in what form—to complete his mission, to liberate Israel from foreign rule, and to celebrate with the disciples the inauguration of the promised kingdom of God.[84]

What they still lacked was scriptural proof, an explicit prophesy in the Holy Scripture. But even here inventiveness came to their rescue. Did not Isaiah 42:52 and 53 speak of a repudiated servant of God whose sufferings and death were an act of atonement for Israel? And did not Psalms 18:22 and 69 depict God's anointed one, seemingly overcome by enemies, whom God at the last moment lifted up from deep, dark waters in order to establish him, on the day of deliverance, as King of the entire world? In Psalm 110 the disciples found the certainty that this Messiah king would sit "at the right hand of God," and in other psalms they read of a Son of Man who came to God on clouds of heaven and was vested with power, glory, and royalty everlasting. They took all these passages to refer only to their executed rabbi.

Jesus' followers within the Jerusalem community were orthodox Pharisaic Jews. Their meeting place was the synagogue. That their executed rabbi was a heavenly being would have been an impossible concept for them; he was a teacher and example whose instructions were to be followed and whose teachings were to be believed.

> After all they knew who Jesus was. They knew him through their many years of constant association with the Master. No matter how highly they still thought of the Risen One, how deeply they may have liked to link their remembrance of the man Jesus in their consciousness to the prevailing conceptions of the Messiah, in no way did they go as far in following the prevailing theological view, namely the boundless deification of their Lord and Master as Paul undertook relatively so soon after Jesus' death.[85]

Even the most devout Christian would be suspicious of the notion that Jesus enjoined his disciples to worship him, or to ponder over whether he was similar to or consubstantial with God. Porphyrius (whom Wilcken[86] called the most educated and penetrating critic of Christianity) and Emperor Julian (of whom Bishop Cyrillos is said to have acknowledged that "none of our doctors can refute his works")[87] had already shown on the basis of the New Testament "that Jesus had not called himself God, that he did not preach about himself but about a God of all men. It was his followers who abandoned his teaching and introduced a new doctrine (their own) in which Jesus became an object of divine worship and veneration."[88] There is hardly any difference between the early Christian controversy and the modern discussion.

The famous Protestant theologian von Harnack coined the phrase, "not the Son, but the Father alone belongs to the Gospel as Jesus proclaimed it."[89] And Küng asks this:

> Would it not perhaps correspond more to the New Testament evidence and to modern man's historical way of thinking if we started out like the first disciples from the real human being Jesus, his historical message and manifestation, his life and fate, his historical reality and historical activity, and then asked about the relationship of this human being Jesus to God, about his unity with the Father?[90]

John 20:11–17 relates that the risen Jesus met Mary Magdalene who at first took him for a gardener. But the Risen One identified himself to her. In her joy she managed to utter only a single word, which cannot be found in the Hebrew or Aramaic language, *Rabbuni!* Possibly that was a pet name with which Mary Magdalene was wont to address Jesus. (Ben-Chorin once put forward this theory in a lecture.) It means something like "my little rabbi."[91] In any case, Mary did not stiffen in awe and adoration as before a divine being; for her all that mattered was that her good and trusted rabbi was there again.

The family members and disciples could believe only that Jesus, capable as he was of working wonders, had been chosen by God and vested with special Messianic gifts. God could not simply let such a one die and forget him. To suppose that James considered his brother as a Son of God who existed with the Almighty in heaven before his birth would be absurd.[92]

Anyone who had preached, in the Temple of Jerusalem or a synogogue where Jesus' followers gathered, that the recently executed Jesus of Nazareth had not been a human being but a god, would have been either uproariously laughed at or stoned to death. The notions that God is a Trinity, and that God would take someone to heaven and delegate to him definite functions of divine rulership, would have been as inconceivable to any Jew of two thousand years ago as it is today.

When the disciples and other followers of Jesus occasionally used the expression "Son of God," it must have been in the Jewish-Oriental sense[93] of a human being who leads an especially pious and God-fearing life, a life pleasing to God. Caiaphas certainly could also have claimed to be a "Son of God." The epithet is characteristic of the Jews' vivid, pictorial language; Jesus himself is quoted as having used it. Matthew's account of the Sermon on the Mount has him say, "Happy the peacemakers: they shall be called Sons of God" (5:9).[94]

"Son of God" was an intensification of "children of God." The Jews must all have felt themselves to be children of God; the notion that they are God's chosen people was fundamental to their religion.[95] God rules these children of His people, but God Himself begets no children! Jesus preached wholly in this spirit: "But I say this to you: love your enemies and pray for those who persecute you; in this way you will be sons of your Father in heaven" (Matt. 5:44-45).

To the Jewish religious understanding the notion that God could have a biological son is by definition one of unparalleled tastelessness. Thus the high priest's question, "Are you the son of the Blessed One?" was not about a physical kinship but sought to determine whether Jesus aspired to Messiahship. Assuming that it is true that Jesus answered, "I am and you will see the Son of Man..." his answer would not have sounded odd to Jewish ears. The dialogue makes sense only if interpreted in terms of Jewish thought and language. If it is assessed based on a language conditioned by Christian consciousness, Jesus' answer was contradictory and utterly meaningless. On one hand, he stated he was God's earthly son; on the other, he gave as proof that he as a human being would have a place at the side of God. According to the correct philosophical and linguistic interpretation, the high priest and Jesus (if they actually did have a verbal exchange) spoke to each other on the same level, and not at cross-purposes. It must be borne in mind that both participants in the dialogue were Jews, not Christians. Even the evangelist makes this clear by paraphrasing the name of God with "The Blessed One."

Misapplication of the Blasphemy Clause?

Jesus could never have committed blasphemy by answering the high priest's question affirmatively. The evangelists (particularly Mark) employ the word "blasphemy" readily and loosely. When Jesus forgives the sins of a paralytic (a wholly different matter than that being dealt with by the Sanhedrin), the scribes are said to have "thought to themselves" that it was blasphemy: "How can this man talk like that? He is blaspheming. Who can forgive sins but God?" (Mark 2:7-8). Kolping[96] considers it possible that the entire concept of blasphemy is historically unfounded and that it originated within the Christian community.

An exact definition of a blasphemer is found in Leviticus 24:11: anyone who curses or reviles the name of Yahweh. The incident that prompted this determination is of interest: During a quarrel a young man whose mother was Jewish and whose father was Egyptian cursed the Israelite God.

But how could Jesus have committed blasphemy by replying to a question pertaining to Messianic status? The name of God was not touched upon, never mind slandered in any way.[97]

> Neither the claim to the title of Messiah or self-designation as the Son of God, indeed, not even the combination of the two, according to Jewish law, constitutes grounds for the charge of blasphemy. To sum up: the Gospels do not give us any exact description of the charges in the trial of Jesus which the Jewish authorities would have been obligated to consider proven and deserving of the death penalty.[98]

Mark and Matthew nevertheless place in Caiaphas' mouth the utterance: "What need of witnesses have we now? . . . You heard the blasphemy" (Mark 14:63-64). No historical veracity can be attributed to it. There is no reason to assume that he did not know the most basic legal precept, that the established facts of the case should be examined on the basis of the relevant laws. Caiaphas was not alone, but the president of a judicial body comprised of the country's best and most prominent jurists. No reasonable doubt exists that they were well able to analyze and correctly apprehend the facts of an essentially simple case.

The evangelists wrongly accuse Caiaphas and the entire Sanhedrin of an absolutely false interpretation of a decisive legal point (within the framework of an illegal proceeding). In so doing they make it even plainer that they are arguing toward a foregone conclusion and trying to divert sole responsibility from the Romans. They expected their public to be unfamiliar with Jewish law and thus prepared to accept the misrepresentation unreservedly.

The ancients' ideals of historiography explain why things are narrated by the evangelists that seem utterly absurd. The assertion that both the court servants in the presence of the judges and the judges themselves spat in Jesus' face, pummelled him with their fists, and played cruel practical tricks on him, as is said also of the Roman soldiers (Matt. 26:67–68),[99] was calculated to make the reader angry at Caiaphas and the Supreme Council. The intent was to create a situation that compared negatively with the allegedly distinguished comportment of the Roman judge Pilate, who at the beginning of his session engaged in a philosophical discussion with the accused on the nature of truth. And at the end of the session he washed his hands instead of spitting.

Jesus' passing himself off to Caiaphas as the Messiah of the House of David could at most be construed as boastful usurpation of office. Perhaps, in view of Pilate's known severity, such behavior from one individual did pose a danger to the whole Jewish people; but even that would not have constituted a punishable offense under Jewish law.[100] The Protestant New Testament scholar Günther Bornkamm sums it up:

> Precisely this question, constituting the climax of the synoptic accounts, is historically contestable because the sovereignty title Son of God clearly stems from the profession of the Christian faith, but was not an attribute of a Jewish Messiah. On the other hand, the claim of being the Messiah as such in Judaism was not considered a blasphemy deserving of the death penalty.[101]

The Catholic New Testament scholar Peter Fiedler states, "Even if Jesus had professed that he was the Messiah in line with the synoptic version, no Jew would have considered that a basis for a death sentence on account of blasphemy; after all it involved a matter relating to Israel's hope for salvation!"

It would never have occurred to anybody in the original Jerusalem community that claiming Messiahship could be a blasphemy. James, the Lord's brother, had proclaimed that Jesus was the Messiah for years without suffering the slightest harm. What plunged Paul into conflict with Judaism was not his profession of faith in the Messiah Jesus and his divine status as Son of God, but his attitude to the Law. Haenchen writes,

Only when the Christians no longer feel bound to the Law does Judaism begin to feel Christianity as an alien religion. Only now does the belief in the Messiah, Jesus, who is understood as the Son of God, become an alien religion that now has to reckon with persecution. Only now does the declaration "Jesus is the Messiah!" become a blasphemy.[102]

If anyone in Jesus' time fancied himself to be the Messiah, that was his own business so long as he observed the Law. Several Messiah-pretenders, pseudo-Messiahs, appeared in Jewish history. Bultmann writes:

> In fact, there was a whole succession of prophets who, according to the account of Josephus, "behaving as if they were chosen by God, caused disturbances and revolution and drove the people insane with their oratory, and enticed them into the desert, as if God might there announce to them the miracle of their deliverance." All these Messianic insurrections the Romans suppressed, and crucified their instigators or executed them in other ways whenever they could get their hands on them.[103]

To be sure, the Sadduccees had an interest in maintaining security and order, but the pseudo-Messiahs were never persecuted by the Jewish authorities. They were the resistance fighters of their day. In the final analysis, the only reason they were denied recognition as Messiahs was that they did not succeed in liberating Israel from Roman domination.

Bar Kochba was the last of them. He was preceded by, to name the most prominent, Simon Bar Giora, Menachem, and Eleazar Ben Dinseus.[104] Bar Giora, clad in the royal robe of a Messiah, was taken prisoner by the Romans after the siege of Jerusalem, brought to Rome, and publicly strangled at the height of the victory celebration. Menachem was the leader of the Zealot uprisings; he let himself be worshiped in Jerusalem as a Messiah, fell into the hands of the Romans, and was crucified. Eleazar Ben Dinseus (not to be confused with Eleazar the defender of Masada, who committed suicide with all his people in order not to fall into the hands of the Romans) was taken prisoner as a pseudo-Messiah by the Roman procurator Antonius Felix in A.D. 53 and brought to Rome for a public execution.

Of interest in this connection is the fact that the highly respected Rabbi Akiba Simon proclaimed Bar Kochba to be the Messiah after his initially successful uprising had made a final military victory seem possible for a brief period (it was crushed by the Romans in A.D. 135). Military victory was sufficient to merit the title Messiah; even descent from the House of David was relegated to the background. Nobody ever claimed that Bar Kochba was a scion of the House of David.

To sum up: If the high priest and Sanhedrin were of the opinion that the rabbi from Galilee deserved the death penalty because he had designated himself Messiah, it could mean only that his guilt was according to the Roman occupation statute—thus Caiaphas had no reason to rend his robe.

Ten

TRANSGRESSIONS OF JESUS NOT MENTIONED IN THE INDICTMENT?

As David Flusser[1] points out, the Synoptic Gospels never say that Jesus' religious life disregarded any precept of the Law. On the contrary, the texts indicate that he accepted and espoused the Halacha as it was represented by the Pharisees. The Gospels often comment on Jesus' strict fidelity to the Torah.[2] The best-known example comes from the Sermon on the Mount:

> Do not imagine that I have come to abolish the Law or the Prophets. I have come not to abolish but to complete them. I tell you solemnly, till heaven and earth disappear, not one dot, not one little stroke, shall disappear from the Law until its purpose is achieved. Therefore, the man who infringes even one of the least of these commandments and teaches others to do the same will be considered the least in the kingdom of heaven; but the man who keeps them and teaches them will be considered great in the kingdom of heaven. (Matt. 5:17–19)

Nevertheless Jesus probably could have been charged with concrete infringements of the Law, and if he had been condemned accordingly nobody could have asserted that the court had bent the Law. Later the Inquisition courts managed to decree burnings at the stakes—in the name of Jesus—on much flimsier evidence.

Theological writings even highlight the legality of the death penalty imposed by Caiaphas and the Sanhedrin, based on Jesus' actual breaches of the Law. Strobel writes:

> Caiaphas' role and point of view derive from his unconditional bond and loyalty to the Law. Hence, in a tragic way, he perforce also had to carry out the Law's provisions against Jesus. Caiaphas was not at all prey to base human envy, human vindictiveness or human bloodthirstiness, as a Christian misunderstanding asserts. Blinzler must also be contradicted on this point. For without any understanding of the duress under which the high priest stood, he calls into question the integrity of Caiaphas' character.[3]

Küng comes to the following conclusion:

> Jesus, having frequently risked his life by his talk and action, must have reckoned with a violent end. . . . From the standpoint of the traditional religion of the law and Temple, the Jewish hierarchy had to act against the heretical teacher, the false prophet, blasphemer and religious seducer of the people, if they were not to undergo a radical conversion and put their faith in the message with all its consequences.[4]

To "save the honor" of Caiaphas, Stauffer thinks that the following must be said:[5]

> The death sentence handed down by the great Sanhedrin was not judicial murder, but juridically completely correct. Jesus' infringements of the Sabbath were so massive and demonstrative, while his other violations of the Torah were laden with possible punitive consequences. Under these circumstances his authoritative deeds, wonders and signs were bound to be stigmatized as pseudo-prophetic seduction tricks.

I cannot share so ironclad a judgment. Did Jesus often risk his life on the basis of his sayings and acts? Were the Sabbath violations really so massive, so shockingly demonstrative? After all, the core of his sayings and deeds, at least, had always been the proclamation of the Good News of the approaching kingdom of God, together with a summons to repentance. This was not a punishable offense. And where is the other factual evidence that could designate him a "blasphemer" or "seducer of the people"? There had been a great number of nonconformist itinerant preachers and miracle workers. Even John the Baptist was not denounced as a teacher of false doctrine or a false prophet but was a victim of political skullduggery.

And yet some violations of religious laws in one way or another there certainly were. Infringements of the Sabbath and purity regulations are to some extent documented. Distinctions between civil offenses and transgressions of the religious law were unknown to the ancient world. Moreover, all secular spheres of life also had a religious relevance, especially in Judaism. Jesus could just as well have been acquitted as condemned in a religious trial, depending on whether a liberal or an orthodox court passed judgment on him.

Sabbath Violations?

Jesus was reproached for violations of the Sabbath; this is emphasized in all the Gospels.[6] We may assume that the evangelists did not arbitrarily invent them. The Mosaic Law prescribes the death penalty for Sabbath violations. According to Numbers 15:32–36, a man was stoned because he had been found gathering wood on the Sabbath. The Sabbath is divine service par excellence, created not only for man but also for God. Precisely this concept differentiated Israel from the pagan world: God himself celebrates the Sabbath to impose it on His people of Israel as a binding religious observance.[7] Strict observance of the Sabbath prescriptions was evident even in the military. It is said that a Jewish uprising against the Syrian King Antioch IV failed because of the Sabbath observance.[8] And in 64 B.C. when Pompey besieged Jerusalem the Jews allegedly refused to bear arms on the Sabbath, thereby ensuring a Roman victory.[9]

This must be qualified with the knowledge that Jewish jurisprudence did allow for states of emergency. Israelites were to observe the laws in order to live, not to die because of them. Resorting to arms for self-defense in the event of an attack was justified at any time. When Israel was attacked by Egypt on Yom Kippur 1973, even the most orthodox did not question the need for speedy and full response.

Flusser[10] contends that Jesus never violated Jewish legal practice, that he committed no proven transgressions of the Sabbath law (except permitting his disciples to pluck a few ears of corn from a field when they were hungry). But this opinion is not shared by most other authors. For example, caring for the sick on the Sabbath was allowed only if a life was at stake; but none of Jesus' healing activities were such that they could not have been postponed one more day. On the other hand, healing was allowed on the Sabbath as long as no medications were used, and Jesus never employed medications of any kind.[11]

Whether observance of the Sabbath commandment had already been somewhat relaxed by Jesus' time (specifically under the influence of the liberal school of the great Rabbi Hillel), so that minor infringements did not automatically incur the death penalty, is another question. The Sabbath violations for which Jesus was rebuked were certainly minor.[12] Lehmann,[13] who maintains that Jesus was an Essene, notes the following interesting circumstance: For the Essenes Wednesday rather than Saturday was the Sabbath day. Accordingly when Jesus was rebuked by the Pharisees on the usual Sabbath he could have contended that for him, as an Essene, it was a regular workday. But no reference to a Wednesday by Jesus is to be found anywhere.

The crucial point in connection with the Sabbath violations is that Jesus expressly contradicts a strict Sabbath observance: "But he said to them, 'If any one of you here had only one sheep and it fell down a hole on the sabbath day, would he not get hold of it and lift it out?' " (Matt. 12:11–12). The fact remains that Jesus was here propounding and acting on views that must have been perceived as a challenge by the conservative mentality. Against only one validation of the Sabbath observance, namely the concern that the disciples might be forced to flee on the Sabbath of all days (Matt. 24:20), stand many striking discussions in which Jesus was forced to defend his attitude: "And he said to them, 'The sabbath was made for man, not man for the sabbath; so the Son of Man is master even of the sabbath' " (Mark 2:27–28).

Jesus apparently is not prepared to discuss what conditions constitute exceptional cases (for example, rendering emergency aid) for Sabbath violations. His view is that a reasonable person would always render emergency aid on a Sabbath. In this he goes far beyond the rabbinical principle, "The Sabbath is entrusted to you, but not you to the Sabbath." He extrapolates a kind of common law: The performance of a really good deed must also be allowed on the Sabbath. Küng writes:[14]

> But for Jesus the Sabbath is not a religious end in itself: man is the end of the Sabbath. It is not a question of not doing anything on the Sabbath, but of doing the right thing; if even beasts can be saved, then still more human beings. But in this way it is left in principle to man to decide when he will keep the Sabbath and when not. This is important also for the observance of the other commandments. Certainly the law is not opposed, but in practice man is made the measure of the law.

All this would of course be intolerable to an orthodox Jew, but none of it contributed to Jesus' indictment or conviction. There is no causal connection between Sabbath infringements and the trial as it was described.

Rejection of the Purity Regulations?

Another glaring offense is that Jesus appears to have denied the purity regulations laid down in the Old Testament: "Listen to me, all of you, and understand. Nothing that goes into a man from outside can make him unclean; it is the things that come out of a man that make him unclean" (Mark 7:14–16). Many of his hearers may not have understood the exact meaning of this. Even the disciples hardly understood and Jesus, waxing indignant over their reservations, becomes more explicit:

> He said to them, "Do you not understand either? Can you not see that whatever goes into a man from outside cannot make him unclean, because it does not go into his heart through his stomach and passes out into the sewer?" (Thus he pronounced all foods clean.) "For it is from within, from men's hearts, that evil intentions emerge.

". . . All these evil things come from within and make a man unclean." (Mark 7:18–23)

According to this, all foods were considered clean; Jesus disavowed any difference between clean and unclean animals and foods. It is not merely a matter of whether he may have neglected the custom of washing hands before eating (Mark 7:5).

Trilling writes:

> Whoever breaks bread with tax collectors, sinners or pagans is an apostate of the unpleasant sort in the eyes of the Torah Jews. Jesus, however, is more than an apostate, he is a defector priest. For he does not content himself with ignoring the Mosaic food laws privately and on social occasions, but in principle repeals them (Mark 7:15, 19) and seduces his disciples to apostasy even on this decisive point.[15]

The contraventions of the purity regulations take up far less space in the Gospel accounts than those of the Sabbath, yet many scholars opine that the rejection of the purity regulations was the more significant. Jesus' attitude to the Sabbath, as documented in the Gospels, is merely a relativization of the regulations. Here, by contrast, an entire legislative code is cast to the winds and revolutionary new rules are formulated (Mark 7:14–16).[16] Mussner writes,[17] "For the lengthy pericope in Mark 7:1–23 bluntly depicts the 'watershed' of the Marcan Gospel: the 'waters' of the Church, as regards the theme of 'clean' and 'unclean' flow in a different direction than the 'waters' of Judaism."

To the extent that the evangelist's account is historically reliable, a question remains. Why should such a law-abiding Jew as Jesus give up his beliefs on so important a point? His socializing with tax collectors and pagans, who might have tempted him to enjoy forbidden food, would likewise have been inconsistent with a patriotic outlook. The evangelist's intention may have been to make Jesus the forerunner of a society that knew no distinction between clean and unclean food. Paul had already prepared the way: "Do not hesitate to eat anything that is sold in butchers' shops: there is no need to raise questions of conscience; for the earth and everything that is in it belong to the Lord" (1 Cor. 10:25–27).

Be that as it may, the possible transgression of purity regulations cannot be linked to Jesus' condemnation. Even if Jesus was "an apostate of the unpleasant sort in the eyes of the Torah Jews," as Trilling puts it, the fact is that these Jews did not resort to court proceedings against him.

In the history of Jewish law there is no known case of anyone being condemned to death for infringing the food laws. Chaim Cohn who, as a Jewish jurist, has conducted probably the most thorough inquiries into the trial of Jesus of Nazareth,[18] wrote to me that violations of dietary laws were never prosecuted. The punishment for enjoyment of forbidden foods was left to the discretion of God *(Karet)* who could "exterminate" the soul of the sinner at will or shift his punishment to the next world. A hundred years after Jesus' death *Karet* was replaced by beating, probably in order to restrain sinners. The question of whether two penalties (a human one and a divine one) could be meted out for the same sin met with the response that the matter should be left to the justice of God, which would probably be satisfied with the human punishment.

BLASPHEMOUS PRESUMPTION?

Sabbath infringements and the violations of the purity regulations are more or less petty offenses compared to what is attributed to Jesus in the Johannine Gospel, specifically such pronouncements as the following:

"No one can come to the Father except through me."

"For the Father judges no one; He has entrusted all judgment to the son."

"I am the resurrection . . . and whoever lives and believes in me will never die."

"Anyone who does eat my flesh and drink my blood has eternal life, and I shall raise him up on the last day."

"You are from below, I am from above. You are of this world; I am not of this world."

"I tell you most solemnly, before Abraham ever was, I am."

These words are so blasphemous that they would have gone almost beyond the powers of comprehension of a Jewish priest or judge, had Jesus actually spoken them. The charges of instigating defection from the true faith and seeing visions (Deut. 13:2–8),[19] plus the charge of false prophesy (Deut. 18:20) and that of blasphemy, would together have been surpassingly grave. Or would these words have led to Jesus' salvation if he really had been prosecuted by Jewish authorities? Perhaps, but only if the judges—like those in the well-known case of his namesake, the son of Ananias[20]—had "no longer assumed that the Rabbi from Galilee was of sound mind." This question is never asked because the uncontested view is now that these sayings in the Johannine Gospel are not Jesus', but a later Christian proclamation of the faith.[21]

Eleven

SUFFERED UNDER PONTIUS PILATE

THE SITUATION OF THE PRISONER

Whether the Romans took Jesus into custody or whether he was "delivered up"[1] to them by the Jewish authorities may be considered later. At all events, Jesus was not condemned to death by a Jewish court or executed by Jewish hangmen.

Under Roman jurisdiction, Jesus still had a chance to escape with his life. Of course, paradoxically, it was a much slimmer chance than the Gospels described; according to them, Pilate would have preferred to acquit him. All Jesus had to do was to convince the Romans that—despite his sharp criticism of social conditions, despite his commitment to the oppressed, persecuted, and suffering among his people (Luke 12:49; 22:36; Matt. 10:34–36)—he was essentially a peaceful man and had nothing to do with the Zealot rebels. Whereas the Zealots strove to overthrow the Roman occupation force and establish Israel within the borders of David's kingdom, Jesus advocated nonviolence:[2]

"To the man who slaps you on one cheek, present the other cheek too; to the man who takes your cloak from you, do not refuse your tunic." (Luke 6:29-30)

"I say this to you who are listening: love your enemies, do good to those who hate you." (Luke 6:27)

"Put your sword back, for all who draw the sword will die by the sword." (Matt. 26:52-53)

Here too, it becomes necessary to point to the parallels between Jesus' teaching and that of John the Baptist. Josephus Flavius[3] refers to John as "a good man, [who] had exhorted the Jews to lead righteous lives, to practice justice towards their fellows and piety towards God, and so doing to join baptism." Despite the peaceful character of his sermons, "when others too joined the crowds about him, because they were aroused to the highest degree by his sermons," Tetrarch Herod Antipas, the loyal ally of Rome, judged him to be a political agitator who might lead his followers to "some form of sedition" and on the basis of this suspicion he was carried off to the Machaerus Fortress and there put to death.

There has been much speculation as to what might have happened had Pilate been convinced of Jesus' peaceable character and set him to continue his teaching activity, and had Jesus successfully advocated nonviolence to the Zealots in A.D. 40 and 50. Christianity could not have come into being. Nor would the armed, suicidal Jewish resistance against the Romans that ended in A.D. 70 with the destruction of the Temple, the subjection of Israel, and the expulsion and enslavement of the Jewish population have occurred.

Of course, on the momentous day itself the situation seemed much more ordinary; Jesus was suspected by the occupation force of agitation. The chances of escaping with his life were already reduced because the Romans under the procurator[4] Pilate were responding to the constant threat of Jewish uprisings with especially drastic measures. No other people had ever put up such resistance against the Romans. The Roman garrison in Jerusalem was on special alert because the Passover was imminent. The Romans were vastly outnumbered as a consequence of the masses of pilgrims streaming into Jerusalem from all over the known world. (These must have included numerous Galilean Zealots.) The pilgrims came not only from the great Jewish Diaspora—communities in Babylon and Alexandria—but also from Britain, the Rhine and Danube regions, and all the Mediterranean countries. Under such circumstances a tiny spark would have sufficed for an uprising to break out.

Josephus Flavius writes[5] of a riot that occurred several years later during a Feast of Tabernacles when Cumanus was procurator. It cost the lives of three thousand Jews. The riot broke out when a Roman guard entered the Temple precinct and expressed his contempt for the Jews in an obscene gesture.

To forestall such an eventuality, Pilate had come up to Jerusalem from his seat at Caesarea on the Mediterranean. He probably brought along a cavalry detachment to reinforce the Jerusalem garrison. As we learn from the synoptics, a minor uprising does seem to have taken place, in the course of which the two rebels crucified with Jesus were apprehended.

Just where Pilate's residence (the Praetorium, as John calls it) was located is a controversial point. The word is a military term for the official residence of the procurator. It could have been a villa or even a barracks or a tent. Josephus Flavius[6] reports that the procurator Gessius Florus, installed as the prefect of Judea by the Emperor Nero in A.D. 64, lived in Herod's former palace, specifically in one of its three towers. (One, the so-called Tower of David, still stands in the Jaffa Gate.) Many authors believe Pontius Pilate did likewise. Others opine that Pilate lived in the Antonia Fortress, an equally grandiose structure north of the Temple that Herod had ordered built in honor of his patron, Mark Antony. The Antonia Fortress was a combination of palace, fortress, barracks, and prison.[7]

Since the thirteenth century, Christian tradition has accepted the Antonia Fortress as the site where Jesus was condemned by Pontius Pilate. Pilgrims have started from there to walk the "Via Dolorosa" in commemoration of his martyrdom, to the Church of the Holy Sepulchre erected on the presumed site of Golgotha. Of course there is no historical confirmation that this was the site of the execution.

Excavations from 1927 to 1932 revealed striking stone slabs in the inner courtyard of the Antonia Fortress. These could be the "Pavement" mentioned in John's Gospel as the site of the hearing: "Pilate had Jesus brought out, and seated himself on the chair of judgment at a place called The Pavement, in Hebrew Gabbatha" (19:13). But one could just as well assume that Gabbatha signifies the upper part of the city (*Gabbatha* means "hump"). Josephus speaks of the "upper marketplace" and the "upper city" where Herod's palace stood. The Greeks called the courtyard *lithostratos* because it was paved with stone slabs.[8] This, of course, would mean that both the beginning and end of the Via Dolorosa must be unhistorical.

Pilate, like all tyrants, operated through intimidation. In any case Jesus, accused of being a subversive, had fallen into his hands. If Jesus was handed over to the Romans by the Sanhedrin after Caiaphas had obtained his statement that he was the Son of God, there must have been a confession by the accused of his role as a rebel. According to Roman criminal law (in contrast to the Jewish law), a confession carried great weight. "Son of God" would have meant that the person concerned had claimed the status of the anointed king of the House of David, had said he was the promised Messiah.[9] For the Romans, if they took him at all seriously, anyone who designated himself as such would have presented a threat of the first order. The Messiah was supposed to be a militant figure who before reconciling his people with God had to drive the occupation power from the country.[10] Paul expresses this: "After that will come the end, when he hands over the kingdom to God the Father, having done away with every sovereignty, authority and power. For he must be king until he has put all his enemies under his feet" (1 Cor. 15:24–25).

It is possible that Jesus had aroused real Messianic hopes in sectors of the population; this could easily have happened given the general anticipation of a Messiah's arrival. Bultmann writes:

> Here it must be emphasized that some of these mob movements had no political character. The crowds stirred with Messianic hopes often used no violence, but expected the end of the Roman rule and the coming of the Kingdom of God to be achieved purely by a miracle of God's working. The Romans did not distinguish, and indeed they could not; all these movements were suspected as hostile to the Roman authority.[11]

The enthusiasm of Jesus' followers might have further fueled this feeling. Moreover, the Nazarene entered Jerusalem on a Messianic animal, a donkey, in keeping with a prophesy of Zechariah 9:9—and for a high Jewish holiday at that. This in itself would have made him a suspected revolutionary in the eyes of the occupying power. Goguel writes, "In the synoptic gospels the entry into Jerusalem is the crowning event of those elements of the previous narrative which present the coming of Jesus into Judea as the triumphant march of an aspirant to Messiahship."[12]

Jesus was burdened with a further disadvantage of a personal kind: He was a Galilean rabbi. This automatically made him suspect in the eyes of the Roman procurator. Luke 23:6–7 reports that Pilate is somewhat shocked to learn in the course of the hearing that Jesus is a Galilean; that would have been a typical reaction for a summary court-martial. In a civil trial proceeding, then as now, the personal data of the accused would have been established beforehand, but such formalities are dispensed with in a summary court-martial. Circumstances that prove exonerating or incriminating, as in Jesus' case, often become known only by chance as the facts of the case are set out.

Galileans were considered especially patriotic and reputed to be troublemakers. Strobel writes, "Pilate, here, of course, knew that Galilee was the native heath of fanaticism, of anti-Roman groups in particular."[13] In A.D. 6–7, when the imperial census (mentioned in the Christmas story of Luke's Gospel) was ordered by Quirinius, an uprising took place in Galilee under the leadership of Judas of Gamala ("Judas the Galilean," as he is called in Acts 5:37). This was ruthlessly suppressed by the Romans. In addition, they took revenge by dispatching a reprisal force to various Galilean villages—an event that must have deeply influenced the child Jesus.

The Zealots had much in common with the Pharisees. The Pharisees were likewise avowed patriots. They rejected the Zealots' use of violence to alter prevailing conditions; instead, they trusted that God would bring about change. But many Pharisees, probably those who constituted the militant wing of the sect, sympathized with the Zealots.[14] Judas of Gamala is said to have been a Pharisaic rabbi initially. Zealots and Pharisees alike regarded the land of Palestine as a personal gift from God to the children of Israel. In their eyes the presence of Roman occupation troops was a sacrilege. Consequently, they interpreted the First Commandment as a prohibition from recognizing the emperor or paying tribute.

For the sake of this principle, the Zealots revolted against the tax increase ordered by Augustus at the beginning of the first century. The same reasoning was behind the revolt in A.D. 66 that ended with the tragedies in Jerusalem and Masada.

In Jerusalem, where the Sadducees were the leading Jewish sect, great pains were taken to come to terms with the Romans.[15] In Galilee, the trend was toward violence. The Zealots (or *sicarii*, literally "dagger-men," as the Romans called them), as guerrilla fighters, were often branded simply as "Galileans."[16]

Neither the Essenes nor the Zealots are mentioned in the Gospels. There have been many speculations on the reasons for this silence. Most of the explanations contend that the evangelists wanted to keep secret either that Jesus had been an Essene or that he and his followers wanted to unleash a Zealot uprising with the mass participation of the population.[17] Jesus' followers, even the narrower circle of his disciples, must have included a few Zealots. In the literature Judas Iscariot is mostly called a Zealot. The nickname Iscariot does not mean "the man from Kerioth" as is widely assumed (for example by Lapide), but is an Aramaic bowdlerization of *sicarii*. Thus Judas may have been given the nickname Dagger-man.[18] The disciples James and John (sons of Zebedee) were nicknamed "sons of thunder," a pointed indication that they were also Zealots. Possibly Simon Peter was also: He is said to have unsheathed a sword at the moment of Jesus' arrest and to have cut off the ear of the Jewish servant Malchus. His nickname *Barjona* ("son of Jonah," Matt. 16:17) could also suggest membership in the Zealot fellowship.[19] Kolping writes, "The designation Barjona for Simon Peter is tantamount to identification as a member of a terrorist group."[20] In the list of apostles of Luke 6:15, "Simon called the Zealot" is introduced as a disciple. And assuming that the disciple Andrew, the brother of Simon Peter, was also a Zealot, there was a sizable number of Zealots among the disciples.[21] The mistrust of the Romans cannot be rejected out of hand as being unfounded.[22]

That Jesus was himself a Zealot is very improbable. True, many of the words placed in his mouth—for example, that he is not come to bring peace but rather fire and sword (Luke 12:49; Matt. 10:34), and the direct order to the disciples to arm themselves with swords (Luke 22:36)—could suggest membership in a Zealot fellowship. But that absolutely does not fit in with his answer to the disciples after they pointed out that they had only two swords: "That is enough!" (Luke 22:38). A Zealot uprising could hardly have been started with two swords. Especially Luke underlines Jesus' abhorrence of any violence, although a certain militancy can be inferred from this Gospel. When Peter cuts off the ear of "the servant of the high priest" Jesus immediately puts a stop to any further action, touches the wounded man's ear, and heals him on the spot—his last miracle. No acts of violence were to be committed for his sake or in his presence.

Speculations of such authors as Carmichael or Lehmann that Jesus was the tool of a Zealot detachment are none too convincing. An exponent of the Zealot theory, of course, could object that the numerous Gospel indications of Jesus' peaceable disposition do not in themselves warrant the conclusion that he was exclusively pacifist. For the obvious political intent of the Gospels was to ensure that Jesus appeared as having no connection whatever to any protest movement against Rome. But there is Jesus' rejection of any use of force and his readiness for unconditional reconciliation, which runs like a red thread through all the Gospels. This is not emphasized with respect to the Roman occupation force (which would be suspect), but only regarding Jesus' relationships with his fellow Jews. Nor is there the least indication as to why Jesus should have deviated from the attitude of his teacher John. The eminently reliable parallels drawn by the evangelists between John and Jesus[23] point to the opposite. Furthermore, if Jesus really had been a Zealot rebel, this alone would have given him a greater prominence and he would also have been mentioned as a Zealot in contemporary writings, just as the names of the leaders of the insurrectionary movements are mentioned by Josephus Flavius.

Jesus seems to have belonged to the moderate wing of observant Jews of his time, which placed its trust in the Lord of Hosts alone and endured the Roman domination until He was ready to usher in the kingdom of God on earth. Therein he differed from the Zealots "who were determined to establish this heavenly kingdom with their own hands and who felt assured of the assistance of the Lord of hosts in their pious work."[24] Küng writes:[25]

> He avoids all titles such as Messiah and Son of David which might be misinterpreted in a political sense. In his message of the kingdom of God there is no trace of nationalism nor of prejudice against unbelievers. Nowhere does he speak of restoring David's kingdom in power and glory. Nowhere does he show any sign of acting with a political objective, to seize worldly power . . . What we do find is quite the reverse (and this is socially relevant): renunciation of power, forbearance, grace, peace; libera-

tion from the vicious circle of violence and counter-violence, of guilt and reprisal.

The parable of the seed growing by itself (Mark 4:26–29) could be a good example of this.

It is nonetheless noteworthy that Jesus has also exercised a decisive influence on radical and militant figures of history such as Thomas Müntzer or Che Guevara, who symbolized a worldwide revolutionary youth movement with his "Jesus look." Overall, however, Jesus is presented as the "Prince of Peace," someone who wanted to bring about change only from within, though he was confident that Israel's Savior, the Messiah, would appear in the immediate offing to dispatch the foe. Gandhi and Martin Luther King could more rightfully cite him than Thomas Müntzer and Che Guevara.[26] Forty years after Jesus' death, the Jewish Christians thought and acted as had their rabbi from Nazareth: They did not participate in the Zealot uprising against Rome, but moved to Pella, in east Jordan, to establish a new community of their own.

It is misleading to think that Pilate resolved the question of membership in the Zealot party in a thorough hearing, that he went to the trouble of mounting a regular trial of a presumed rebel in his custody, or that he would have been inclined to let the suspect off. A man seized as a rebel, particularly in the seething city of Jerusalem a few days before Passover, A.D. 30, would have had to be more lucky than clever to go free.

Nevertheless it is undeniable that Jesus could at least have attempted to convince the Romans that his activity was not political but exclusively religious, that he was proclaiming love among men—and in a much milder form than did John the Baptist, who addressed even penitents with invectives such as "brood of vipers"—exhorting them to repentance and inner conversion, and that he intended only to continue this activity. Only a few months before he is said to have spoken in such a manner in Galilee: "Come to me, all you who labor and are overburdened, and I will give you rest. Shoulder my yoke and learn from me, for I am gentle and humble in heart, and you will find rest for your souls. Yes, my yoke is easy and my burden light" (Matt. 11:28–30).

In his "speech from the throne," as Bishop Scarf once described the Sermon on the Mount, Jesus is said to have showered special praise on the peaceful (correctly translated, "those who make peace"), calling them not only "blessed," but also "Sons of God"

(Matt. 5:9). He admonished his hearers to "come to terms with your opponent" (Matt. 5:25), and charged those who had been harmed by another not to seek revenge but, if struck by anyone on the right cheek, to "offer him the other as well" (Matt. 5:39). A Jew asked by a Roman soldier to supply forced labor[27] was not only to oblige but to exceed the obligation: "And if anyone orders you to go one mile, go two miles with him" (Matt. 5:42).

Of course Jesus was a good Israelite;[28] he could not have been indifferent to the fact that the Holy Land was occupied by foreign troops; he longed for the kingdom of God, and that implied the end of the occupation. But he had never incited anyone to rise against Rome. Obviously he considered it proper in the given political and military situation to "Give back to Caesar what belongs to Caesar" (Mark 12:17).[29] He understood the precept to love one's neighbor in such a way that he did not unconditionally despise tax collectors as collaborators of the Romans, though he was not friendly with them. He had confidence in their capacity to mend their ways. Nowhere is it reported that he spoke out against the occupying power. On the contrary, when bitter complaints were voiced against them he is said to have defended them:

> It was just about this time that some people arrived and told him about the Galileans whose blood Pilate had mingled with that of their sacrifices. At this he said to them, "Do you suppose these Galileans who suffered like that were greater sinners than any other Galileans? They were not, I tell you. No; but unless you repent you will all perish as they did." (Luke 13:1–4)

Such a pro-Roman attitude as the evangelists suggest to the reader must be taken with a grain of salt. But why should Jesus not have pointed out to Pilate at least that he had never advocated any anti-Roman activity? Why would he have passed himself off as king of the Jews, a militant Messiah who had set out to overthrow Roman rule?

It is the evangelist John who reports that Jesus had decisively rejected five thousand of his countrymen who spontaneously wanted to make him king: "Jesus, who could see they were about to come and take him by force and make him king, escaped back to the hills by himself" (6:15). Here, of course, we are not dealing with historical fact. Yet the problem shines through the legend.

Pilate's question as to Jesus' kingship must have been an allegorical reworking of the earliest (pre-Pauline) version of the historical facts: that the Roman occupation force saw Jesus as a Zealot agitator and executed him accordingly.

READINESS FOR DEATH OR WILL TO LIVE?

There is certainly no obvious reason why Jesus should not at least have made an attempt to save his life. Threatened with the cross one would presumably grasp at any straw, nor does anyone foolishly risk his life, especially if he has been unjustly accused of a crime. In Gospel accounts Jesus is presented as prepared to admit to any charge leveled against him, no matter how farfetched. Of the little we know of Jesus one thing is pretty certain: He was not a yes man. Nor is there anything to suggest that while in custody he was brainwashed, in the manner of Stalinist show trials.

Jesus could not really have been as fatalistic as the Gospels portray him; that would be tantamount to saying that he had a crucifixion wish. Such a masochist trait is certainly incompatible with a man who wants to proclaim the Good News of the approaching kingdom of God, who is on a familiar footing with his God and addresses Him not as "Father" but affectionately as "Papa." The assertion that Jesus "willingly took upon himself" the crucifixion death strikes me as absurd, quite aside from the fact that the idea of a death wish is alien to Jewish thought.[30]

An especially beautiful maxim, typical of Jesus and Judaism, states, "You must love your neighbor as yourself" (Matt. 22:39). Love your neighbor as yourself! Then why should this still young and sensuous man, fond of good food, wine, and women, want to die? And precisely at a time when he had just launched his public ministry and it was showing the first signs of success?[31] Of course he clung to his life. There is simply no reason to assume otherwise.[32]

Even on the way to Gethsemane, after the paschal meal, he made a sensational announcement to his disciples: He did not intend to go to the city the next day to participate in the festivities. He had decided to set out for Galilee—after staying in Jerusalem had become dangerous, it may be inferred. He wanted to flee alone; the disciples were to follow him later: "And Jesus said to them, 'You will all lose faith, for the scripture says: I shall strike the shepherd and the sheep will be scattered, however after my resurrection I shall go before you to Galilee' " (Mark 14:27–29).

The words *meta to egerthenai me* ("the moment I awaken"*) were later translated as "but when I rise again," for the edification of the faithful. Jesus cannot have been referring to his own resurrection; even the disciples did not understand him thus. The evangelist's report that the women closest to Jesus brought fragrant oils with which to anoint the corpse (Mark 16:1) on Easter Sunday would be incomprehensible. Nor would there be any reason for them to be "frightened out of their wits" because of the angel's words in front of the empty tomb (Mark 16:8). Flusser[33] points out that a Passover regulation required everyone to remain within the Jerusalem city walls after the paschal sacrifice. Jesus' infringement of this rule could only be explained as a flight.

Jesus was afraid in the face of suffering and persecution; he probably also feared for his life. But this was precisely because he wanted to go on living. He constantly prayed God to protect him and preserve his life. And, of course, as a believer, he hoped that his prayers would be answered: "My Father,"[34] he said, "if it is possible, let this cup[35] pass me by. Nevertheless, let it be as you, not I, would have it" (Matt. 26:39).

This prayer to be allowed to go on living is addressed to God without any reservation.[36] In Klausner's[37] view the words "as you, not I, would have it" were later interpolations of the evangelists, who could not imagine that a Messiah's prayer offered imploringly to God, as a son pleads to his father, would not be heard. But there is another interpretation: Küng[38] advocates the view that the formula "Let it be as you, not I, would have it" parallels Judaism's Eighteen Benedictions. It is the typical formula of a petitioner and appears also in the Lord's Prayer. The mystery of the prayer's being heard is precisely that only God's will, not that of the person praying, will be done.

The evangelist Luke embellishes this human situation of fear and hope: "Then an angel appeared to him, coming from heaven to give him strength. In his anguish he prayed even more earnestly, and his sweat fell to the ground like great drops of blood" (22:43–44). This passage directly contradicts the image of Jesus that the Church presents as being the one above death, who feels himself sheltered in God's guiding hand at all times and knows that

---

*Literally, in the original Greek.

his death will be only temporary, that he will be raised up to eternal life on the right hand of God in Paradise. In the synoptic Gethsemane scene, and explicitly in Luke's depiction, we see a man "forced to his knees," so to speak, terrified and close to despair.[39] Prayer is the only remaining hope. Craveri writes:[40]

> Throughout Christian history, this passage of the Gospels has been sharply attacked because it shows a human weakness of Jesus, unworthy not only of the Son of God but even of a philosopher who disciplines himself to disdain death. In many Codices, including that of the Vatican, the whole passage has been eliminated. But it has been observed that its very incongruity attests to the authenticity of the Gospels.

On the other hand, the reports of Jesus' fear in Gethsemane as expressed in the prayer naturally encounter historical objections. What witnesses are to be examined here? Jesus was alone, having turned away from his disciples, who in any case were fast asleep. Nevertheless the Gethsemane scene as it is depicted is not without historical value. Jesus' agitation and fear stand in sharp contrast to the calm ascribed to him in the Gospel narratives. Goguel[41] concludes that this part of the tradition as handed down could only have originated at a time when it was actually known that Jesus had experienced a real fear of death at that moment.

Viewed thus, the Gethsemane event is true in the higher sense that it expresses allegorically what was transpiring in Jesus' soul. Ben-Chorin writes:[42]

> Here stands no hero, no demigod, no myth! Here is a man who trembles for his life. And Jesus is especially close to us in this hour of fear. Here before us stands the true man, in the grip of the fear of death, born with the fear of death, whose life is always life toward death and whose meaning and striving always revolves around flight in the face of death.

Jesus did not want to die. And if he had to die, why a Roman death, and that in its cruelest and most disgraceful form? After all, the Romans had played no role in his activity. Jesus, like any other man in such a situation, would have defended himself and set things straight had such an opportunity been granted to him. But unfortunately we must assume that he had no such opportunity, let alone any chance of talking with Pilate about the meaning of being or philosophizing about the nature of truth (John 18:34-38). Goguel: "The fate of Jesus was sealed not at the Praetorium but ... when the Procurator decided to arrest him."[43] Pilate is reported to have limited himself to a few words: *"Tu est le Roi des Juifs? Eh bien, tu seras crucifié!"*[44]

Be that as it may, it is unclear whether Pilate had Jesus in custody having ordered his arrest (on his own initiative or on the basis of Jewish reports) or whether Jesus had been handed over to him by the Jewish authorities. It is likewise unknown whether Jesus was actually questioned about the pretentious title "King of the Jews." But the fact remains that he was suspected of being a political subversive. Political rebels were crucified without much ado, without a formal hearing or an interpreter at hand. Jesus' case would not have proceeded differently than those of other rebels, real or alleged. The *lex Julia maiestatis* provided sufficient legal grounds. To such a Jew-hater as Pilate, one Jew more or less who died on the cross mattered not a bit.

Twelve

THE PROCURATOR AND THE JEWS

The Alleged Collective Guilt

It cannot be true that the people who initially received Jesus so enthusiastically and espoused his message later, in a sudden and unexplained shift, sided with his adversaries—the potentates in the Sanhedrin—and demanded in chorus his crucifixion because he had allegedly designated himself "King of the Jews." Such a change of mood cannot be accounted for, even given the well-known fact that crowds are fickle and initial mass enthusiasm can swiftly recede. Even if Jesus had completely lost his popularity with the people in the span of a few days, this would normally have meant only that he was no longer celebrated as a hero, but was treated with indifference or disdain and finally sank into oblivion. But this whole premise remains improbable, since there would have been no cause for it; Jesus had remained faithful to the message that had won him popularity. Why should an acknowledged prophet suddenly, from one day to another, be persecuted with bloodthirsty hatred and denounced to the occupation force with demands for his execution? Besides, why should the Jews, who suffered under the oppressive Roman yoke and yearned for nothing more than to get rid of this foreign rule, suddenly have changed into loyal subjects of the Roman emperor? "We found this man inciting our people to revolt, opposing payment of the tribute to Caesar, and claiming to be Christ, a king" (Luke 23:2). "From that moment Pilate was anxious to set him free, but the Jews shouted, 'If you set him free you are no friend of Caesar's; anyone who makes himself king is defying Caesar' " (John 19:12).

This is strikingly at variance with the synoptics, who all cite the fear of the high priests that if they arrested Jesus publicly it might spark a popular uprising in his favor: ". . . the chief priests and the scribes were looking for some way of doing away with him, because they mistrusted the people" (Luke 22:2).

Even the evangelist John, otherwise especially intent on accusing the people as a whole, cannot escape the people's bond with Jesus: "If we let him go on in this way everybody will believe in him" (11:48). The evangelist Mark pointedly highlights the opposition between the people and its leaders, placing Jesus clearly on the side of the people. When Jesus carried on discussions with the Sadducees and exposed them through parable-like sayings, they wanted him arrested but did not dare carry out their plan for fear of the people's reaction: "And they would have liked to arrest him, because they realized that the parable was aimed at them, but they were afraid of the crowds" (12:12).

This fear of a popular uprising is chronicled again a few days later: "The chief priests and the scribes were looking for a way to arrest Jesus by some trick and have him put to death. For they said, 'It must not be during the festivities, or there will be a disturbance among the people' " (Mark 14:1–2).[1]

According to the synoptic accounts, Caiaphas and his closest followers acted deviously *(en dolo)* toward their subjects in order to eliminate Jesus inconspicuously. For an arrest "among the festive crowds" might have provoked not only demonstrations of sympathy for the prisoner but also a violent popular uprising. How does all this square with the reports of hate-filled crowds demanding Jesus' death?

Even disregarding this, if the fear of pro-Jesus demonstrations was unfounded, all that can be concluded is that the clique around Caiaphas—in collusion with the Roman military authorities—wanted to do away with Jesus. What part then would "the Jews" have had?[2] The people had no voice in the decisions or political subterfuges of their authorities. Klausner[3] cites a folk song of that time, "a kind of street ballad" in which the little people ridicule their rulers. The high priest Annas mentioned in the Gospels crops up in the ditty:

> Woe is me before the House of Boethius:
> Woe is me before their "clubs"!
> Woe is me before the House of Annas:
> Woe is me before their denunciations . . .
> For they are high priests,
> And their sons are treasurers,
> And their sons-in-law administrators,
> And their servants hit the people with sticks.

Accordingly, it may be asked, what did the ordinary citizens of Jerusalem and the pilgrims have to do with the death sentence against Jesus of Nazareth, these people whose thoughts and feelings were wholly and exclusively attuned to the paschal feast in the offing? What part, for example, did the citizens of Jerusalem, Hebron, and Bethlehem, the entire population of the countryside, the shepherds and peasants in the fields, the fishermen from Lake Gennesaret, play in the death of Jesus of Nazareth?[4]

Pontius Pilate has gone down in history as an especially cruel character. A writing of the Jewish philosopher Philo of Alexandria contains a letter of King Agrippa I to Emperor Caligula. In it Pilate's misdeeds are denounced: "bribery, acts of violence, pillage, maltreatment, insults, non-stop executions without verdicts and endless and unbearable cruelties."[5] Lapide[6] writes, "The rabbinical literature calls him a kind of Haman, the pagan despot who had planned the extermination of the Jews (Esther 3)."

In A.D. 26 Pilate was appointed by either Emperor Tiberius or his highest government official Sejanus as procurator (or more correctly, prefect) of Judea. The origin of his name is shrouded in speculation. One theory is that he was the son of an officer who was honorarily entitled to carry a javelin *(pilum)*. He is even said to be the son of Marcus Pontius, who had commanded the army under Augustus during the crusade against the Cantabrians (26–19 B.C.).[7] In any case Pilate, like all the procurators in Judea, was a knight and so belonged to an aristocratic stratum, just below the senatorial order in rank. Our knowledge of the careers of other Roman knights permits the assumption that Pilate was already active in the military sphere before he came to Judea. Within his province, he had life and death power over his subjects. Josephus Flavius noted that[8] Pilate, unlike his predecessors, never troubled himself about the religious feelings of the Jews. It is historically verified that Pilate was deposed by Emperor Tiberius in A.D. 36, at the instigation of his superior Vitellius, the governor of Syria. Nothing more is known concerning his fate. Tiberius died shortly before Pontius Pilate next set foot in Rome. It is considered likely that Pontius Pilate had been banished to Vienne in Gaul.[9] The reason for his removal was that he had allowed a protest demonstration by Samaritans to be crushed especially brutally. His notorious hatred of Jews, his total lack of empathy, and his lack of consideration toward the subject peoples had become an unbearable burden for Rome.

It is absurd to believe that a man known for his stubbornness who, furthermore, looked down on the Jews with utter contempt like a colonialist master, would have let himself be influenced by, of all things, a mob in front of his residence, or would have felt compelled to pronounce a death sentence against his will!

As a result of archaeological excavations it has been estimated that, at most, three thousand people could be jammed into the inner court of the Antonia Fortress, which was the site of the trial according to the Christian tradition. Assuming that such a mob really existed, that it was neither invented by the evangelists for political reasons nor simply a legendary fulfillment of Psalm 31:13,* it represented, at most, 2 percent of the residents and pilgrims in Jerusalem at the time, a thousandth part of all the Jews alive at that period.[10] Yet the entire people of Israel is blamed.[11] The evangelist John has Pilate say, "Am I a Jew? It is your own people and the chief priests who have handed you over to me" (18:35).

Further on in his account, John presents things as though Pilate had defiantly stood up for Jesus' acquittal but had yielded in the end to the demands of the Jews. On this point Lapide[12] comments:

> Only one who can visualize the thousands of crosses to which Pilate, his predecessors and his successors had let countless Jews be nailed after a brief trial or none at all, understands the bloodsoaked irony of these lines, the aim of which is to publicly deride the humane Jewish administration of justice to which crucifixions are unknown.

*"I hear their endless slanders, threats from every quarter, as they combine against me, plotting to take my life."—Tr.

Matthew lets the Jewish people, in a chorus of self-recrimination, implore God to revenge himself on the Jews for Jesus' death: "And the people to a man, shouted back, 'His blood be on us and on our children!' " (27:25–26). He too wants to saddle the entire Jewish people with collective guilt for the violent death of Jesus.[13] This is tantamount to downright infamy on the part of the evangelists—or, to be more exact, of those who later interpolated this pericope.[14] Against it, unequivocally, leaving no room for doubt, stands the Torah's clear text in Deut. 24:16 prohibiting consanguineous guilt: "Fathers may not be put to death for their sons, nor sons for fathers. Each is to be put to death for his own sin."

The prophet Ezekiel expressed a similar admonition, which has been counted among the fundamentals of Jewish jurisprudence for about three thousand years: "The man who has sinned is the one who must die; a son is not to suffer for the sins of his father, nor a father for the sins of his son. To the upright man his integrity will be credited, to the wicked his wickedness" (Ezek. 18:20).

The thesis of the so-called "self-damnation of the Jews" goes back to Matthew's Gospel and is absolutely contradictory to the fundamentals of Jewish legal thinking. The idea derived from it of collective guilt of the Jewish people, "consanguineous liability up to the thousandth member," was most unfortunately taken up by Christian teaching and the frightful consequences of that have ensued under the protection of the Church. Origen, the most important theologian of the third century, wrote in his commentary on Matthew, "The Jews nailed Jesus to the cross . . . therefore the blood of Christ falls back not only upon the Jews of his time, but on all the generations of Jews until the end of the world."[15]

Augustine, Thomas Aquinas, and Martin Luther shared the very same view on this matter:

> And thus it will come to pass that the blood of Christ demands to be ransomed to this day. What is said in Genesis 4:10: "Listen to the sound of your brother's blood, crying out to me from the ground." But the blood of Christ is more effective than Abel's blood. The apostle to the Hebrews 12:25: "We have blood which pleads more insistently than Abel's."[16]

At the Nuremberg trial Julius Streicher, editor of the Nazi propaganda sheet *Der Stürmer,* declared that Luther, were he still alive, would have been made to appear before the tribunal like himself. *Der Stürmer* allegedly contained no more than what can be read in Luther:[17]

> Here in Wittenberg at our parish church there is a sow hewed in stone; under it there lie young piglets and Jews who suckle. Behind the arse of the sow stands a rabbi who raises the sow's right leg with his left hand and bending down he makes room for himself and fixes his gaze diligently on the Talmud as if he wanted to read and learn something profound and unusual. . . . This is why we Germans say of anyone who flaunts wisdom without proper warrant: Where did he read that? In the sow's arse, stupid.[18]

A publication of the archdiocese of Freiburg issued on March 27, 1941, is a pastoral letter written by the then archbishop under the title *Man of Sorrows*. In it the Easter message was transmitted in a special exegesis:

> Their eyes were blinded by their Jewish lust for world domination. . . . Misled by the Pharisees, now also the people rose up against Him. The Pharisaic secret service, through lies and calumny, had aroused the beast in them and they thirsted for macabre excitations and blood. . . . "Rabble-rouser!" Some hissed and shouted, "False Messiah, Imposter!," epithets confirmed from the roadside by excited women screaming louder than the men. The Savior, however, beheld them with his bloodshot eyes. A look that they will never forget in eternity. A look of shaming sadness over men, deep under the beast. . . . The beast had smelt human blood and wanted to quench its raging thirst on it. It will be sufficiently sated only when he dies nailed to the crossbeams. . . . Meanwhile over Jerusalem rings out the terrible but prophetic self-damnation of the Jews: "His blood be on us and on our children!" The curse has been terribly fulfilled up to this very day.

Up to this very day: On March 27, 1941, Jewish descendants of Jesus went by the thousands to their deaths, as they did on any other day of that time. To the archbishop this was no obstacle for directing a greeting to the "suffering Savior": "We greet Thee, we Christians of a new, German epoch": Such was German exegesis, not quite fifty years ago. It could just as well have appeared in a Protestant Church publication.

Leaving aside the genocide inflicted on the Jews, the fateful thesis of self-damnation is espoused up to the present day by theologians of both confessions. The Protestant Stauffer writes, "And in chorus the assembled people declaimed the frightful formula of the anticipated self-damnation.... Jewry was made to pay for this decision a few decades later with the destruction of Jerusalem."[19] The Catholic Blinzler writes, "Whereas Pilate most expressly refused to assume responsibility for Jesus' death, the Jewish people took that responsibility upon itself with sacrilegious exuberance. ... Matthew, writing for Jewish Christians, is clearly concerned to make the monstrous guilt of their people clear to his readers."[20] As for those who dare highlight the Romans' part in Jesus' death, Blinzler cannot "rid himself of the impression that they want to diminish as far as possible the guilt of the Jews in Jesus' death." For him, "the Jews remain those who out of hatred and wickedness clamored for the death of God's envoy."[21]

Such theologians argue not much differently than a typical visitor—who has remained nameless, thank God—to the Oberammergau Passion Play of 1970: "Just as we do not deny that Hitler destroyed millions of Jews, likewise can the Jews just as little deny that they nailed Jesus to the cross."[22] The difference between the two views is that, for example, Blinzler assumes an indirect responsibility of the Jews; the Oberammergau visitor, a direct responsibility.[23]

The facts were turned on their head from the outset, and theologians like Blinzler and Stauffer have striven mightily to keep this madness alive and well to counter any attempt at mitigation. The roots of anti-Semitism lie in this attitude and this teaching. For two thousand years they have served as justification for Jews being considered as people of limited rights and subjected to discrimination, expulsion, and slaughter.[24]

So Jesus' death certainly did not bring grace and salvation to all people. For the Jews, from Titus to Hitler, Jesus has brought only disaster and torment. His forgiving words,[25] "Father, forgive them; they do not know what they are doing" (Mark 23:34), surely include all people who have violated the precept of love of neighbor, whether Jews, Romans, or Christians (still unknown to Jesus). Those who as "Christians" preach love of neighbor, but in reality, in Jesus' name, have deliberately caused unspeakable wrong and sorrow, would have done well not only to have felt themselves doubly committed through the Savior, but also to have felt most deeply ashamed of themselves!

Today, an overwhelming number of Christian theologians voice this view. I shall cite four of them:

> Karl Rahner:[26] "Christians have repeatedly done the Jews the most serious, appalling injustice. We must face up to this accusation, we must let the plaintiff who tells us what Christians have done to Jews keep on speaking."

> Hans Küng:[27] "Nazi anti-Judaism was the work of godless, anti-Christian criminals. But it would not have been possible without the almost two-thousand-years' pre-history of 'Christian' anti-Judaism, which prevented Christians in Germany from organizing a convinced and energetic resistance on a broad front."

> Karl Barth:[28] "The Church, which as a whole owes everything to the Jews, still remains indebted to them to this day."

> Cardinal Bea:[29] "To damn the whole Jewish people of that time, most of whose members had not even heard of Jesus, would be just as wrong as if sixty million Germans—myself included—were to be punished for Hitler's crimes."

THE JUDGE AS A GOOD MAN

In the evangelists' efforts to ascribe Jesus' violent death to the Jews, Pontius Pilate is presented as a charming man, who owing to a tragic entanglement could not have acted otherwise: "The Jesus... you handed over and then disowned in the presence of Pilate after Pilate had decided to release him" (Acts 3:13).

Stauffer[30] comments accordingly:

> Pilate, however, not only abhors bloodshed, he also shrinks from a serious conflict with the Jewish accusers. The three attempts that Pilate undertakes to rescue Jesus are all designed not to offend the Jews.... This man fights

with all the means at his disposal for a proper dispensation of justice and protection of the innocent.

It is easy to see that Pilate is exonerated more and more from Gospel to Gospel. Already in Mark 15:12-14 the tribunal becomes the site of a public opinion poll; the Jewish people demand the crucifixion. . . . Indeed the people are the primary movers from beginning to end:[31] " 'But in that case,' he said to them, 'what am I to do with the man you call king of the Jews?' They shouted back, 'Crucify him!' "

In Matthew 27:25, Pilate shifts the blame onto those present before him: " 'I am innocent of this man's blood. It is your concern.' " According to Luke 23:15, Pilate declares that Jesus is innocent: " 'As you can see, the man has done nothing that deserves death.' " John's Pilate even made desperate attempts to avoid having to condemn Jesus: " 'Take him yourselves, and try him by your own Law. . . . I find no case against him. . . . Look, I am going to bring him out to you to let you see that I find no case' " (John 18:31, 38; 19:4).

Mark states that Jesus was crucified already at nine o'clock in the morning, hence the proceedings could not have dragged on for very long. The fourth Gospel, by contrast, states that he was condemned to death by Pilate at twelve o'clock noon; hence the crucifixion took place at one o'clock at the earliest.[32] John was trying to show that Pilate had resisted Jewish pressure for a long time.[33] Here, as with the date of death, Church teaching prefers the Johannine hour.

In contrast to the allegedly uninformed procurator, the Jewish accusers respond from the outset in a surly, demanding tone when Pilate politely inquires about the nature of the charge:[34] "So Pilate came outside to them and said, 'What charge do you bring against this man?' They replied, 'If he were not a criminal we should not be handing him over to you' " (John 18:29-31). Although Pilate receives no answer to his question and asks the Jews to stop bothering him with the case, he knows exactly what the matter is all about. He calls Jesus to him in the Praetorium and asks him frankly, "Are you the king of the Jews?" (John 18:33). The reply is an evasive question from Jesus, "Do you ask this of your own accord, or have others spoken to you about me?" (John 18:34-35). A conversation ensues between them in the course of which Pilate is increasingly convinced of Jesus' innocence: " 'Mine is not a kingdom of this world. . . . Yes, I am a king, I was born for this, I came into the world for this: to bear witness to the truth; and all who are on the side of truth listen to my voice.' 'Truth?' said Pilate. 'What is that?' " (John 18:36–38).

When the judge steps out of the Praetorium to announce the result of his interrogation, he is made unsure of himself by the mob. Then, after he goes back and forth from the Praetorium a few times—"from Pontius to Pilate," as the phrase goes—the pendulum swings in favor of the mob: Pilate yields to the demand that Jesus be crucified.

The unhistorical character of this Johannine account is evident on many counts. First, it should be noted that if it were true Pilate would seriously have violated trial procedure. Roman criminal law prescribed that the presiding judge must make the parties involved confront each other, must not deal with them separately (Acts 25:16). Secondly, we must ask ourselves who could have overheard the alleged conversation between Pilate and Jesus inside the Praetorium and reported it to the Christian community. It is impossible that the accounts of the conversation between Pilate and Jesus are based on historical facts. No further proof is needed to point out that the procurator would not have let himself be drawn into a philosophical dialogue by a Jew suspected of instigating an uprising against Rome. A statement like "Mine is not a kingdom of this world" out of the mouth of a Jew is in any case fictional; only a Christian could speak thus. Here is John's typical Gnostic-tinged theology; this dialogue also stands in fundamental opposition to the portrayal in Mark and Matthew. Their descriptions of the hearing highlight precisely Jesus' stubborn silence, which they say amazed Pilate: "But to the governor's complete amazement, he offered no reply to any of the charges" (Matt. 27:14).

The wife of the Roman—she is said to have been named Claudia or Procula and to have been a granddaughter of Emperor Augustus—is introduced into the trial event by Matthew: "Now as he was seated in the chair of judgment, his wife sent him a message, 'Have nothing to do with that man; I have been upset all day by a dream I had about him' " (Matt. 27:19).

Although the procurator pronounced a misjudgment, his wife was more farsighted: She is revered as a saint by the Orthodox Church. Blinzler writes,[35] "Even a pagan woman recognized Jesus' innocence and makes an attempt to save him from his fate that his people had intended for him."

All the efforts of the presiding judge to let Jesus off run aground in the face of Jewish bloodthirstiness. As a lone fighter for the right, Pilate wages a hopeless battle against the *vox populi*. First he tries this, as Luke depicts it, pragmatic solution. He ignores the Sanhedrin's charges that Jesus is a rabble-rouser, a tax dodger, and a traitor (Luke 23:2) without comment. Then when he deals with the charge that Jesus claims to be king of the Jews, he dismisses it as of no consequence: "Pilate put to him this question, 'Are you the king of the Jews?' 'It is you who say it,' he replied. Pilate then said to the chief priests and the crowd, 'I find no case against this man' " (23:3–5).

When the Jewish authorities and people press further for Jesus' condemnation and Pilate is again forced to make a decision, he turns cunning. Although it is allegedly a matter of rebellion against the Roman emperor, he abruptly denies his jurisdiction and hands Jesus' case to the Jewish sovereign, Tetrarch Herod Antipas.[36] He, with his retinue, is sojourning in Jerusalem as a pilgrim on this significant Passover—a welcome coincidence for Luke to insert in his narrative. But Pilate's calculation backfires. Antipas likewise cannot find Jesus guilty of any capital crime, and will have nothing to do with the case, despite the fact that it was a good opportunity for him to revenge himself. Only a few hours before the Nazarene is said to have publicly called him a fox (Luke 13:32). Yet Antipas[37] restricts himself to expressing his contempt for Jesus: "Then Herod, together with his guards, treated him with contempt and made fun of him; he put a rich cloak[38] on him and sent him back to Pilate" (Luke 23:11).

When Pilate has to take over the case again he has yet another argument for releasing Jesus: After all, he is not the only judge convinced of the innocence of the accused. A very prominent Jew, no less than the sovereign of Galilee, has convinced himself of Jesus' innocence:

> Pilate then summoned the chief priests and the leading men and the people. "You brought this man before me," he said, "as a political agitator. Now I have gone into the matter myself in your presence and found no case against the man in respect of all the charges you bring against him. Nor has Herod either, since he has sent him back to us. As you can see, the man has done nothing that deserves death." (Luke 23:13–15)

The pigheaded people respect no reasoned argument but demand the death of the accused: "But as one man they howled, 'Away with him!'" (Luke 23:18–19). The Jesus-Pilate-Herod meeting is reported only in Luke 23:7–15. It is typical of post-Easter narrative. Enemies at first, now Pilate and Herod are presented as the first people to be reconciled through Jesus' sacrificial death. Here again, Luke is at pains to stress that Christianity presents no danger to the state: Jesus is politically harmless and is so judged by the Jewish sovereign and the Roman procurator alike.

Who Was Barabbas?

Pilate takes pains to save Jesus if possible. A brigand named Barabbas is also in his custody awaiting execution. Pilate has him brought before the people to ensure that, when he gives them a choice between the brigand and Jesus, they will decide in favor of the rabbi and not the brigand: "Pilate said to them, 'Which do you want me to release for you: Barabbas, or Jesus who is called Christ?'" (Matt. 27:17).[39]

But his hope is dashed; the crowd prefers the brigand: "They all said, 'Let him be crucified!'" (Matt. 27:23). "But as one man they howled, 'Away with him! Give us Barabbas!'" (Luke 23:18). "'Would you like me, then, to release the king of the Jews?' At this they shouted, 'Not this man,' they said, 'but Barabbas'" (John 18:39–40).

The name Barabbas raises problems, because it means nothing more than "son of the father"; hence it is not a proper name. There are texts that say this man is not named Barabbas but—of all things—Jesus. This, of course, is suppressed in most editions of the New Testament (surprisingly, also in the ecumenical Herder Bible edition). In the Greek original text of the New Testament,[40] the Bible published by the German Bible Society in 1982, and the New English Bible,[41] he is presented as "Jesus Barabbas." Barabbas is not part of the actual name but is used to designate this particular Jesus: "Now there was at that time a notorious prisoner whose name was Jesus Barabbas. So when the crowd gathered, Pilate said to them, 'Which do you want me to release for you: Barabbas, or Jesus who is also called Christ?'" (Matt. 27:16–17).

The similarity of names could have been coincidence, since the name Jesus was very common. Origen opined that the evangelist must have been mistaken about the names. But perhaps that imprisoned partisan leader[42] really named Jesus has been renamed Barabbas so as not to allow such a man to bear the holy name of Jesus.

But there is also an altogether different exegetical variant: Two persons were made of Jesus Barabbas and our Jesus only several decades later; and both are really identical. Since Barabbas is not a real name it would also fit Jesus: Son of God is the same as Son of Abbas. Jesus addresses God as "Abba." A special theological opinion holds that Matthew wanted to get across the point that "the Jews" had decided in favor of the bad and against the good Jesus.[43]

Those arguing thus must, to be fair, also allow the possibility of an altogether different conclusion: If this identity exists, then the Jews pressing for the release of Jesus Bar-Abbas were demanding not Jesus' execution but his release. This would be natural in regard to a prophet who only a few days before had aroused enthusiasm among the people upon his arrival, and likewise in regard to a Jew in Roman custody as an alleged rebel and earmarked for execution. It would make perfect sense that, when the demand for release proved unsuccessful and Jesus was led to the execution site, "large numbers of people followed him, and of women too, who mourned and lamented for him" (Luke 23:27). Anyway, why the people should have regarded the sentence as a grievous misfortune if they themselves had demanded it is insoluble.

The Barabbas incident[44] and the Lucan report on the mourning crowd could stem from the one and same source of an initial transmission of the Passion story. In the later versions Jesus "Bar-Abbas," alias Jesus "Son of God," was split into two persons and the mourning crowd was changed into a hostile Jewish mob. Here, the reason for the alteration would be that the evangelists sought to disseminate their writings in a manner pleasing to the Roman authorities, and to conceal the fact that the one whom they regarded as their Lord was really a Galilean whom the Romans had executed as a rebel rabble-rouser.

If one does not accept the thesis of identity between Jesus-Barabbas and Jesus-Son of God, then one thing may be established about Barabbas, assuming that he really existed. He was a resistance fighter who enjoyed the sympathy of the people and was possibly also close to the patriot Jesus and his disciples. Matthew 27:16 calls Barabbas a "notorious prisoner."[45] An attempt, as far as possible, to secure the release of this folk hero would be an understandable concern on the part of the Jewish people. But the Gospels pursue an altogether different aim in their depiction of the Barabbas incident. It is designed to show the monstrous guilt of the Jews: A brigand and a murderer is preferred to Jesus. "It was you who accused the Holy One, the Just One, you who demanded the reprieve of a murderer" (Acts 3:14–15).

Martin Luther[46] comments, "Matthew means to say that Pilate wanted to propose the most dreadful murderer so that the Jews could not ask for him. But they would have sooner pleaded for the Devil himself before they would have had the Son of God released." *Sic et hodie agitur et semper.* *

Pesch, in his commentary on Mark,[47] says the Barabbas episode may actually present the decisive feature of the conclusion of the trial before Pilate. He says Jesus' fate was "rather unwittingly" decided in the frame of the amnesty discussion. Pilate, who did not regard Jesus' guilt as proven, made a grave tactical mistake by including Jesus in the amnesty discussion, thus depriving him of the possibility of an acquittal. The crowd mentioned in the Gospels was a special group "that was interested in the release of Barabbas" and had probably never heard of Jesus. These people suddenly appeared before Pilate and demanded the release of their favorite Barabbas. They had been encouraged by the high priests to hold to their demands. At any rate, they were talked into believing that Jesus (who was unknown to them) had been justly found guilty by the authorities and deserved the death penalty. Pilate, committed to the amnesty promise, supposedly released Barabbas and "consequently, Jesus had to be delivered to the crucifixion." Thus a sentence could no longer be arrived at. Like many dogmatic theologians Pesch is also dominated by the view that the descriptions of the Passion story are absolutely historically verifiable.[48] I fully agree with him as regards the fundamental "guilt question." The rest, however, is sheer speculation, a "story" for which no serious leads exist anywhere.

Aside from the fact that no one can determine exactly the details of a trial against Jesus of Nazareth—and that no one should venture to do so—I consider the whole story of a traditional Passover prisoner's amnesty to be a legend. Neither such a law nor such a custom ever existed; if it had, this would certainly have been re-

---

*It happens thus today and always.

ported in historical sources. The Jews no more enjoyed the right to release a rebel every year than did any other peoples ruled by the Romans.

As a judicial institution, amnesty certainly existed in Roman law. There was the widespread custom to discontinue or squash penal proceedings on high holidays or for special joyous events *(abolitio publica)*.[49] There was also a special Easter amnesty. Significantly, however, the Easter amnesties began first with the later Christian emperors,[50] and these always excluded those guilty of high treason and murder. The Romans never viewed holidays of their subject peoples as occasions for amnesty.[51]

Pilate at the End

Despite the failure of all his efforts to release Jesus, Pilate does not give up. Now he tries to achieve his goal by appealing to pity. He lets Jesus be scourged by his soldiers (John 19:1)[52] in the hope that this will calm the screaming mob. Once more, his calculation goes awry. The sight of the bleeding Jesus vested with a crown of thorns[53]—"Here is the man" Pilate is supposed to have said compassionately (John 19:6)—infuriates the mob even more: "When they saw him the chief priests and the guards shouted, 'Crucify him! Crucify him!'" (John 19:6). Thereupon Pilate supposedly advises the Jews that if they are determined to kill Jesus they should eliminate him in the Roman fashion by crucifying him on their own: "Take him yourselves and crucify him" (John 19:6). From now on the Jews literally muddle everything in their doggedness and pigheadedness. They again stray from the political charge originally raised and revert to the religious charge, only to renew the political argument shortly thereafter: "'We have a Law,' the Jews replied, 'and according to that Law he ought to die, because he has claimed to be the Son of God.' . . . the Jews shouted, 'If you set him free you are no friend of Caesar's; anyone who makes himself king is defying Caesar'" (John 19:7, 12).

No argument is too perfidious for the mob. In a grandiose reversal of all national and ethical values, the people renounce their own credo; they deny their holiest principle that God alone is the king of their people[54] and profess that Emperor Tiberius is their only ruler.[55] They play "their last and most important trump card," as Blinzler puts it:[56] "We have no king except Caesar" (John 19:16).

Pilate, for his part, is the equal of the Jews in his mental disarray; he, too, turns his world view on its head. When he suddenly learns of the religious charge, that Jesus has supposedly passed himself off as the Son of God, it is said that "his fears increased" (John 19:8). The evangelist John obviously does not use this appellation in the sense of a Messianic claim to royalty, since that would not have been news to Pilate. Here we are to understand that Jesus had passed himself off as a supernatural being which—the confusion becomes complete!—would be inconceivable for Jews on the basis of their religious understanding. Blinzler writes, "The news that Jesus passed himself off as a Son of God makes a deep impression on Pilate. Might this accused man really be a higher being?"[57]

Previously there had even been an attempt to put Pilate under personal pressure by threatening to blacken his reputation in Rome because of his overindulgence toward a Jewish rebel like this Jesus of Nazareth: ". . . but the Jews shouted, 'If you set him free you are no friend of Caesar's' " (John 19:12). And this was the man who was to be denounced for his great intolerance, who was notorious in Rome for his cruelty and inflexibility toward the Jews, and who several years later was to be removed from his office in response to a Jewish protest![58]

But the evangelists describe the scene as follows: Pilate cannot cope with the continuous pressure, the nerve-racking shouting and howling. In the end he gives in—reluctantly—to the demand of the Jews.[59] Yet before he hands Jesus over to his soldiers to be executed, this representative of the Roman Empire miraculously recalls and emulates a gesture of Psalm 26 of King David from the Bible of the Jews. He washes his hands in innocence:[60] "Then Pilate saw that he was making no impression, that in fact a riot was imminent. So he took some water, washed his hands in front of the crowd and said, 'I am innocent of this man's blood' " (Matt. 27:24–25).

In view of all the mercy and goodness imputed to the procurator Pontius Pilate, it is not surprising that this Roman should have received a place of honor in later Christian representations.[61] He is venerated as a saint by the Coptic Church, as is his wife Procula by the Orthodox Church.[62] Every year, on June 25, Coptic Christians celebrate St. Pilate's day. The Church Father Tertullian had already asserted the procurator was a "secret Christian."[63]

Sympathy for Pilate is manifest in many places. Even theologians of our day attest to his "righteous judgment and protection of the innocent." Many novelists[64] have written engagingly about him. And when the tourist looks down from Mount Pilatus, seven thousand feet high, on the imposing landscape that is the city of Lucerne and Lake Lucerne, a breath of the sublimity that suffuses his soul perhaps may also gently fall upon the procurator.

EPILOGUE

THE only sources at our disposal—the Gospels—provide scant information on the historical course of events. On the one hand, they want to make the Jesus of the Passion appear as an instrument of the redemptive deed of God. On the other, they aim to lay the burden of the guilt for Jesus' death on the Jews so as not to create, from the outset, an irreconcilable conflict with the world power Rome.

The Jews appear as Jesus' enemies. At the same time non-Jews were to share in the God of the Jews, the sole true God, who had revealed himself as the God of Abraham, Isaac, and Jacob, through Jesus' mediation. All people must be called, through Jesus, to become members of a community, of the believing community of Jesus. But this community is the people of Israel.

> Do not forget, then, that there was a time when you who were pagans physically, termed the Uncircumcised by those who speak of themselves as the Circumcision by reason of a physical operation, do not forget, I say, that

> you had no Christ and were excluded from membership of Israel, aliens with no part in the covenants with their Promise; you were immersed in this world, without hope and without God. But now in Christ Jesus, you that used to be so far apart from us have been brought very close, by the blood of Christ. (Eph. 2:11–13)

The Jewish people is the "good olive tree," as the apostle puts it, from whose roots the Christian community draws its nourishment. From Pope Pius XI stems the highly significant instruction that all Christians are "spiritually Semites." Regardless of this declaration, and many years after Auschwitz, the worldwide collective Good Friday prayer of Catholics reads, "Let us also pray for the perfidious Jews."* Pope Gregory the Great had introduced this prayer in A.D. 600. Pope Pius XII, in 1945, had recommended that it was "in need of improvement." Pope John XXIII took up the cudgels for its abolition on Easter of 1959.[1]

Up to the present day, however, incorrigible Christians still reproach "the Jews" for being "the murderers of our Savior." Not until the Second Vatican Council was the concept of "deicide" officially rejected. Then it was defined as "unseemly" and "theologically questionable," a choice of words that in its reserve unfortunately leaves much to be desired. Lapide writes:

> Anyone who has the numerous papal bulls and church documents in front of him in which there is mention of "the herd of deicidal Jews," "the pestilential sect of Deicides," and Cain, "the archetype of the bloodthirsty Jew," will find it difficult to understand the sudden fastidiousness of the Council Fathers from whom nothing less is expected than a clear and unambiguous condemnation of the oldest and most unfair weapon in the arsenal of religious hostility to the Jews.[2]

In the "Declaration on the Jews" the Council deplores all persecutions of Jews and decisively condemns every form of anti-Semitism. But it cannot manage to go so far as to recognize the guilt and shared responsibility of Christians. Such a confession, in the name of the Church, was made by John XXIII shortly before he died:[3]

---

*The Roman Missal, conforming to the latest decrees of the Holy See on the Good Friday Mass, now reads, "Let us pray also for the unbelieving Jews." "Perfidious" has been expunged.—Tr.

> We acknowledge now that many centuries of blindness have covered our eyes so that we no longer see the beauty of Thy Chosen People and no longer recognize in its face the features of our firstborn brethren. We acknowledge that the mark of Cain stays on our foreheads. For centuries long Abel has lain in blood and tears because we forgot Thy love. Forgive us the curse that we unjustly pronounced on the name of the Jews. Forgive us, for in cursing them, we crucified Thee for the second time. For we knew not what we were doing.

If Jesus' death was decided beforehand in God's plan for salvation, then there is no one against whom a charge of deicide could be directed. In the Letter to the Romans 8:32 Paul writes, "since God did not spare his own Son, but gave him up to benefit us all." Without this death, according to Christian understanding, there would be no forgiveness of sins and no resurrection from the dead. Darkness would still envelop humankind. Hence Jesus' death is fundamentally an act of divine providence, an act of God's love for humankind: "We wish you the grace and peace of God our Father and of the Lord Jesus Christ, who in order to rescue us from this present wicked world sacrificed himself for our sins, in accordance with the will of God our Father, to whom be glory for ever and ever. Amen" (Gal. 1:3–5).

Whatever Jesus said are words of a Jew, not of a Christian. Anyone who believes that the Christian faith enjoins a hatred of Judaism turns away from him who was the first to proclaim the Good News of the New Testament.

In fact anyone who believes in Jesus' divinity, who sees in him the second person of the triune Deity, who understands the deed of the redemption to mean that God's "only begotten Son" took upon himself the fate of human beings, namely birth, life, and death, does not need to accept the notion of a violent death that Jesus suffered at the hands of the Jews. The kernel of Christian faith can only be this: Because death came into the world through a human being, the Son of God become a man therefore also had to die. The overcoming of death, however, the resurrection, is the fulfillment of the act of redemption:

> ... and if Christ has not been raised, you are still in your sins. And what is more serious, all who have died in Christ have perished. If our hope in Christ has been for this life only, we are the most unfortunate of all people.

> But Christ has in fact been raised from the dead, the first fruits of all who have fallen asleep. Death came through one man and in the same way the resurrection of the dead has come through one man. Just as all men die in Adam, so all men will be brought to life in Christ. (1 Cor. 15:17–22)

It has been shown that the charge of deicide raised against Jews is historically false, theologically superfluous, and ruinous from a moral point of view. If my book contributes to the demise of this nonsensical and vicious charge and reproach, if, in other words, it can be a stone in the mosaic of the Christian-Jewish dialogue, then my aim has been achieved.

NOTES

One

1. Other religions have far greater difficulties in this regard than Christianity. The teachings of Buddha were first committed to writing half a century after his death; those of Confucius, seven hundred years following his death.
2. Jesus is mentioned only once by Josephus Flavius, in passing. But even this mention is not historically beyond doubt. Klausner (p. 67 ff.) provides a detailed and exhaustive compilation of the extra-Christian sources.
3. Dautzenberg, p. 63. The claim that there were eyewitnesses stems from Augustine, who said Matthew and John were eyewitnesses whereas Mark and Luke received their information from the formers' "reliable" accounts (Wilcken, p. 156). Despite all scholarly findings to the contrary, claims to this effect are still made, very rarely, some even go beyond Augustine. F. May, a believer in Jesus, in *Die Wahrheit uber Jesus Christus* (Moers, 1982), is interested solely in an "edifying interpretation" of the Scriptures, and dismisses historical facts as "cluttering up . . . the heads of many modern theolo-

gians." Occasionally May even cites these "modern theologians," but only to refute them with "surprising and convincing answers."
4. The two letters of Peter were penned by an author who proclaims the Gospel in a wholly Pauline sense. But this is precisely what the disciple Peter did not do. The letters, in their final version, probably go back only to the beginning of the fourth century. The typical Jesuanic expectation of the approaching kingdom of God contained in 4:7 supports the theory that there was an earlier version of the first Petrine Letter. The legend of Christ's descent into hell (3:19–20) became known only after the Council of Nicaea of A.D. 325. The author of the first Petrine Letter also reports that Christians are being persecuted "all over the world." Such indeed was the case, not under Nero (in whose reign only a few police raids on Christians have been documented), but only much later under Marcus Aurelius and especially Diocletian. On the other hand, it was only at this later time that Christians felt strong enough to resist these persecutions publicly.
5. On the formation of this circle, see Mark 3:14–19. The terminology varies. Mark and Luke use the word "disciple" only for those who belonged to Jesus' narrower circle or who accompanied him on his wanderings. In Matthew and John, those who believed in Jesus' message and revered him are sometimes also called disciples (Matt. 27:57; 28:19; John 7:3; 8:31; 9:28; 13:35; 15:8).

Whether a closed group of disciples already existed during Jesus' lifetime, or arose only later in Jerusalem (when the disciples received the title "apostle" [1 Cor. 15:5]), out of their common faith in the resurrection, is an open question. Cf. Conzelmann, *Religionen*, p. 69, and Simonis, p. 55 ff. Simonis argues convincingly that the Circle of Twelve cannot be regarded as having existed in Jesus' lifetime, but came into being only after his death. The number twelve must not be taken literally; it symbolizes the twelve tribes of the chosen people: "You will eat and drink at my table in my kingdom, and you will sit on thrones to judge the twelve tribes of Israel" (Luke 22:30). In Jesus' time only the tribe of Judah still existed; the others survived only in mythic memory.
6. Landmann, *Jesus und die Juden,* p. 263
7. Wilcken dates it thus.
8. Mayer, pp. 158, 176
9. Mayer, p. 158, in a reference to Landmann
10. Pagels, p. 44
11. On Marcion, see chapter 2 of this book.
12. Isaiah 61:1–2, on which Jesus bases his sermon in his hometown synagogue (Luke 4:18–19), is impressive and evocative.
13. On this point, see chapter 2 of this book.

14. Quoted from Augstein, pp. 106–7.
15. P. 146
16. See among others Schillebeeckx, p. 38.
17. Theological writings frequently mention the "Seven words of Jesus on the Cross." What are meant are the three "words" in John 19:26, 28, and 30, the three "words" in Luke 23:34, 46, and one "word" in Mark 15:34 and Matthew 27:6.
18. In general ancient Greek-Roman historiography was not especially concerned to provide information to the reader. Its aim was to impart an ethical or religious view of reality. Thus heroes are idealized and fictive evil deeds are ascribed to cowards. The Roman historian Titus Livius articulated this as the ideal historiographic method (cf. Schillebeeckx, p. 67).
19. P. 336
20. Ben-Chorin (*Bruder Jesus*, p. 109) describes the testimony of the Berliner Provost Grueber at the Eichmann trial. Eichmann had once asked Grueber why he had risked his life to assist Jews, when he would receive no thanks for it. Grueber believed that Eichmann would recognize the meaning of the parable of the Good Samaritan because of his former connection with the Knights Templar. He replied, "A Jew once lay half dead on the road between Jerusalem and Jericho after being attacked by brigands. Then a man who was not a Jew came upon him and helped him. That, Herr Sturmbannführer, is my answer."
21. Dibelius, quoted by Deschner, p. 34
22. Cf. Schillebeeckx, p. 45
23. See chapter 9 of this book.
24. The historicity of the Sermon on the Mount, at least as a formal discourse with a beginning and an end, is doubtful. First of all, it is striking that the Sermon on the Mount as it is best known is found only in Mark. In Luke (where the site is described as "a piece of level ground") it is greatly abbreviated, and Mark and John are silent about both a Sermon on the Mount and the precept to love one's enemies, among other things. Thus they are silent about what is considered the loftiest and noblest of Jesus' teachings, the quintessence of Christianity. Mark 12:31 rather pointedly highlights only the love of neighbor, without a whisper of love of one's enemies. The words of the Sermon on the Mount are probably merely an editorial legacy of the evangelist Matthew.
25. Kolping, p. 653, footnote 124; p. 667. The situation is clearly expounded in the *Encyclopedia Judaica*, vol. 10:

> Both of the chief sources of the Synoptic Gospels, the old account and the collections of Jesus' sayings, were produced in the primi-

tive Christian congregation in Jerusalem, and were translated into Greek from Aramaic or Hebrew. They contained the picture of Jesus as seen by the disciples who knew him. The present Gospels are amalgams of these two sources, which were often changed as a result of ecclesiastical tendentiousness. This becomes especially clear in the description of Jesus' trial and crucifixion, in which all Gospel writers to some extent exaggerate Jewish guilt and minimize Pilate's involvement. As the tension between church and synagogue grew, Christians were not keen to stress the fact that the founder of their faith was executed by a Roman magistrate. But even in regard to Jesus' trial, as in other cases, advance toward historical reality can be made by comparing the sources according to principles of literary criticism and in conjunction with the study of the Judaism of the time.

26. In passages of the Lucan account, especially Acts 2:23, 4:10, and 5:30, the facts are presented from the exact opposite viewpoint, as amounting to personal guilt laid upon the whole Jewish people. The Jews are made responsible for both Jesus' crucifixion and Judas' betrayal.
27. *Die letzten Tage Jesu in Jerusalem*, p. 172
28. The Jewish writer Maccoby presents another version:

> The Nazarenos as loyal Jews took part in the defense of the city, and most of them perished in the subsequent massacre. A few survived and continued to exist, much weakened, but were no longer able to resume missionary activity or exercise any influence outside Palestine. That the Jewish Christians betook themselves to Pella during the siege of Jerusalem has been convincingly refuted by S. G. E. Brandon. (*Jesus and the Zealots*, p. 208 ff.)

Both Maccoby and Brandon could be wrong. They overlook the fact that during the Jewish War both the leader of the Zealot revolt and the Jewish governor of Jerusalem Bar Giora were revered as Messiahs. This must have been so distasteful to Jesus' followers that it is hard to imagine they would have fought for the cause of these "Messiahs," or accepted their military authority.

29. Some of the Jewish Christians returned to Jerusalem at the end of the war. But Bar Kochba received no Jewish Christian support in his revolt against the Romans (132–135), not on pacifist grounds, but because Jesus' followers must have sensed in him competition they could not withstand (Schoeps, p. 33).
30. Schoeps, p. 17. James, the "Brother of the Lord," was not personally included in the defamation.
31. Acts 13:45–48. Cf. also Schoeps, p. 10
32. Ruether, p. 90

33. On the other hand, there is no mention in the Synoptic Gospels of Jesus baptizing anyone. The accounts in John are contradictory. Whereas John 3:22 has Jesus performing the baptismal rite, the evangelist in John 4:2 stresses that only his disciples baptized, not Jesus himself.
34. In the theological rewrite, this saying attributed to Jesus is designated "words of the Risen Lord."
35. 1 Kings 8:41–43; Isaiah 49:6
36. *Bruder Jesus*, p. 58
37. *Encyclopedia Judaica:*

> The liberal Pharisaic school of Hillel was not unhappy to see Gentiles become Jews. In contrast, the school of Shammai made conversion as difficult as possible because it had grave reservations about proselytism, most of which Jesus shared (Matt. 23:15). As a rule he even did not heal non-Jews. It should be noted that none of the rabbinical documents says that one should not heal a non-Jew.

Two

1. Mark 7:3 gives the reader instruction on Jewish customs.
2. The prevailing view is that the Marcan corpus of Chapter 16 consists only of 16:9–20.
3. This description has also been written into the last chapter of Matthew (which also originated later). Luke and John, on the other hand, mention only localities around Jerusalem, Emmaus, for example, as sites where the Risen One appeared.
4. P. 39
5. Shortly thereafter, another Matthew was admitted to the circle of disciples as Judas' successor (Acts 1:26).
6. To the Roman Catholic Church it was very important that *ecclesia* be translated as "church" here. Luther, by contrast, translated it as "community."
7. Shalom Ben-Chorin (*Bruder Jesus*, p. 38) describes how the Catholic theologian Joseph Schnitzer was removed from his teaching position at the University of Munich and excommunicated because, as an incorruptible scholar, he felt that he was unable to oppose the Protestant theologian Adolph von Harnack and attest to the authenticity of the Gospel passage concerning Peter's power of the keys.
8. P. 192
9. Luke 13:33–35; 19:39–44; 21:22–24; 23:26–31; cf. also Kolping, p. 297
10. Pp. 121 ff., 135, 149
11. But it has classic models in the Old Testament; Ps. 147:6; Job 5:11; 12:19; 1 Sam. 2:7.

Perhaps this pericope allows yet another interpretation, that the "princes" and the "rich" are a reference to the Romans whom God, through the Messiah, will drive from the land in order to raise his humiliated people again.

12. It should be noted that the crib, Mary and Joseph, and the infant Jesus are mentioned in Luke's Gospel, but not an ox or a donkey. The latter two beasts owe their place to the prophet Isaiah 1:3: "The ox knows its owner, and the ass its master's crib, Israel knows nothing, my people understand nothing." Lapide writes (*Flüchtlingskind*, p. 18), "These reprimands of the prophet were torn out of context and adapted by the Church Fathers to an animal homage to Jesus solely for the purpose of illustrating Israel's alleged stubbornness." Francis of Assisi was one of the first to present the manger scene in detail, and he added to it his own friendship for animals, a tradition that lives on to this day.

13. For example Mark 3:31–35; Matt. 13:55; John 2:4. Even regarding Mary's presence at the cross, the evangelist John's depiction 19:26 is a negative report of a sadly distant relationship between mother and son.

14. Kolping, probably mistakenly, writes, "The fact that Jesus had women in his entourage is to be explained on the basis of the domestic services they performed" (*Theologische Revue*, p. 271).

15. Acts 12:2, where mention is made only of the beheading of James. Since John's name no longer crops up in Acts after this, it may be concluded that he shared the same fate.

16. A decree issued by the Reich Ministry of the Interior in 1938 instructed school authorities to see to it that this pericope was deleted from the bibles used in religious instruction classes.

17. Cf. John 11:47 f.; 12:19

18. *Der Jude Jesus*, p. 73. In the same publication the Protestant theologian Lutz adds (p. 135), "In John's Gospel the real Jew becomes a theological symbol and later the theological symbol again became a scapegoat for the real Jews."

19. John 5:19–47; 7:28; 15:21; 16:3

20. John 12:37–40

21. *Grundriss*, p. 27. The statement appears in somewhat moderated form in the fourth edition revised by Andreas Lindemann.

22. Kolping, p. 301

23. Quoted from Augstein, p. 45

24. Ben-Chorin, *Paulus*, p. 91

25. Bornkamm, *Paulus*, p. 18

26. The pagans were disappointed by the emptiness that had overtaken their faith, which offered them no consolation or escape from their worldly afflictions. They flocked in great numbers to Christianity,

the more so because Paul spared them proselyte status. They were attracted by the monotheistic principles, but also by a general faith in mysteries, and a deeply human longing for redemption in the Beyond through a God who promises eternity (cf. also Bleicken, p. 113 ff.).

27. Ben-Chorin, *Paulus,* p. 184 f.
28. Ben-Chorin, *Paulus,* p. 196: "Was love really the driving motive in Paul's life, of which he has so splendidly sung, or was it the hate that emerges from many sentences of his letters?"
29. *Paulus,* p. 47
30. In an ecumenical spirit I would like to judge the apostle's statements according to their "objective value." But some critical exegeses come to another result: The real Israel is the spiritual Israel, the Israel of the Promise, not the Israel of the Sinai covenant. Only the believers in Christ are the real children of Abraham and his Promise. The people of Moses' covenant are doomed to destruction through the wrath of God. Only a small number, those who have arrived at faith in Christ, can be saved. Thus (and only to this extent) God has not rejected his people (Ruether, p. 101 ff.).
31. The second stanza of the well-known hymn "O Sacred Head Now Wounded" reads: "O Lord what Thou hast suffered is all my burden, I myself am guilty for what Thou hast endured. I, Jesus, am the wretched one who hath deserved this."
32. Only the Hellenist wing of Jesus' followers was persecuted; the Hebraic wing was accepted as a loyal sect. The Hellenists had to flee and carry out their missionary activity outside Palestine (Acts 8:1); the Hebraic apostles and the "churches throughout Judea, Galilee and Samaria were now left in peace" (Acts 9:31).
33. Lapide, *Paulus,* p. 53. A change of name because of a religious experience was not unusual. For example, the fisherman Simon was renamed Peter when he became a disciple of Jesus (Mark 3:17; Luke 6:14). In the Catholic Church it is still customary to take a new name when one enters a convent or a monastery, or after being elected pope.
34. There was, however, an Essene community in Damascus. On occasion it has been conjectured that Paul carried on a campaign against the Essenes.
35. Whether Paul, who had traveled much through desert regions, perhaps experienced a hallucination is a wholly different question. Lonely wanderers frequently experience mirages and sometimes even hear voices calling. Paul may have recounted such a vision, and the pious chronicler subsequently elevated it into an experience of salvation.

A much simpler explanation would be that Paul suffered a severe heatstroke and then, as reported in Acts 9:12, was healed by a certain Ananias. Ananias was a follower of Jesus living in Damascus. Paul owed his life to him and this circumstance may have won him over to the faith.

36. The number forty, of course, has a symbolic character. The Flood lasted forty days (Gen. 7:4); the Jews wandered forty years through the wilderness (Num. 14:33); the purifying period of a woman after parturition lasted forty days if she had given birth to a boy, and twice as long if the baby was a girl (Lev. 12:1–15). Jesus is said to have fasted forty days in the wilderness (Matt. 4:2; Luke 4:2). When questioned about the reason for the war of aggression against Lebanon in 1982, Israeli Prime Minister Menachem Begin declared that he wanted to create "forty years of peace from the PLO."
37. Cf. Lehmann, *Jesus-Report*, p. 207, footnote 11
38. Ben-Chorin, *Paulus*, p. 51
39. The Church went much further, even: *Extra ecclesiam nulla salus* ("No salvation outside the Church"); or, "Anyone who does not love the Church as a Mother cannot love God as the Father."
40. P. 64
41. The quotation is from Deschner, p. 181
42. *Die geistlichen Übungen* ("The spiritual exercises"), ed. Weinhand (1921), p. 187
43. But Küng (p. 409) strongly counters the view, frequently propounded by theologians, that Paul is the true founder of Christianity. "Paul then—a man not of hatred but of love, a genuine bearer of 'glad tidings'—did not establish a new Christianity." But the apostle certainly founded Christology, this "stepsister" of Christianity, as Küng would agree.
44. Quoted in Lapide, pp. 55, 59
45. Cassius Dio, *Historia Romana*, 56:46. Not even Barbarossa's death was believed. When he did not return from the Crusade the faithful, anticipating a resurrection, maintained he was in a cavern in the Kyffhäuser Mountain in Thüringen.
46. In Mark 16:19, which originated at the end of the second century, the Lucan depiction of the Ascension is taken over in the form of a mere mention.
47. Ascension Day has been fixed at forty days after Easter Sunday. According to an old tradition, the faithful gazed up at a mannequin representing Christ being pulled through "the hole of the Holy Spirit of the Church." From the direction in which the puppet looked, the worshipers divined whence the storms would come the next year. Ascension Day is always a Thursday.
48. The profession of faith is certainly not of apostolic origin. Its earliest manifestations date back to the latter half of the second century

(probably to combat Marcionism). It later underwent several variations, and achieved its present form in the Middle Ages.
49. Landmann counters this persuasively.
50. Craveri, pp. 424–25
51. Quoted in Goguel, p. 186. Similarly in Mack and Volpert (p. 31 f.), the originator of this fantastic story is not Marcion but the Church Father Basilides of Alexandria.
52. Some centuries later this legend came to Muhammad's attention. He found it so interesting that he incorporated it into the Koran. In Sure 4:158 it is said that the Jews did not really kill or crucify Jesus. They mistook someone who resembled him for Jesus, and put that man to death (cf. also Mack and Volpert, p. 32, and Pagels, p. 122).
53. The formula "resurrection of the flesh," on the other hand, reverts to a definition coined by the Church Father Tertullian at the end of the second century. He pointed out that he was not speaking of the soul's immortality, since this was not denied even by heretics. What is in fact said to be resurrected is "this flesh overflowing with blood, with its osseous frame, transversed by nerves, wound together by veins" (quoted in Pagels, p. 61). Only in the apocryphal gospel of Peter, of which fragments were found at the end of the nineteenth century, is the unfolding of the Resurrection described as such.
54. *Jesus*, p. 165
55. Quoted in Trilling, *Fragen nach der Geschichtlichkeit Jesus* ("Questions Regarding Jesus' Historicity"), p. 145
56. P. 350
57. Pagels, p. 43
58. See Mackey, p. 115

Three

1. On the other hand, the Essenes knew that as the sons of Light they were enjoined to hate the sons of Darkness (the so-called sacrilegious priests in Jerusalem and their adherents). Love of the enemy also crops up repeatedly in the Old Testament (for example, Exod. 23:4–5; Lev. 19:18; Prov. 25:21–22), in a wholly opposite sense to its current meaning. It is quite wrong to assert that Jesus substituted "Love your enemy" for the Old Testament maxim, "An eye for an eye, a tooth for a tooth." Many do not know that the phrase "eye for an eye, tooth for a tooth" has a positive connotation. The Old Testament *Lex talionis* asserts metaphorically that for an eye and a tooth only an eye and a tooth can be demanded, and that the death penalty should not be applied indiscriminately in cases involving bodily injury (the principle of the punishment fitting the crime). In practice this meant that the offender had to pay compensation as well as

any damages. The same applies to the contention that the God of the Old Testament is a God of severity and of wrath and the Christian God, a God of love. Of course there is no difference between the Gods of the Old Testament and the New Testament; Jesus did not want to create a new concept of God. The Old Testament God does not come across to the impartial reader as a "good" God, but might seem a frightening deity with his jealousy and destructiveness. But surely this requires exegetic and theological interpretation, to mitigate that impression somewhat (for example, as Lapide does) with the observation that in the Old Testament God's wrath occurs perhaps five times, whereas God's grace is mentioned more than fifty times. It should be viewed as altogether wrong to pit the New Testament against the Old Testament. Several passages from the apostle Paul's letters, for example, Romans 1:18, also require interpretation and toning down. Too often persecutors and executioners have cited Paul to give a "Christian" justification to countless operations against dissidents, and even to the extermination of entire peoples. At all events, it would be historically dishonest to assert that Christians were the only ones to conceive the precept to love one's enemy.
2. Speculations have suggested that the Essenes were perhaps close to those to whom the letter to the Hebrews was addressed; the letter may have been penned by a colleague of the apostle Paul or Paul himself. (This is discussed in greater detail in Ben-Chorin, *Paulus*, p. 163 f.) Pliny the Elder, Philo, and especially Josephus Flavius reported on the Essenes: In Jesus' time they were said to number between 4,000 and 5,000, as many as the Pharisees. The number of Sadducees was estimated at about 2,000.
3. *Encyclopedia Judaica:*

> Apparently the beginnings of Christianity attracted no greater attention than did the many other sects that sprung up toward the close of the Temple period, and it is certain that the incidents connected with its founder were not at the center of events of the time, as the Gospels would lead one to believe.

4. Cf. Suetonius, *Vita Neronis*, 16
5. Christian historiography strives to set the number of martyrs as high as possible in order to buttress the thesis that the Christian faith became a state religion through the blood of its martyrs. No less a figure than Origen puts this legend into perspective, declaring that the number of Christian martyrs was "small and easy to count" (Deschner, p. 344, with documentation). If Nero really persecuted Christians it was surely not because of their faith but because he

blamed them for the burning of Rome. Another possible explanation for the passage in *Annals* xv:44 could be that Tacitus invented the persecution of Christians under Nero to document the contempt he felt for Christians. For he obviously relished describing the tortures to which they were subjected:

> First, Nero had self-confessed Christians arrested, then, on their information, large numbers of others were condemned—not so much for arson as for their antisocial tendencies. Their deaths were made farcical. Dressed in animal skins, they were torn to pieces by dogs, or crucified, or made into torches to be ignited after dark as a substitute for daylight. Nero provided his gardens for the spectacle.

6. Quoted from Aufhauser, p. 9
7. See Mendelssohn, p. 116
8. Craveri, p. 20. See Landmann (p. 310): "It is not exonerative that some rabbi without a knowledge of Greek should have invented the stupid plot of an affair between Mary and a Roman soldier named Panthera or Pandera and tactlessly and senselessly sullied the honor of this undoubtedly honest woman." Klausner (p. 25) espouses the view that the name Pandera or Panthera is simply a distortion of *Parthenos,* the Greek word for virgin, which in a further bowdlerization allegedly led to the nickname "son of the panther."
9. Landmann, pp. 53, 312
10. No original manuscripts (autographs) of any ancient author have been preserved, not even of Josephus. The recent papyrus finds are not autographs but early transcripts. The oldest transcripts of Josephus' works stem from the tenth century.
11. *Antiquities of the Jews,* Book xviii, 3:1, 4:1. That Josephus describes the Essenes as exclusively peaceful and makes no mention of their influence on the Jewish revolt is an error of the chronicler, probably arising from the fact that the Essenes were enjoined to keep their codex strictly secret.
12. *The Jewish War,* Book vi, 5:3
13. Book xx, 9:1. Ananos is the Greek form for Annas. The Ananos cited here is the son of the high priest mentioned in Luke 3:2 and John 18:13. Josephus speaks of Ananos the Younger and Ananos the Elder.
14. Klausner (p. 74), however, challenges this view: "A Christian would never have spoken of Jesus 'who was called the Messiah.' Such an interpolation would be all too 'sly.' It could have been written only by the Pharisee Jew Josephus."
15. P. 276
16. Flusser (*Die letzten Tage Jesu in Jerusalem,* p. 155 f.) who bases himself on a newly discovered Arabic version of the Josephus passage in

question. See also Klausner (p. 69) referring to Origen. The Josephus passage quoted by Eusebius was unknown to Origen.
17. Vespasian is variously judged. Mommsen (p. 343 f.) described him as a levelheaded commander in chief and a prudent tactician.
18. A bit of Nicodemus' family history is known. He had been one of the wealthiest patricians in Jerusalem. In the Jewish-Roman war rebellious Zealots set his grain elevator afire. His son Gorion, at the beginning of the revolt, took part as a Jewish officer in the negotiations that culminated in capitulation to the Roman occupation force in Jerusalem. His daughter lived in extreme poverty after the war (Flusser, *Selbstzeugnisse*, p. 20, with documentation).
19. Paul bases his entire theology directly "on the cross," but he is silent about it. Only in his very first letter (1 Thess. 2:15) does he mention Jesus' violent death. In a polemical way he accuses the Jews of putting Jesus to death and strives to give the impression that the Jews even carried out the execution.
20. "Natural events of this kind belong to the deaths of great men," judges Kolping (*Fundamentaltheologie*, vol. II, p. 661). Moreover here we are obviously dealing with a legend fulfilled according to Amos 8:9: "That day—it is the Lord Yahweh who speaks—I will make the sun go down at noon, and darken the earth in broad daylight."
21. Benz, p. 24
22. Cf. Craveri (p. 407), who in turn refers to Harnack. Even Blinzler (p. 41) concedes the falsification.
23. Quoted from Ben-Chorin, *Bruder Jesus*, p. 213
24. P. 353
25. P. 550
26. Cf. Lapide and Lutz, p. 136
27. P. 17
28. P. 157
29. Schweitzer, Foreword to 6th ed. of *Geschichte der Leben-Jesu-Forschung*
30. Drews, Foreword (p. xii): "The disavowal of an historical Jesus can justifiably base itself on the insights of the progressive religious-historical studies of our time so that, at least, it can claim the same degree of probability as is enjoyed by the usual manner of presenting the beginnings of Christianity from the theological side." Küng, p. 154: "Karl Barth and with him Bultmann and Tillich, as a result of the conclusion of the early liberal quest for the historical Jesus, took up an attitude of historical skepticism (which Schweitzer by no means shared) and linked this up with Kierkegaard's conception of faith that is historically uncertain (or dogmatically insured against history) as true faith."
31. See Drews, Foreword
32. P. 396

33. E. Bloch, *The Principle of Hope*, p. 1256
34. Simonis, p. 23 ff.
35. Matt. 11:19; Luke 7:34
36. Cf. Kolping, p. 336
37. There is no doubt that the words placed in the mouth of the Baptist in Matthew 3:11 and John 1:29–30 have an avowedly kerygmatic content, obviously because of the necessity to come to terms with the odd situation.
38. Luke 4:28–29; Mark 3:21
39. John 6:60–67; 7:7
40. P. 149 f.
41. The crosses were not as high as they are represented in most paintings of the Golgotha scene. They were about the height of a man; the feet of the victims were only a few inches above the ground.
42. Quoted in Blinzler, p. 368 f.
43. P. 155 ff., 163
44. Blinzler, p. 405 f.
45. On the contrary: According to Zechariah's prophesy (Zech. 13:3–4) it is precisely the "false" prophet who will be "run through." It is nevertheless understandable that some ancient Church Fathers occasionally attempted to link the death on the cross to a cryptic prophesy, in view of the great importance attached to the fulfillment of prophesies. One referred to Isaiah 53, the so-called Deutero-Isaiah, where mention is made of the "suffering servant of God" as a figure who had already appeared but whose importance remained unknown, who had been despised and died ignominiously, but who would one day rise again in order to fulfill the splendor of the divine promise.
46. To these should be added the deliberate inconsistencies. I am referring to the not infrequent juxtaposition of sayings that lack an internal connecting logic, as in the pericope on the dispute among the disciples as to who would occupy first place (Mark 9:33–37). Here we are probably dealing with authentic sayings of Jesus that were placed together, despite their disjointedness, because for once they were definitely from the source.
47. Some dogmatic theologians, however, refuse to admit Jesus' error. They revert to the four words contained in the second Letter of Peter 3:8–13, which, in turn, cites the well-known Psalm 90:4 according to which a day is like a thousand to the Lord and a thousand years are like a day. On the other hand Küng states: "To err is human. And if Jesus of Nazareth was truly man, he could also err."

Four

1. In the unified translation of the Bible published by Herder in 1980, there is no mention of "his wife" but of "his betrothed." Both translations are possible on the basis of textual variations. The same applies to the Jerusalem Bible, the source of all biblical quotations in this book, as well as to the King James version of the Bible. The biblical quote in German reads *seinem vertrauten Weibe* (his promised wife) [Tr.].
2. This is the Greek translation of the Old Testament ordered by the great King Ptolemy II (305–204 B.C.) in the wake of the Alexandrian conquest and the consequent hellenization of Palestine. It was said to be the work of seventy translators, but this number may be apocryphal. Its special importance lay in the fact that it allowed Jews living in the Diaspora to read their Bible.
3. P. 456
4. Kolping (p. 322): "The dispatch of an angel to a virgin was alien to the Jewish sensibility of that time."
5. Cf. also Lapide, *Ein Flüchtlingskind*, p. 69 f.:

    > It is certainly not due to blind chance that, for example, Mithras, the "Savior" and sun-god of the Romans after whom the first day of the Christian week is still called Sunday, was born of a virgin in a crib, of all days, on December 25, and adored by shepherds; promised peace to the world only to be crucified later; and rose again on Easter and, finally, journeyed to heaven, to mention only the most striking similarities with the Christ of the Greek Gospel.

6. I remain unconvinced by Knoch's reference (p. 221) to Acts 1:14 to show "an indication of an early Christian Marian veneration." The very opposite is the case. Apart from the fact that Mary is mentioned only subordinately in Acts 1:14, many other people, for example Mary Magdalene, must be placed on the same level if these passages are to be considered veneration.
7. The Church Father Ignatius of Antioch was the next to mention the virgin birth, citing Matthew and Luke.
8. Craveri, p. 26. However the Proto-gospel of James, composed presumably at the end of the second century, was "written for the glorification of Mary, who is now also of Davidic descent (already asserted by Justin anyway), whose virginity is understood in the sense of 'inviolability'; and Jesus' brothers are children of Joseph by an earlier marriage" (Kolping, p. 321, footnote 42).
9. Craveri, p. 27
10. The Holy Inquisition called one of its torture racks the "Iron Maiden" or "Our Lady of Sorrows." It was a tall female figure of

11. To be precise, in A.D. 274 Emperor Aurelian voluntarily relinquished his status as a god and proclaimed the *sol invictus* the titular god of the empire, with himself as the god's earthly representative.
12. During the Crusades, notwithstanding all the knights' barbarities, there were periods when the war was fought only from Monday to Thursday. The enemies' holidays, the Muslim Friday, the Jewish Saturday, and the Christian Sunday, were respected.
13. In any case, dates were not taken all that seriously until the sixteenth century. Often the year was presumed to begin at Easter; March 25 was the agreed date. Hence it is frequently difficult to fix the year of events that transpired in January, February, and March. At times the beginning of the year was determined by the accession to the throne of the reigning monarch or pope. The religious calendar compounded the confusion, determining religious events not by the date of the month but, for example, as "three days before the birth of the Virgin" or "the third Sunday of Lent."
14. The dates debated by ancient and modern scholars range from 9 B.C. to A.D. 12 (cf. tabular diagram in Edwards, p. 25 f.).
15. In Luke 1:5, on the other hand, Jesus is said to have been born "in the days of King Herod of Judea" (i.e., 27–4 B.C.).
16. This area was known as Canaan in the Old Testament, but is generally referred to as Palestine. After the defeat of the Bar Kochba revolt Hadrian wanted to nullify the area's associations with Israel, and it was then named Palestine officially. Jerusalem was renamed Aelia Capitolina until the reign of Emperor Constantine. Israelites usually spoke of the land Juda, after the southern province of Judea, rarely of Israel or the Holy Land. Linguistically, Palestine is derived from "Philistine Land." The Greek seafarers applied the name of the coastal strip once inhabited by the Philistines to the whole country.
17. The title Procurator Augusti probably dates from Claudius. A stone slab found in Caesarea in 1961 designates Pontius Pilate "praefectus Judaeae."
18. Claudius became emperor in A.D. 41 after Caligula was murdered. He was a schoolmate of a grandson of Herod the Great, Agrippa I. Through Claudius, Agrippa managed to depose the procurator, and under his leadership Palestine was once more a vassal kingdom. In 44, after Agrippa's death, Claudius reinstated the post of procurator.
19. Thus, only Luke describes a pilgrimage to Jerusalem made by the twelve-year-old Jesus with his parents. On the way home his parents suddenly missed him. They returned anxiously and found him in the Temple engaged in a discussion with scribes. When they re-

(Note: Item 10 context continues: cast iron into which suspected heretics were forced to climb. They were then pierced by iron thorns or squeezed to death.)

proached him for causing them so much concern he snapped at them (2:41–50). Further elaborations on Jesus' childhood can be found in some apocryphal gospels, the best-known being the so-called Childhood Gospel of Thomas. Here Jesus appears as a divine rascal; for example, it describes the school pranks that he played on his teachers (cf. also Wolff, p. 157 f.).

20. Craveri, p. 48
21. A further point of reference for Jesus' date of birth is provided by Luke 3:23: "When he started to teach, Jesus was about thirty years old." Jesus began his public ministry after being baptized. According to Luke 3:1, John had begun to proclaim his baptism of repentance in the fifteenth year of the reign of Emperor Tiberius. Bearing in mind that the calculation starts not from January but from the Jewish spring month of Nisan, this would be A.D. 28 or 29. If Jesus was thirty years old at that time, he was born in 2 or 1 B.C.

    Yet Luke does say that Jesus was *about* thirty years old when he began his public ministry. A precise dating is thus not possible, especially since Luke and the other Synoptic Gospels all say that Jesus began his mission only after the arrest of John the Baptist by Herod Antipas in A.D. 29, i.e., not immediately after his own baptism. Nor is it known how Luke arrived at his dating.
22. Possibly John did not know the Synoptic Gospels (see chapter 2 of this book).
23. In King James version, Isaiah 9:11. Conzelmann (*Religionen*, p. 624) points out that Galilee had been isolated after the deportations carried out by the Assyrians, but that the Maccabees later settled there, making it Jewish once more. In Jesus' time its rural population was predominantly Jewish.
24. Kolping, p. 314
25. The observance of this is Candlemas, celebrated on February 2; in the Catholic Church it marks the official end of the Christmas season.
26. Actually the child himself, as firstborn, belonged to God and should have been consecrated to him (Exod. 13:1–2). But when Jesus was born, this custom was no longer practiced and instead parents made an animal sacrifice or paid a suitable sum of money.
27. Lapide, *Ein Flüchtlingskind*, p. 21
28. Lapide, *Ein Flüchtlingskind*, p. 16 ff.
29. This passage does not appear in the English translation of Schweitzer's *Geschichte der Leben-Jesus-Forschung*. It can be found on p. 512 of the second German edition (Tübingen, 1951).
30. Bultmann, p. 24
31. Schoeps, p. 37: "It is not Peter who appears as the leader of the community, but the brother of the Lord, James, who is said to have

been installed as the Bishop of Jerusalem. Peter was obliged to submit to James written yearly reports on his sermons and activities."
32. Quoted from Deschner, p. 154. Cf. also Schoeps, p. 23.
33. Ben-Chorin, *Mutter Mirjam*, p. 33 f.
34. P. 452

Five

1. Kolping (p. 320) counters as follows: "By giving the son born of his lawful wife his name, Joseph, a descendant of David, recognized his son and irrevocably inserted him in the genealogy and the hereditary titles linked to it. Thus the strange exception of the last member of the genealogy is fully explained and substantiated, namely as an event announced and decreed by God."
2. Lapide, *Ein Flüchtlingskind*, p. 27:

   > For bible-attuned ears the fact that Mary was already in a state of advanced pregnancy as a "betrothed" is no slander, the less so as the four female forebears in Jesus' family tree—Tamar, Rachel, Ruth and Bathsheba—though world-famous, were not exactly models of chastity. In Judges 11:1 we read that Jephthah, the judge who freed Israel from the hands of the Ammonites, "was a valiant warrior. He was the son of a harlot," which did not adversely affect his work as a liberator.

3. The unreality is further heightened by the fact that the genealogy is taken even further back: to the archfather Abraham (Matthew) and to Adam (Luke). In Matthew, Joseph has twenty-six forebears before David; in Luke, forty-one.
4. Lapide, *Ein Flüchtlingskind*, p. 22: "What is striking here is that all five are good Jewish Bible names, without the least Hellenic influence such as can be found in Philip, Andrew and Nicodemus."
5. Kolping (p. 319) points out that in Judaism every first son bears the title "firstborn" whether or not he is followed by siblings. The brothers mentioned in Mark and Matthew must have been older than Jesus; otherwise their protective attitude (as expressed in Mark 3:21, for example) is incomprehensible. But if they actually were older, they could not have been Mary's sons since Jesus was the firstborn.
6. Blinzler (p. 392), for example, places the word "brothers" in quotes. In the Proto-gospel of James, Jesus' siblings are presented as Joseph's children by a previous marriage.
7. Pesch, *Markus-Evangelium*, p. 22
8. Flusser, *Selbstzeugnisse*, p. 22

Notes

9. Kolping, p. 316; Stauffer, p. 23
10. See Craveri, p. 18
11. P. 20
12. *Bruder Jesus*, p. 86
13. Egon Friedell, p. 72: " 'Woman, why turn to me?' If the passage were only an apology, such a phrase would surely have been suppressed since it could easily be misunderstood. But how realistic it sounds! The eternal theme—the genius and the 'family'—is brought to life in this shattering description."
14. Landmann, p. 310. The author continues (p. 311):

> The enormous importance of the mother-goddess cult for the "acceptance" of Christianity, especially in the southern Mediterranean lands, can be inferred, for example, from the solid conviction of the simple people of Naples that Jesus deserved death on the cross because of his consistently dismissive attitude to his mother and for having said, "Woman, why turn to me?"

Six

1. This abridged summary has been taken from Pöhlmann, p. 91.
2. Küng, pp. 192–93
3. Augstein (pp. 183–84) has compiled the principal opinions now current concerning Jesus' outer appearance.
4. Craveri, p. 163
5. Stauffer (p. 50 f.) attempts a reconstruction:

> Ancient Palestinian Jews had a light brown complexion; the color of their eyes was predominantly brown. The gospels tell us nothing about the color of Jesus' eyes. We do know, however, that from his appearance one could take him for a man of forty (John 8:57). Are we to assume, therefore, that Jesus did not look very young, and that at that time his face was already tired and careworn? Then we may roughly imagine Jesus as the Christ of Rembrandt's so-called "Hundred Gilder Print" or of the painting "Christ at Emmaus" in the Louvre. The ancient Palestinian Jews were black-haired. In Jesus' time and homeland men wore their hair down to their shoulders, parted in the middle, combed and salved with a light, delicate oil. Disorderly hair was taboo. A beard or a moustache formed part of the male image.

6. Stauffer, p. 50
7. A travelogue of an expedition that set out at the beginning of our century (under the direction of the Old Testament scholar Gustav Dalman), quoted in Bätz and Mack (p. 32), contains the following observation: "Locusts are cooked in salt water, dried, ground and

8. The expression "bridegroom" in the Luther translation misleadingly implies a kerygmatic content to the effect that Jesus was likening himself to the bridegroom of the parable of the foolish and wise virgins (in which the bridegroom represents the Messiah). St. Jerome chose *filii sponsi*, which makes no sense, for his Latin translation. The Greek original contains *nymphon* which is equivalent to "bridal chamber." Jesus was evidently comparing a place where delicacies are eaten to a bridal chamber.
9. P. 323
10. Mark 14:3–9; Matt. 26:6–13; John 11:2; 12:1–8. These women are called by their names only in John.
11. Craveri, p. 295
12. Doubts have been cast on the authenticity of Jesus' words. It is improbable that the execution was prevented simply by his command. Even Jesus' justification of his intervention seems questionable, as Haenchen (p. 373) says: "If earthly justice is to be administered only by men without sin, then the administration of justice will cease to exist."
13. Wolff, p. 53
14. Gospel of Philip, 32:55b; quoted in Vardimann
15. Ben-Chorin, *Bruder Jesus*, p. 127 ff.
16. Quoted from Vardimann
17. P. 135
18. The tax collectors collaborated with the occupying Romans. They were entrepreneurs who, alone or jointly, acquired a lease on districts, from which the taxes flowed into their pockets—in exchange for a solid down-payment. They could do more or less as they pleased. When collections were good they enjoyed a profit; when collections were bad, they risked failure.
19. Cf. Wolff, p. 121
20. Cf. also Matt. 25:14 ff.; Mark 13:34; Luke 12:42 ff. On the other hand, the authenticity of the parable of the entrusted pounds (or talents) has been questioned by some scholars. A. Mayer (p. 251) writes: "To imagine God as participating in exploitative business deals in my view borders on blasphemy. With Jesus one is more liable to meet God in the slums than in rich financial districts. At any rate, in order to follow his word one doesn't need a bank." "Give to anyone who asks, and if anyone wants to borrow, do not turn away" (Matt. 5:42). Lapide views the matter differently. He accepts the core of the parable as authentic but opines that Jesus was speaking with "mor-

(then placed in sacks thus providing a week's nourishing food for men, camels and horses in arid, barren terrains. Raswan (one of Dalman's guides) liked their taste after roasting but found them stale after the boiling and nasty after eating for too long a time . . ."

dant irony" meant for Archelaus, Herod's son, whose tax collectors had behaved so ruthlessly toward the Jews while he was visiting Rome that he extolled the usury as a "profitable business" upon his return (cf. Lapide, *Er wandelte*, p. 38).
21. P. 70
22. Bodo Volkmann, a professor of mathematics at the University of Stuttgart, was mirthfully and roundly applauded at an evangelical gathering held in Stuttgart on June 6, 1988, when he declared:

> Anyone who would want to interpret the Sermon on the Mount politically should also, to be consistent, abolish the judicial organs (Judge not!) and the police ("Resist not evil!"), as well as insurance policies ("Worry not about the morrow"), bankers ("Do not store treasures for yourself on earth!"), and trade unions ("If someone hires you to work for forty hours a week for him, work willingly eighty hours for him for the same wages!"). Not only must the German Army be abolished, but also all the other institutions that protect the citizenry from harm.

23. Craveri, p. 170
24. Paul and his followers condoned slavery in even clearer terms (1 Cor. 7:20–22; 1 Pet. 2:18–20).

Seven

1. Conzelmann, *Religionen*, p. 646
2. According to Mark 9:19 he must have spoken similarly to the disciples: "How much longer must I put up with you?"
3. Mussner writes, "At first Jesus claimed to offer the eschatological kingdom of God. After Israel rejected the offer, he presents himself as having been rejected along with the offer." (This is quoted in Kolping, p. 630.) The formulation "Israel rejected the offer" has a reproachful ring, and points toward the Church's contention that Jesus had been rejected by his countrymen and that therein lies the "guilt" of the Jewish people. This is stated as though it were impossible to establish, wholly objectively, that Jesus had simply enjoyed less success than his more popular predecessor John the Baptist.
4. One glib interpretation of Jesus' curses would be that, although both evangelists want to emphasize Jesus' disappointment at his meager results in Galilee, the curses themselves are purely symbolic. Then again, expressing oneself in strong and exaggerated language is typical of the Oriental region.
5. Kolping (p. 620) writes, "At that point Jesus certainly had no Messianic ambition."
6. P. 265

7. The following Talmudic tale (quoted from Bätz and Mack, p. 76) is typical: "A Gentile asks Schammai to be converted to Judaism on condition that the teaching of the Torah take place 'while I stand on one foot.' Schammai chases him away. When the Gentile repeats his request to Hillel, he is told: 'Do not do what you hate to your neighbor! That is the whole Torah. All the rest is commentary on it. Begone and learn it.'"
8. Kolping (p. 620) writes, "What can be known about Jesus' intentions in journeying to Jerusalem is that whereas up to then he had dealt with simple folk, he now had to reckon on a confrontation with the leaders of his people."
9. According to Mark 6:17–29, John the moralist had pilloried Herod Antipas for marrying the wife of his brother Philip and thereby embarking on an ostensibly incestuous relationship. The wife, with her daughter's cooperation, supposedly revenged herself by inducing Herod to behead the Baptist. This is almost certainly legend.
10. See Landmann, p. 68.
11. To date the event close to Easter, the absurd assertion has occasionally been made that the Jews were in the habit of eating fig buds. It is much more probable, of course, that the textual passage is a later Christological interpolation of a symbolic character.
12. Ben-Chorin, *Bruder Jesus*, p. 137
13. *Jesus*, p. 137
14. Mackey, p. 71
15. There are authors, for example, who assert the contrary.
16. Neither Jesus' trial before the Jewish Supreme Council nor the one before the Roman procurator corresponds to any Old Testament prophesy as such.
17. The extra month was added for a purely practical reason. Rabbi Gamaliel wrote a friend about this matter around A.D. 50: "We would like to inform you that the doves are still tender and the lambs are still young and the corn is not yet ripe, so it was found advisable to add another thirty days to the year" (quoted in Edwards, p. 17).
18. The Christian Easter observance reflects this tradition: Easter falls always on the Sunday following the first full moon after the beginning of spring.
19. *Jesus*, p. 142
20. But Jesus probably celebrated the Seder according to the rules of the Essenes; hence, it was appropriate that men only were present.
21. Kolping (p. 596) expresses doubt that the Last Supper was a Passover meal: "That any doubt can exist as to its Passover character indicates that positive proof is not so easy to come by . . . the synoptics' intention was to make as close a connection as possible between the early Christian communion and the Passover meal."

22. Kolping, p. 341
23. The historical truth of the passage concerning Simon of Cyrene is confirmed in that Mark even mentions the sons of Simon (Alexander and Rufus) by name—an otherwise irrelevant piece of information, which the other evangelists do not report.
24. See chapter 3 of this book.
25. Ben-Chorin, *Bruder Jesus,* p. 161
26. See the tabular diagram in Edwards, p. 81 f. Edwards, an anthroposophist, postulates a death date which is different from that of most researchers; like Rudolph Steiner, he accepts April 13 of A.D. 33. John 2:20 states that when Jesus entered Jerusalem, the Herodian temple was already forty-six years old. If this dating (which I do not accept) is taken at face value, A.D. 28 was the year of Jesus' death. Herod had decided to build the Temple in the eighteenth year of his reign (Josephus Flavius, *Antiquities of the Jews,* Book XV 11:1), i.e., in 20–19 B.C.
27. Blinzler observes (p. 372): "This much is clear: Jesus was completely conscious up to the last moment and his thoughts belonged to his heavenly Father." Blinzler, of course, does not substantiate this; he confuses historicity and preachment.
28. The absence of testimonies was emphasized by the Berlin church historian H. Lietzmann. This conviction was widely adopted by critical theologians such as Bornkamm, Dibelius and Haenchen. See also Strobel, p. 31, footnote 6, and Blinzler, p. 23, footnote 58, p. 174.
29. P. 70
30. The fruits that naive faith can yield are still etched in my memory from a debate in which I had been invited to participate by a Protestant pastor. When I touched on the absence of witnesses a—relatively young—listener reproached me as follows: The accused, Jesus Christ, risen from the dead, heard everything; he briefed his followers on the proceedings so that they could commit them to writing. The speaker was applauded loudly by most of the audience.
31. The Marian cult refers to this passage. For through her alleged presence at the foot of the cross, Mary is accorded a role in Jesus' public life.
32. Bultmann (quoted in Augstein, p. 302) refers to the symbolic sense of this scene. Jesus' mother would represent Jewish Christianity; the favorite disciple, the pagan Christians. Jewish Christianity allegedly aspired joining the great Christian community.
33. Luke speaks in a general way: "All his friends stood at a distance. So also did the women who had accompanied him from Galilee, and they saw all this happen" (Luke 23:49).
34. The correct translation is in the ecumenical unified translation of the Bible (Herder, 1980). See also H. Merkel (cited in Kümmel, p. 399).

35. Bornkamm, *Jesus*, p. 145
36. P. 491
37. Conzelmann, cited by Strobel, p. 10, footnote 22.

Eight

1. The Syrian mercenaries probably did not understand Hebrew; their language was Aramaic. It can be presumed, of course, that they had no biblical knowledge; so Mark 15:36, "Wait and see if Elijah will come to take him down," is surely without historical basis.
2. At any rate, this was so during the epoch in question. In the Hellenist-Hasmonian epoch crucifixion may also have been a Jewish form of execution (Hengel [p. 176] bases his assertion on Yigael Yadin and the Temple scrolls). The crucifixion, or "hanging on wood," of living persons, as was occasionally practiced by Jews, was apparently abolished by Herod (Hengel, with commentary in Kümmel, p. 410).
3. Related in Craveri, p. 406, with documentation
4. The simple soldier's pay was miserable. His annual income, paid in three installments, amounted to 227 denarii. A Palestinian day-laborer, by comparison, earned 1 denarius a day (Bätz and Mack, p. 27). When the four soldiers assigned to a crucifixion were allowed to share the clothing of the crucified, no matter how shabby, this was deemed a pay supplement. On the other hand, it is more probable that the pericope of the sharing of the clothes was to demonstrate a prophesy fulfillment according to Psalm 22:18: "They divide my garments among them and cast lots for my clothes."
5. Cf. Hengel, commented on by Kümmel, p. 409
6. Drews, p. 74
7. Scholars ascertained that these remains of the crucified were laid in a private grave only later (Kümmel p. 411).
8. The description was reprinted by Bätz and Mack, p. 96, illustration on p. 113.
9. "Blood and water," the sacrament of Holy Communion and baptism! And the lance fulfills the prophesy of Zechariah 12:10.
10. No crucifixion ever took place in Greece itself.
11. Aurelius Victor, *De Caesaribus*, I, 414
12. Goguel (p. 470):

> If the course of events was as here described, Pilate would not have needed to enquire whether Jesus had committed acts which could be punished by Roman law; all he would have had to do would have been to find out whether he had committed offenses which were punishable under the Jewish law, and whether that law was being correctly applied. In this case, however, there is no question of a Jewish sentence sanctioned by the Roman authority;

both the sentence and the execution were carried out by the Romans in accordance with Roman Law.

13. Schillebeeckx, p. 165: "All Jews at that time knew that the Romans had the right to carry out crucifixions, that Herod Antipas had the *ius gladi** . . . Finally the Sanhedrin had the right to sentence persons to death by stoning."
14. The cause of Stephen's stoning is shrouded in obscurity; the description is ambiguous. The original charge was heresy, but a heresy that was typical of Jews' internecine controversies. Paul had taken it to an even greater extent. The tumult broke out when Stephen insulted the members of the Sanhedrin by calling them "stubborn," "betrayers," "murderers," and "law-breakers." It cannot be excluded the lynching was instigated by the infuriated mob, although Paul's mention of the presence and participation of the members of the Sanhedrin speaks against such an assumption. It might have been Hebrew Christians who felt spurned by the Hellenist Stephen. In this case Stephen would have been put to death by fellow Christians, as a result of the tension between the Hebraists and the Hellenists.
15. See chapter 6 of this book.
16. Illustration in Flusser, *Selbstzeugnisse*, p. 107; Bätz and Mack, p. 29
17. Josephus Flavius, *Antiquities of the Jews*, Book xx, 9:1
18. Strobel provides an overview of the arguments (p. 23 ff.). Cf. also Schnackenburg, p. 23 ff., John 18:11 accompanied by a plethora of bibliographical references. Schnackenburg assumes that there was no Jewish competence to carry out a death sentence, but leaves the question open. Karlheinz Müller dealt especially thoroughly with this question at the conference of German-speaking Catholic New Testament scholars, held in Gerz in the spring of 1987 (*Quaestiones Disputatae*, p. 41 ff.). Müller argued forcefully against the existence of this death sentence competence, but in my opinion he did not succeed in refuting the many opposing arguments.
19. Special constructs must be attempted. Thus, for example, Strobel (p. 88 and footnote 233) writes: "Stephen . . . hardly differs as a legal case from that of Jesus. . . . Since the Roman authority at that time recognized the judgment of the Sanhedrin on Jesus, obviously this time the Sanhedrin took the execution upon itself after the Roman procurator declined, but followed the Old Testament law stipulating stoning."
20. Goguel, p. 523
21. In his book, *Pontius Pilate Defensus;* see Blinzler, p. 24. A recent thesis, especially despicable though quite isolated, holds that the Jews delivered Jesus to the Romans for crucifixion so that the Savior would

---

*The law of the sword.

suffer the most ignominious possible death, as opposed to the relatively dignified death by stoning. This idea was propounded (as related in Schlotheim, p. 21) by the Protestant theologian Bornhaüser in 1947, three years after Auschwitz! The Catholic theologian Blinzler argues along similar lines (p. 346): "The Jews attached a great importance to having him draw his last breath on the cross as a 'curse of God.' " Mussner, who gladly cites Blinzler in discussing the trial narrative, obviously took this from Blinzler: "That he was not hanged, but crucified, was connected with the fact that his Jewish enemies at the trial expressly demanded the shameful execution on the cross from Pilate." In contrast to Blinzler and other theologians, Mussner is a prominent spokesman in the Christian-Jewish dialogue who has been awarded the Buber-Rosenzweig medal; he is no advocate of anti-Judaism (*Die Kraft der Wurzel*, p. 134).

22. Detailed summary in Blinzler, p. 241
23. Doerff (citing Mommsen), p. 53
24. Cf. also Josephus Flavius, *The Jewish War*, Book ii, 8:1.
25. Josephus Flavius, *The Jewish War*, Book ii, 20:5: "Josephus [Caiaphas] chose the wisest elders from among the people and raised them to the highest authority for all of Galilee. In every city he installed seven judges for minor matters, whereas for matters of greater import and homicides, he ordered that they be submitted to himself and the seventy Elders." The special role of the number seventy has its model in Exodus 24:1.
26. Mark 14:53: "all the chief priests and the elders and the scribes." Only someone unfamiliar with the judicial mind could think that all members of a large judicial body would willingly appear at a late-night session—and just before a feast to boot. This does not even take into account their alcohol consumption.
27. The mockery of the Roman soldiers is missing from Luke's account. His purpose, as ever, is to show that Rome was never anti-Christian.
28. Whereas Matthew is silent as to the hour of the execution, time problems crop up in Luke, deviating from Mark and equally insoluble. In Luke the Jewish Council assembles just before daybreak so that Jesus can be handed over to Pilate as soon as possible in the morning (22:66; 23:1). Luke says nothing about the actual moment of the crucifixion; nevertheless, he like the other synoptics mentions noon as the hour of the solar eclipse and the agony of Jesus. This would have allowed no time for a hearing before Pilate. Yet this hearing, an especially long one according to Luke's account, is alleged to have taken place. The Johannine account (19:14; 19:16) is utterly different. According to him the sentence was handed down at noon; the crucifixion could not have taken place before 3 o'clock. Only Rudolph Pesch, in *Der Prozess Jesu* (p. 56), can give more exact

information: "Jesus of Nazareth was crucified at 9 o'clock in the morning of the Passover festival day, on Friday, April 7, A.D. 30."
29. Haenchen (p. 540) describes the strictness of the prescriptions regarding the burial of the dead just before a festival day as follows: "A man who lay dying on a Friday said to his relatives: 'I already know why you close my eyes and keep my nose closed, you don't want to violate the Sabbath. Neither do I, therefore take leave.'"
30. *La date de la Cène* (1957); see Blinzler, p. 109 ff.
31. Kroll, p. 375
32. Goguel, p. 481
33. These words, "Am I a brigand?" have meaning only if they are addressed to a Roman arresting officer. Moreover, only Romans were allowed to carry swords, never Jews. Hence the Jews were present, if at all, as bailiffs of the Romans. Thus Mark 14:49: "I was among you teaching in the Temple day after day and you never laid hands on me. But this is to fulfill the scriptures" must be viewed as a later Christological interpolation.
34. Pesch (in *Der Prozess Jesu*, p. 15) interprets it as a "guerrilla band." He uses the vocabulary typical when an occupation force has brought freedom fighters into being in the occupied country. Thus, for example, special units of the German *Wehrmacht* in Poland, France, Yugoslavia, or Russia were to fight "guerrilla bands." Naturally the Roman occupation force also viewed the Jewish Zealots as "bandits" or guerrillas.
35. According to Mark 15:32 and Matthew 27:44, both "robbers" mocked Jesus.
36. Jesus reportedly promised this man, "Today you will be with me in paradise" (Luke 23:43). The "today," this "ascension to heaven directly from the cross" (Kolping, p. 660), does not make sense: Do not the grave and the descent into hell come first, followed on the third day by the resurrection? (Cf. also Luke 24:50.)
37. Only Luke reports that the Jewish authorities had supplied Pilate with this specific charge; according to Mark and Matthew, Pilate surmises as much without having been informed.
38. *Antiquities of the Jews*, Book xvii, 10:8
39. Violation of *lex Julia maiestatis* is explained in the *Corpus iuris Dig.* 48:4, 1:1: *Maiestatis autem crimen illud est, quod adversus populum, Romanum, vel adversus securitatem elus committitur.** Roughly, this is the definition of high treason. The offense can be punished, depending on the status of the culprit, by crucifixion, killing by wild beasts in the circus, or deportation to an island (*Dig.* 48:19, 38).
40. A Roman pro-consul, Seneca's brother

*However that particular treason is perpetrated versus the Roman people or constitutes a threat to their security.

41. Klausner writes (p. 490): "The sly Roman tyrant does not let himself be deprived of the pleasure of making fun of the whole Jewish people with the inscription placed above the cross: Behold what an ignominious death the Romans impose on this so-called King of the Jews!" On the other hand, Haenchen writes (p. 514): " 'King of the Jews' could only have been written if Pilate's intention was to play a nasty joke on the Jews."
42. Haenchen, quoted in Kolping, p. 663
43. Probably in the center of the crossbeam. The text was legible because the head of the crucified hung forward or sideways.
44. Blinzler (p. 77), referring to a passage in Josephus Flavius, points out that the members of the house of Annas "conducted an active trade in accessories for the sacrifices in the manner of unscrupulous stock exchange jobbers."
45. The Johannine account is especially sensational here, although he inverts the time given by the synoptics, having the incident occur at the beginning rather than at the end of Jesus' public activity (John 2:13).
46. Lohse and Haenchen, cited in Kolping, p. 265
47. Kolping, p. 265
48. Acts 21:31–33 describes how swiftly the Romans responded to potential riots. Pesch propounds a rather ingenuous explanation in *Der Prozess Jesu* (p. 35): "The procurator was personally in Jerusalem specifically on the Passover festival day in order to carry out his duty as protector of the Temple that Jesus seemed to be attacking."
49. On the basis of Matthew 21:46, the assumption that the Pharisees and scribes would gladly have had Jesus arrested because they were offended by his parables of the two sons and the wicked husbandmen is untenable.
50. Bethany is mentioned as a place where Jesus sojourned only in Matthew 21:17 and John 12:1. On the other hand, we read in Luke 21:37: "In the daytime he would be in the Temple teaching but would spend the night on the hill called the Mount of Olives." According to the chronology of the evangelist John, which does not agree with that of the synoptics, Jesus did not appear in public between his return to Jerusalem for the Passover (supposedly on the Monday of Passover) and his death. The presentation in John's Gospel suggests that Jesus returned on the eve of the Passover only in order to die there (Goguel, p. 412).
51. Haarenberg, p. 89
52. Cf. Jens (p. 48 f.). He cites a fictitious vote of the members of the Dominican Order in 1962, according to which "not only the kiss in the garden of Gethsemane, but also the death, the suicide in potter's field, is proof that the betrayal was really a labor of love."

Notes

53. P. 41
54. P. 566
55. I Cor. 15:5. The election of Matthew as the new twelfth disciple, replacing Judas, actually took place forty days later (Acts 1:21–26).
56. P. 59
57. Ben-Chorin, *Bruder Jesus*, p. 193
58. Goguel, pp. 497–98
59. See Jens, p. 85 (cf. also Landmann, p. 260).
60. Trilling, "Gegner Jesu," p. 203
61. Goldschmidt and Limbeck, p. 9
62. Ben-Chorin, *Bruder Jesus*, p. 154. Whether Judas has really addressed him as "my friend" seems questionable because of the likelihood that this is a fulfillment legend; cf. Ps. 41:9 and Ps. 55:13–15.
63. Jens, p. 57
64. Luther *(Von den Juden und ihren Lügen)* finds satisfaction in anger. I quote from Jens (p. 88):

> I, accursed goy, cannot understand where the Jews have learned such a sublime art. Otherwise I must think that Judas Iscariot hung himself, that his innards burst, that, as happens to the hanged, his bladder exploded, and that the Jews then ordered their servants to collect the piss of Judas together with the other relics in golden pitchers and silver plates, and then shared the shit and filth, because they saw things in the scriptures that neither Matthew nor Isaiah nor all the angels, not to mention us accursed goyim, can see.

65. Cf. also Jens, pp. 15 f., 58 ff. In a fictional vein he argues (p. 60): "What does Jesus care about the noose and the hemp that will knot Judas? After all, he has his cross!"
66. Jens, p. 5 ff.; quotation from Limbeck, p. 85 f. The Franciscan monk is fiction, as is Jens' entire report—see p. 95 of this report.
67. Jens, pp. 24, 37
68. All the exegetes agree that the means of betrayal was not the notorious kiss of Judas. The kiss is obviously to be understood in relation to the allegory of the deadly kiss that appears in 2 Sam. 20:9; cf. Ben-Chorin, *Bruder Jesus*, p. 188.
69. In Luke 22:52 the chief priests and the Council members are present.
70. Acts 21:31, 22:24, 23:10, and 24:7. For details, see Blinzler, p. 90 ff.
71. Mark speaks likewise of "a number of men" (14:43); Matthew, of a "large number of men."
72. P. 90 f.
73. P. 468
74. P. 92

75. Besides Blinzler (p. 96), this novel interpretation is also taken up by Kroll (p. 357) and—with evident reserve—by Kolping (p. 637):

> There is no consensus on who actually carried out the arrest. Bultmann, with others, considers the arrest by the Romans to be historically verified. . . . Nevertheless it is easier to view the arresters as the court functionaries of the Supreme Council. In John 18:12 there is mention of a "cohort" and "Jewish guards." That the arrest was carried out by the Roman cohort is highly improbable since Pilate learned about Jesus only later. . . . The initiative lay with the Jews.

76. According to Luke 22:51, the right ear was cut off.
77. Naturally, the historicity of this feat—which only John mentions—is open to question. Kolping writes (p. 567): "The historicity of the sword episode is still shrouded in doubts. Jesus' words in Mark 14:48 take no note of the sword-blow and fit very poorly with its having just transpired. It is obvious, however, that the arresters had to stand guard over Jesus."
78. P. 512
79. Blinzler, p. 136
80. Pesch, p. 411
81. Klausner, p. 471, who cites Josephus Flavius.
82. Kolping (*Theologische Revue*, p. 272) proposes that the Johannine report is historically significant to this extent: "The nocturnal hearing before Annas could be the vestige of a tradition that lies at the base of the religious truth in Mark and Matthew."
83. The Jewish author Maccoby takes a somewhat different view. According to him, Caiaphas was a kind of Roman puppet who placed Rome's interests above those of Israel. He believes Jesus' arrest and the delivery to the Romans were ordered by Caiaphas, who viewed Jesus as an agitator against the occupation power. The Sanhedrin, let alone the people, were not at all involved in this operation; full responsibility lies with the traitor Caiaphas.
84. J. G. Sadosam, quoted in Kümmel, p. 402
85. Ben-Chorin, *Bruder Jesus*, p. 194
86. P. 80
87. This view is contested. But if Pilate was not of Sejanus' party, Sejanus' fall should not have troubled Caiaphas.
88. Caiaphas' words to the Supreme Council have not been correctly reported. The words "the whole nation to be destroyed" would not have been uttered when such a danger did not exist. The Romans' devastation of the country began only after A.D. 70 (the destruction of Jerusalem by Titus). That was the time when the Gospels were written.

89. Lapide, *Wer war schuld an Jesu Tod,* p. 402
90. Thus Hans Maas, a member of the Church council from Karlsruhe, expressed it in a letter to me.
91. Bultmann, p. 164. This possibility is also—indirectly—pointed out by Kolping, who refers to Haenchen (p. 668): "Up to this day the hypothesis accorded the greatest probability is that the political leadership of Jerusalem's Judaism denounced Jesus to the Romans, who put him to death for alleged rebellious activity." The same idea is expressed in the *Encyclopedia Judaica:* "The deliverance of Jesus into the hands of the Romans was, it seems, the work of the Sadducean 'high priests,' who are often mentioned in the story. A man suspected of being a messianic pretender could be delivered to the Romans without a verdict of the Jewish high court."
92. The memorandum of the Council of the Evangelical Church of Germany *Christians and Jews* (1975) states: "The upshot of the collaboration between the autonomous Jewish administration and the Roman occupying power—a collaboration that does not come through very clearly in its historical particulars—was the execution of Jesus by the Romans" (quoted in Strobel, p. 4). A detailed and convincing description of the historical situation and the sentence is contained in Kremers, p. 871. Cf. further Hildegard Gollinger (p. 897) who in barely four dictionary columns knowledgeably presents a distinguished exegetic survey of the trial.
93. From Pilate's unconditional release of the body, Blinzler infers (p. 394) that the procurator "had reluctantly pronounced the death sentence." Stauffer (p. 108) provides the following easy explanation: "It may be . . . concluded that Pilate and some Jewish judges no longer had a clear conscience."
94. Luke 23:54 says, "The Sabbath was imminent," meaning the first star.
95. For this reason I cannot see why the so-called Shroud of Turin is taken to be the winding-sheet in which Jesus was wrapped. The fact that this cloth presents great riddles for science—as is undoubtedly the case, given the findings thus far—and that it could have been used to wrap a crucified person does not imply that it had anything to do with Jesus of Nazareth. The shroud will remain controversial as long as the Church authorities refuse to submit it to independent experts for an opinion and insist on making their own selection of experts to be consulted. In any case, the mystery of the shroud is irrelevant to the subject of this book. If it should prove to be "authentic," it could only support the theory that the Romans crucified Jesus.
96. Goguel, p. 547
97. Goguel, p. 548

98. Goguel, p. 550
99. Schmithals, "Wer war verantwortlich für den Tod Jesu?" in *Der Tagespiegel,* Dec. 22, 1987
100. This changed later. After Christianity triumphed over Roman paganism, the Christian emperor felt obliged to declare it the true faith and proclaimed pagan practices a crime against the state.
101. The fact that Christians lost the *privilegia judaica* and thereby, among other things, had to forfeit exemption from emperor worship, is a wholly different question.
102. Mark 12:1-12; Matt. 21:33-46; Luke 20:9-19.
103. R. Ruether, p. 101 ff.
104. See chapter 1 of this book.
105. Maccoby, p. 205
106. Mayer, p. 111. Nero was sentenced to death for his appalling crimes by a decree of the Senate *(Dammatio Memoriae).* He escaped execution by committing suicide. His memory was expunged from the history of Roman emperors.
107. Cf. on this point Mommsen, p. 348 f.
108. Seven types of Pharisees are to be distinguished. Six are bad; only the seventh, the "charitable Pharisee" who obeys God out of love, is the true Pharisee. Cf. in this regard Ben-Chorin, *Bruder Jesus,* p. 21 ff.
109. P. 99
110. P. 268
111. Cf. Matt. 22:35; Acts 5:34. There were also scribes among the Sadducees. Kolping (p. 274) designates the scribes as "one of the three groups in the Jerusalem Sanhedrin."
112. Küng, p. 179
113. Ben-Chorin, *Paulus,* p. 190, with documentation
114. Küng, p. 203
115. Speidel, p. 33
116. Thoma, quoted in Mussner, p. 281
117. Quoted from Lapide, "Jesu Tod," p. 239
118. Cf. also Acts 3:13. There it is given to Peter to charge that the betrayal perpetrated by Judas the disciple is to be equated with the alleged betrayal by the people of Israel.
119. I still remember a remark made during a lecture on the trial of Jesus delivered in the 1960s by Fritz Bauer, the highly esteemed Hessian public prosecutor (now deceased): "The Jews wanted to get rid of the Romans, but not of their own sins!"
120. P. 537
121. P. 427. Or, Haas put it: "One entered in the Roman penal record as guilty of high treason would not have been acceptable to the Roman magistrates as founder of a religion" (p. 234).

122. P. 12 f.
123. P. 139 f.
124. Lapide, *Er wandelte*, p. 44
125. Goguel, p. 98, vol. i. Romans felt a certain contempt for Orientals as long as they did not adopt the Graeco-Roman culture.
126. The first motion was filed in 1948, immediately after the establishment of the State of Israel.
127. Blinzler, p. 15 ff., Ben-Chorin, *Bruder Jesus*, p. 191 f.

Nine

1. In this connection, see the synopsis in Kremers, p. 78 ff. Ruth Kastning-Olmesdahl, p. 91:

   > For many Christians there still is no doubt that "the Jews" wanted and brought about Jesus' death because they did not want to recognize him as the Messiah, their Lord. It often seems central to Christians' perception of themselves that they can distinguish themselves from the Jews, the judges and "killers" of Jesus. For this reason they defend themselves against all attempts to call the guilt of the Jews into question.

2. Kolping, p. 653; cf. also Küng, p. 331; Bornkamm, p. 143 f.; Holtz, p. 128
3. Of the Passion story Dibelius accepts only the following as historically verified: the timing, according to Mark 14:2; the fact of the Last Supper; the nocturnal arrest with the help of Judas; the sentence to death on the cross; and the fact of the crucifixion (cited in Trilling, *Fragen*, p. 132).
4. This is attested to by the numerous reactions to the theories I have put forward.
5. To such a theologian as Blinzler, the expression "councilor" has too favorable a ring. He opts instead for "Sanhedrist" which supposedly has a pejorative connotation (for example, on p. 255). He makes exceptions for Joseph of Arimathea and Nicodemus. He refers to these members of the Sanhedrin respectfully as "councilors" (pp. 394, 397).
6. Flusser, *Selbstzeugnisse* (p. 117), with documentation. Blinzler (p. 220) objects that the "little Sanhedrin" was not yet known in Jesus' time.
7. *Antiquities of the Jews*, Book xx, 9:1
8. ". . . more an aristocratic, religious-political caste-grouping than a party" (Kolping, p. 269)
9. Speidel, p. 34. Kolping (p. 27) appears to view the "scribes" as an independent third faction within the Sanhedrin, but likewise as-

serts, "Mostly they belonged to the Party of the Pharisees." He does not share Speidel's view that the Pharisees were the strongest faction.
10. The nickname obviously was an honorary epithet. It derives, like Kephas, from the Aramaic word *Kepha,* rock.
11. Annas was appointed high priest in A.D. 6 by the procurator Coponius. He founded a real dynasty of high priests, and even after his removal retained his political influence as an *eminence grise.* Caiaphas succeeded Eleazar, the son of Annas; it may be assumed that he was devoted to his father-in-law. After Caiaphas was removed another son of Annas, Jonathan, took over his office. He was followed by his brother Mathias, who was deposed in 41–42. (How long Mathias was in office is not known.) It is known that in 62 still another son of Annas (also called Annas) occupied the post of high priest. It was he who condemned Jesus' brother James in an illegal hearing and so lost his post. In the Jewish War (66–70) Annas was put to death by Zealot rebels.
12. Haim Cohn brought my attention to this in a letter. I can thus correct my earlier statement that the accused in capital cases was entitled to a defense counsel. I erroneously called this person *Baal-Rib,* which really means a litigant party in a civil trial.
13. The three predictions of the Passion in Mark 8:31, 9:31, and 10:33 (the so-called *vaticinia ex eventu*) are not just testimonies of faith but were created wholly as a result of faith. In the first and third, Jesus announces that he will be sentenced to death by the Sanhedrin; in the second, he does not specify who his killer will be.
14. Mark 8:31; 11:18; 14:43, 53; 15:1
15. Cf., for example, Matt. 23.
16. From this Flusser (*Selbstzeugnisse,* p. 120) concludes (with a reference to Josephus Flavius) that scribes here are the Temple secretaries, not, as before, the Pharisaic rabbis. Mark 14:55 suddenly calls those assembled "chief priests and the whole Sanhedrin." In any event, the word "Pharisee," which was applied so frequently to Jesus' accusers, is no longer used anywhere in the Passion story.
17. J. Eckstein, in the transcript of a lecture delivered in Freiburg in the spring of 1986, writes, "A Sanhedrin that condemned a man to death in a seven-year period was considered bloodthirsty. Rabbi Eleazar, the son of Annas, said once every seventy years; Rabbi Akiba and Rabbi Tarfon said, 'If we were members of the Sanhedrin no one would ever be put to death.'"
18. Blinzler (p. 216 ff.) counters with the hypothesis that in Jesus' time the Pharisaic criminal procedure laid down in the Mishna was not in force; instead, the more rigid trial law of the Sadducees was applied. He says the apparently illegal criminal procedure against

256 *Notes*

Jesus was in line with the Sadducee penal statutes. Others, including Strobel (p. 48 ff.), have refuted this hypothesis convincingly.
19. Or so report Mark 14:53–54 and Matthew 26:57–58. In an obviously intentional deviation, Luke 22:6 does not describe a nocturnal session in the high priest's residence, but a meeting of the Sanhedrin on the following morning. Strobel (p. 66) concludes that "there must have been an 'original tradition' in which it seems that the interrogation in the house of the high priest and the decisive hearing in the meeting hall of the Sanhedrin were still separated." He sees as proof of this Mark 14:60, where we read "the high priest then stood up before the assembly," which could only mean the semicircular hall used for Supreme Council meetings.
20. Mendelssohn, p. 67, with documentation
21. Flusser, *Die letzten Tage Jesu in Jerusalem*, p. 92
22. On this point I must also contradict Shalom Ben-Chorin (*Bruder Jesus*, p. 198), who does not derive the argument of nonhistoricity from the manifold of illegalities. He writes, "Political trials that are conducted for reasons of state do not always proceed according to the sections of the rules of the court. . . . All the finesses of the court rules are not adhered to." But this is not a matter of infringement of a section of the court rules or of "finesses"; it concerns a trial that approximates a judicial farce. It would head the list in the world record of such miscarriages of justice, and it would have been committed by a judicial college consisting of the wisest men of Israel.
23. Luke (Acts 6:14) mentions Jesus' words on the destruction of the Temple in connection with the charge against Stephen.
24. Kolping, p. 642, footnote 88: "The death sentence is presupposed, but not mentioned."
25. Blinzler, p. 199. Haim Cohn contradicts him and traces this frequently voiced theory to a misinterpretation of source material. He says the correct reading is that the judges were sent home once they had arrived at a unanimous opinion. Then they had to reassemble for further deliberation.
26. Here is a logical inconsistency in the narrative. Pilate, according to the Johannine account, has obviously permitted the arrest, but only inquires what has occasioned these events once Jesus is in his presence, and then orders the Jewish authorities not to bother him with the case (John 18:29–31).
27. Kolping, however, opines (p. 640) that this charge must have played a role: "If [the cleansing of the Temple] is not expressly mentioned it may be due to the fragmentary and casual character of the particulars that have come down to us."
28. For example, Strobel (p. 81 ff.). He tries to get around the snag of the gross, indeed grotesque, procedural infractions in the trial of Jesus,

to get around its lack of historical credibility. Strobel cites Jewish juridical prescriptions according to which in a "special case"—for example, a seduction case being tried in court—all procedural guarantees in favor of the accused would be suspended so that even arbitrary legal actions could be directed against him. Strobel, of course, contradicts himself when he refers to the Johannine Gospel's frequent mention of "seduction" in regard to Jesus. The "seduction" mentioned in John cannot be that deserving of the extreme penalty as described in Deuteronomy 13:7–12. This is clear from the fact that there was no denunciation, nor was a hearing conducted as prescribed in Deuteronomy 13:14. Pesch (*Der Prozess Jesu*, pp. 31 ff., 41, 45), in an effort to rescue the thesis of the historicity of the Sanhedrin trial, blindly adopts Strobel's view even though only a year earlier, at the convention of the German-speaking Catholic New Testament scholars held in Graz in April 1987, Strobel's thesis was pronounced "downright misleading" ("Prozess gegen Jesus" article by Karlheinz Müller in *Quaestiones Disputatae*, p. 43).

29. Matthew's report is somewhat different. After the appearance of "several lying witnesses" (nothing more is said of their eyewitness depositions), two finally "stepped forward" and made a statement about the destruction of the Temple. Matthew does not say either that they were false witnesses or that their depositions contradicted each other.

30. According to Matthew 26:61 he did not say "I will" but "I have the power to" destroy the Temple.

31. The sight of the monumental Temple must have been overwhelming. Herod the Great had altered and enlarged the structure. In Jesus' time the Jerusalem Temple was among the most spectacular sights in the world.

32. The Temple was in fact in ruins at the time the Gospels were composed. The author of the Marcan Gospel was still affected by his direct experience of the destruction.

33. For the early Christians the Book of Daniel was the preferred source for the prophesy of the destruction of the Temple (Deut. 9:27, as compared with Matt. 24:15). It was no longer referred to in later Church history, after Porphyrius proved that Daniel was not prophesying but merely chronicling past events (Wilcken, p. 152).

34. I do not share Fiedler's view, put forth in writing to me, that Jeremiah was spared (26:23–24) because he enjoyed the protection of a high-ranking person (Ahikam). Ahikam protected him not from a guilty verdict from the Supreme Council, but from a mob threatening lynching. Nor can I agree with Fiedler that there are parallels between the situation of Jesus of Nazareth and that of Jesus "the son of Ananos" whom Josephus Flavius names. The son of Ananos was

a primitive fool who got on the nerves of Jews and Romans alike with his Cassandra-like wailings about the imminent outbreak of war. It was for this reason that he was seized by the Jewish authorities and handed over to the Roman occupation force. This Jesus was soundly thrashed by the Romans (but they did not scourge him, as they would have if he were to be crucified), and released because they believed he was insane. Jesus the son of Ananos had not foretold the destruction of the Temple out of a concern for Israel, but had simply cried war at an earsplitting volume.

35. The evangelist John takes it upon himself to interpret: "But he was speaking of the sanctuary that was his body" (2:21). Obviously this was to show that the resurrection after three days had been foretold.
36. Cited in Mendelssohn, p. 68, with documentation
37. I do not share Schillebeeckx's view (p. 279 ff.) that Jesus' absolute silence before the Sanhedrin could be used to justify his condemnation. Schillebeeckx views Jesus' silence as an infringement of Deut. 17:12: "If anyone presumes to disobey either the priest who is there in the service of Yahweh your God, or the judge, that man must die." I have never read such an interpretation anywhere else.
38. P. 93
39. P. 18
40. Ben-Chorin, *Bruder Jesus*, p. 198
41. Conzelmann, p. 646; likewise Fiedler, p. 13
42. P. 642
43. P. 152
44. The so-called Emmaus disciples (Luke 24:19) in their sadness reiterate quite clearly that they considered Jesus a prophet.
45. Lapide, *Der Jude Jesus* p. 34 f.
46. Lapide, *Der Jude Jesus*, pp. 29, 31 f.
47. Conzelmann, p. 646, and others. It could have been that the Pharisees were trying, respectfully, to give him a well-intentioned warning; the disciples' shouts of joy could all too easily have reached the ears of the occupation force.
48. Schneider, *Taschenbuchkommentar*, p. 387
49. Conzelmann, p. 630
50. Ben-Chorin, *Bruder Jesus*, p. 134
51. Bloch, quoted in Augstein, p. 152. Haim Cohn also wrote me in this sense: "Since the first man was assigned the name 'Adam' and was the father of all men, every man after Adam became 'Ben-Adam,' which suddenly, as 'son of man,' created confusion in the entire Christian theology."
52. Even if this had been the case, no charge could properly have been pressed because of the lack of an accuser as prescribed in Deuteronomy 19:18.

53. Blinzler, p. 192.
54. Klausner, p. 474, with documentation. There are no other grounds that could justify the gesture of tearing his robe. Strobel (p. 99) cites the grounds for such a gesture and gives references: "Because of bad news . . . and because a Torah was burned, and because of the cities of Judah and because of the sanctuary and because of Jerusalem."
55. Ben-Chorin, *Bruder Jesus,* p. 201
56. Kolping, p. 642
57. Kolping, p. 645
58. Kolping, p. 643
59. Ben-Chorin, *Bruder Jesus,* p. 197
60. Blinzler, p. 151: "No unbiased reader of one of the two Gospels can escape the impression that . . . it is on the reply of Jesus that the failure or success of the plans of his adversaries depends. If the reply is 'yes,' then they have won; a 'no' would dash their hopes."
61. G. B. Shaw, in his lengthy preface to *Androcles and the Lion,* also fell victim to this error, cited by Blinzler (p. 189, footnote 15):

> Jesus was condemned to death because of his blasphemous assertion that he was God. . . . Hence he [Caiaphas] treated Jesus as an impostor and as a blasphemer, whereas we would have treated him as one mentally disturbed. If Jesus had appeared before one of our courts, he would have been handed over to two doctors who, after having established that he was possessed by an *idée fixe* and declared him incapable of understanding, would have dispatched him to a nursing home.

62. In the Letter to the Galatians 4:4, however, Paul seems to place the beginning of the divine sonship at another point in time.
63. Haenchen, p. 505, footnote 1. Schneider (p. 10) highlights that the Lucan Christology makes a clearer distinction between Messiah and Son of God than do Matthew and Mark. "According to the Lucan conception Jesus is the Son of God because now—in the time of the Church—he sits at the right of the Power of God. . . . The distinct separation between Messiah and Son of God must be seen as a product of the Hellenistic Christology." On the other hand, the only New Testament passages in which "Son of God" and "Messiah" are used synonymously are Luke's (Luke 4:41; Acts 9:21, 22).
64. Dibelius (p. 74):

> The evangelists look backward. They know that Jesus was not only killed but also resurrected and raised to God. . . . They speak on the basis of the Easter faith, and for this faith the word Messiah, i.e., the Christ, has a new meaning: it designates the dignity that is due to Jesus and to no other: The word received its mean-

ing from history. Before Easter, however, in Jesus' lifetime, the word did not connote events, but expectation. Anyone could read into it a meaning that reflected his hopes.

65. The word *Kyrios* (Latin: *Dominus*) underwent a similar process. The Jewish Christians in Jerusalem occasionally used the dogmatically insignificant honorary formula "our Lord" (Hebrew: *Maran*) for their rabbi. This designation assumed an entirely new meaning when it was translated into Greek as *Kyrios*, "the Lord." In the Septuagint, *Kyrios* is used exclusively for God. The Roman rulers, following the pagan custom, appropriated the title for themselves to reinforce the idea of their divinity.
66. Bultmann, pp. 19–20
67. Lapide and Lutz, *Der Jude Jesus*, p. 28 f.
68. Flusser, *Selbstzeugnisse*, p. 83
69. Bätz and Mack, p. 84
70. Moreover, all cruelty to animals would cease. "When that day comes I will make a treaty on her behalf with the wild animals, with the birds of heaven and the creeping things of the earth; I will break bow, sword and battle in the country" (Hos. 2:20).
71. The question posed in Mark 12:35–37, about the relation of the Messiah to David, is probably along the same lines. This "obscure passage" is an echo of a discussion within the community according to which the Messiah, by virtue of his glorification, is more than David, in fact David's Lord (Conzelmann, p. 630).
72. Cf. Acts 15:1–35
73. In the ancient world, accounts of miracles were the order of the day. The Greek and Roman poets have described an abundance of wonders supposedly wrought by prominent contemporaries. Thus, for example, Tacitus and Suetonius both report that Vespasian, after being proclaimed emperor, healed a blind person in Egypt. Craveri (p. 119) determines that the reliability of a Titus Livius or a Tacitus is certainly not below that of the authors of the Gospels; hence, it cannot be assumed that the miracles described by the evangelists are proofs of Jesus' divinity. Nor have the miracles attributed to Jesus ever occupied a central place in theological teaching; his words can and should stand on their own without the reinforcement of miracles. All that can be believed from the stories of the miracles is that at times Jesus' activity sparked surprise and amazement in people. (Küng presents some convincing arguments in this connection, p. 226 ff.).
74. Cf. Wilcken, p. 189
75. In the Letter to the Galatians 3:20 Jesus was not even assigned a mediator role: "Now there can only be an intermediary between two parties, yet God is one."

76. *Geheimnis des Rabbi J.*, p. 262
77. Shortly before he died in A.D. 337, Constantine had himself baptized and by none other than Bishop Eusebius, the promoter of the Arian faith. Thus the first Christian emperor died a heretic.
78. In Galatians 2:5 Paul proudly reports that he did not let himself be intimidated in Jerusalem, and Acts 22:18 mentions a Pauline vision: "Hurry," he said, "leave Jerusalem at once; they will not accept the testimony you are giving about me."
79. Ben-Chorin, in *Bruder Jesus* (p. 197), points out that when the King of the Jews mounts the throne, he is newly conceived as the Son of God. Psalm 89:20, 26–27, reads: "I have selected my servant David and anointed him with my holy oil. . . . He will invoke me, 'My father, my God and rock of my safety,' and I shall make him my firstborn, the Most High for kings on earth."
80. The English religious scholar Fitzmyer points this out very clearly with the help of a Qumran fragment in which the Messiah is designated as "Son of God" and "Son of the Most High." Fitzmyer's translation, with his interpolations, reads as follows:

> But your son shall be great upon the earth, O King! All man shall make peace, and all shall serve him. He shall be called the Son of the Great God, and by his name shall he be named. He shall be hailed as the Son of God, and they shall call him Son of the Most High. As comets flash to the sight, so shall be their kingdom (taken from Mussner, p. 297).

81. Kolping, p. 641 f.
82. Küng (pp. 354–55) sees indications that the reunion may have taken place at Pentecost the year of Jesus' death:

> It is again only from the late Lucan Acts of the Apostles that we learn of a Christian feast of Pentecost. *Pentekoste* (= fiftieth day) had been a harvest festival for the Jews. . . . On the first Pentecost after Jesus' death, when many pilgrims must certainly have come to Jerusalem, the first gathering of Jesus' followers—returning mainly from Galilee—and their constitution as the eschatological community (with enthusiastic charismatic accompanying manifestations) may well have taken place. Luke perhaps made use of a tradition of the first occurrence of a mass ecstasy under the influence of the Spirit in Jerusalem at the first Pentecost. Oddly enough, neither Paul nor Mark nor Matthew seems to know anything of a Christian Pentecost. For John Easter and Pentecost (gift of the Spirit) expressly coincide.

83. This idea of a reappearance in another form occasioned some confusion. Jesus and some of his followers saw in John the Baptist the born again Elijah; others viewed Jesus as Elijah, and still others saw

in Jesus the resurrected Baptist (Matt. 16:13–14). Herod Antipas allegedly also thought Jesus was the risen John the Baptist (Mark 6:14).
84. Thus the imminence of the apocalypse was mistakenly announced a second time. The followers and apostles in Jerusalem were convinced of the imminent return of the Messiah and the approaching kingdom of God. Paul too believed at first that he would experience fully the return of the Lord. In his first document, the Letter to the Thessalonians (4:15, 17), he assured its recipients that they will all be alive when the Lord comes but that this would not give them any advantage over those already dead. Later he seemed to have a different opinion, developing his theme so that the waiting for the Lord's return is extended indefinitely and eventually rendered irrelevant. Paul proclaimed that, through Jesus' death and resurrection, the great turning point had already occurred (2 Cor. 5:17). And in the second Letter to the Thessalonians (assuming that Paul actually penned the letter) he distanced himself from his promises of the first letter: A whole series of conditions now had to be fulfilled before the Lord's return. Then, when Christianity became the state religion, the expectation of an imminent end to the world receded completely into the background. The bishops had become so comfortably ensconced that a speedy end no longer fitted in with their goals. The *Parousia* (Second Coming) became unimportant. The awaited Messiah gave way to the presence of Christ in the sacraments. Faith in the *Parousia* was replaced by the certainty that humanity is redeemed through the death of Jesus. In the fourth century the author of the second Petrine Letter (3:8) remembered the words of the psalm: "You must never forget that with the Lord, 'a day' can mean a thousand years, and a thousand years is like a day." Then, comfortingly and admonishingly, he continues, "The Lord is not being slow to carry out his promise, as anybody else might be called slow; but he is being patient with you all, wanting nobody to be lost and everybody to be brought to change his ways."
85. Drews, p. 117
86. P. 138
87. Quoted by Wilcken, p. 208
88. Quoted by Wilcken, p. 215
89. Von Harnack, p. 92
90. P. 133
91. I doubt Ben-Chorin is right here. The blind man of Jericho (Mark 10:51) also called Jesus *Rabbuni*, in the original Greek text, at any rate.
92. James led his own community in Jerusalem. Its members, obviously strongly influenced by Qumran, called themselves "the poor" (Ebionites). There were some Pharisees in the group. The Jewish authorities left this community undisturbed, at least in the first century.

Later Ebionite circles were established in the Diaspora. But a mere 150 years later, when Pauline teaching prevailed over that of James and even the ideal of poverty had lost the prestige it once possessed in the Church, the Ebionites were damned as heretics. This was not unfounded since, although they did view Jesus as the Messiah, they did not consider him the Son of God in a biological sense.

93. An experienced judge or lawyer was called "son of the law," and could even receive the honorary title "father of the law."
94. Luther translated this wrongly as "They will be called the children of God," apparently so as not to detract from the later Christian view of Jesus as the one and only Son of God.
95. Wilcken, p. 192

> Julian irritatedly cites the claim of the Jews to be the elect: "Moses says that the creator of the world chose the Jewish people, that he takes exclusive care of them and that he extends his protection exclusively to them. But beyond that he said not a word regarding other peoples and how and by what gods they are ruled." This idea of the chosen people, Julian observes, was taken over by the Christians. For "Jesus of Nazareth as well as Paul, who by far surpassed all the magicians and all the quacks of every place and time, assert that he is the God of Israel and of Judea and that the Jews are his chosen people." In another passage where he speaks of Jesus, Julian wonders why God sent prophets to the Jews "but to us no prophet, no anointed one, no teacher, no precursor in order to proclaim his love of men, a love that one day, albeit belatedly, will also reach us. . . . If he is the God of all of us and the Creator of all, why has he abandoned us thus?"

Julian, despite his reservations regarding Judaism, succeeded in harnessing the Jews to his side against the Christians.

96. P. 633
97. The view that Jesus' blasphemy was not in claiming to be the Messiah and Son of God, but in claiming to sit at the right hand of God and saying that his coming on the clouds would be proclaimed, is also erroneous. It has been rejected by Blinzler (p. 192 ff.); but Mussner continues to state it (*Die Kraft der Wurzel*, p. 129).
98. Mackey, p. 76
99. Strobel "justifies" this act (p. 72): "In certain cases it was absolutely required that zeal for religion be expressed spontaneously and aggressively."
100. Kolping writes (p. 646):

> Only the Christian-Messiah conception which held that Jesus stood very close to God ("on the right of the Power") was bound

to provoke Jewish resistance. . . . Nevertheless Messiah ideas of this sort at that time could not yet constitute an object of controversy between Jesus and the Sanhedrin. From Mark's account of the discussion in the Sanhedrin, we cannot clearly understand just what induced the authorities of his people to repudiate Jesus.

101. P. 144; likewise Küng, p. 331
102. Haenchen, p. 514
103. Bultmann, p. 211
104. Lapide and Lutz, *Der Jude Jesus* (p. 31). Two possible but not definite Messiah pretenders were the resistance fighters Theudas and Judas the Galilean, mentioned in Acts 5:36–37. Theudas claimed to be "someone important," and Judas the Galilean was placed on the same plane with him.

Ten

1. Flusser, *Die letzten Tage Jesu in Jerusalem*, p. 35
2. Paul writes in the Letter to the Galatians 3:13: "Christ redeemed us from the curse of the Law by being cursed for our sake, since scripture says: 'Cursed be everyone who is hanged from a tree.' " This means that those of the Easter faith who no longer adhered to the prescriptions of the Torah were not subject to the curse stipulated in Deuteronomy 28:15.
3. P. 139
4. Pp. 311, 326
5. See Ben-Chorin, *Bruder Jesus*, p. 198
6. John 5:10–16; Mark 3:1–6; Matt. 12:9–14; Luke 6:1–11
7. Braun, p. 81
8. 1 Macc. 2:33–36
9. Salcia Landmann (p. 123) is even of the opinion that the conquest of Masada by the Romans in A.D. 77 was due to the defenders' loyal and steadfast observance of the Sabbath.
10. Flusser, *Selbstzeugnisse*, p. 44
11. *Encyclopedia Judaica*, vol. 10: "According to the Synoptic Gospels, Jesus did not heal by physical means on the Sabbath but only by words, healing through speech having always been permitted on the Sabbath, even when the illness was not dangerous." Cf. also Maccoby, p. 230, with documentation.
12. See, for example, Mark 3:2–6, where the evangelist claims that the Pharisees made common cause with the Herodians trying to justify putting Jesus to death on the grounds of trivial Sabbath violations. This is a historical impossibility. Cf. also Schmithals, p. 192. Haim

Cohn, in a discussion with the present author, declared it a nonpunishable offense.
13. Lehmann, *Jesus-Report*, p. 98 f.
14. P. 208
15. Trilling, *Fragen*, p. 81

> According to Leviticus 11:7, a Jew may not eat pork. In the mass of Torah precepts these prescriptions can seem negligible whereas in Jewish practice they play a decisive role. Hundreds of Jewish men and women faced martyrdom during the Syrian religious persecutions in order to avoid the abomination of eating pork. Millions of Jews in Jesus' time had to endure the mockery of their Greek and Roman neighbors in all the known world because they did not eat a ham sandwich. Even Emperor Augustus found this amusing. Anyone who despised the Mosaic food prohibitions made common cause with the despisers and the executioners of Israel. Presumably even the oft-repeated reproach that Jesus ate with tax-collectors and sinners was connected with the struggle to validate the canonical food prescriptions. For who knows how many times a collaborator like Zachary in pleasure-loving Jericho had gladly sat at table in an officers' club with the leading figures of the occupation power and therefore found himself in no position to observe the Mosaic food prohibitions. This sufficed to defame him as a sinner in the eyes of the Torah-true circles of Jericho (Luke 19:7). And when Jesus, uninvited, sat himself down at a table he certainly could not expect that all the courses served would be kosher.

16. The account of the healing of the leper furnishes further Gospel material on Jesus' attitude to the cleanliness question. Mussner discusses this in great detail in *Die Kraft der Wurzel*, p. 100 ff.
17. Mussner, *Die Kraft der Wurzel*, p. 99
18. Cohn, *The Trial and Death of Jesus*
19. Such a case occurs when a prophet or a visionary begins to announce signs and prodigies coupled with the summons to others to serve and to follow gods unknown up to then.
20. Cf. chapter 3.
21. Käsemann, p. 188

Eleven

1. Strobel, p. 95: "The technical term 'deliver up,' in the context of the Passion story as well as in a judicial sense of being handed over into custody, also has an unmistakable ring of martyrdom and redemption which is a fulfillment of Jesus' prediction in Mark 10:33–34 that the chief priests and scribes would "hand him over to the pagans."

266   Notes

2. But cf. Mackey (pp. 79, 81):

> Jesus—anything but a pacifist—really did incite the people by his activity to carry out revolutionary actions against the military forces in the country. And Pilate, on the basis of his experience with the Zealots, could see a danger in Jesus' activities. . . . Most of those who participate in military confrontation or armed revolt do so in the name of peace and are deeply convinced that they are the only true pacifists while others—like Jesus, perhaps—who never lift a finger to inflict physical injury on another person have been able to introduce radical changes in human society and have lastingly jeopardized its structures, for which reason they draw more violence upon themselves and their proselytes than the best-armed guerrilla groups in the world have been able to do.

3. Josephus Flavius, *Antiquities of the Jews,* Book xviii, 5:2. See also chapter 3 of this book.
4. This is the title by which Pilate is generally known. His actual title was *Praefectus Judaeae* ("prefect of Judea").
5. Josephus Flavius, *The Jewish War,* Book ii, 12:1
6. Josephus Flavius, *The Jewish War,* Book ii, 14:8
7. The Procurator Ventidius Cumanus (A.D. 48–52) was quartered there when an uprising broke out during the Feast of Tabernacles (Josephus Flavius, *Antiquities of the Jews,* Book xx, 5:3; *The Jewish War,* Book ii, 12:1).
8. Speidel, p. 97
9. It is surely true that the claim to royal status also constituted a crime of lèse-majesté in regard to Emperor Tiberius (Ben-Chorin, *Bruder Jesus,* p. 202). In the context of the wide-ranging trial of a prominent personage, this could naturally have been mentioned. But we are concerned with a summary court-martial whose only function was to deter potential rebels—and these, whenever they formed a group, immediately elected a "king."
10. The overanxious reactions of the Romans to any suspicion of Davidic descent is highlighted in an episode that has come down to us from St. Jerome: In A.D. 110, Trajan's governor Atticus even had the Ebionite Bishop Simon crucified after a political charge was made against him. Simon was doomed because the Romans viewed him as a scion of David. The fact that he was an Ebionite, a pacifist who had nothing to do with movements against Rome, was of no avail. (In this connection see Schoeps, p. 32.)
11. P. 224
12. Goguel, p. 409. Whether Jesus really made a Messianic entry into Jerusalem, as related in the Gospels, is historically doubtful, as are

all the events said to be fulfillments of prophetic pronouncements. Kolping (p. 624) writes, "There is strong reason to doubt the historicity of messianic homage to Jesus." Salcia Landmann writes, "If he really rode into Jerusalem on a donkey then, at that very moment, he must have already believed that he was the Messiah." On the other hand, Flusser *(Die letzten Tage Jesu in Jerusalem)* convincingly argues, "At that time riding a donkey was generally common. One could enter Jerusalem either on foot or on a donkey. At that time no Jew in the House of David rode on a horse."

13. P. 111
14. Küng, p. 203
15. The leader of the Jewish uprising against Rome in A.D. 66, Eleazar, the son of the high priest Ananos, was a Sadducee.
16. Augstein, p. 284, with documentation
17. The Gospels do contain occasional allusions to political and nationalist aspirations, for example, Mark 10:37; Luke 19:11–14 and 24:21.
18. A third guess as to the meaning of the nickname "Iscariot" holds that it stemmed from the Aramaic *schekra* or *eschkaria*, deceit or deceitfulness—thus it would mean "Judas the Deceiver" (Goldschmidt, p. 25 f.; Limbeck, p. 46 ff.). This interpretation is supported by the fact that the dagger-men *(sicarii)* were not yet known in Jesus' time. They emerged during the term of the procurator Felix, which began in A.D. 52.
19. Bar Jona is not only translated as "Son of Jona" but can also mean a man who lives out of doors or an outlaw. *Baryonim* (the plural of Bar Jona) was definitely a designation for a Zealot; the great Zealot leader Judas of Galilee was occasionally so called (Lehmann, *Jesus-Report*, p. 127).
20. P. 361
21. Fifty percent, assuming there were twelve disciples.
22. Lehmann *(Jesus-Report,* p. 123) writes, "A zealous believer was always a Zealot against anything alien that he experienced in history. The true believer was by nature the true rebel, whether or not he reached for a sword."
23. Cf. also Renan, p. 153
24. Mommsen, p. 340 f.
25. Pp. 187–88
26. Küng, p. 189
27. The occupation statutes stipulated that a Roman soldier could make any Jew, regardless of social stratum, carry his luggage for a mile, in other words, make him a porter.
28. Mark 7:27; Matt. 10:5–6; 15:26
29. See Mark 12:17 but also Lapide's proposed interpretation *(Er predigte,* pp. 35, 41):

> Give to Caesar what is Caesar's! On the basis of this brief, fateful phrase the doctors of the Church, since Augustine, have provided the theological rope with which to strangle every attempt at religious emancipation. They coupled throne and altar and raised it to the level of a sacred sentinel, and for a millennium and a half, they have made of the Church the bastion of political reaction. There is no "give" in the Greek text, rather, it reads "give back" and it is good Hebraism. It means to say: Give the accursed silver back to the imperial master of the mint which according to Roman law is his property! Refuse not only to pay the imperial tax, but refuse to accept the Bible-hostile coins! Purify yourselves by returning his sinful money, so that you again can give to God what is of God: the recognition of his exclusive rulership over the world.

30. The death wish was typical of the later Christian martyrs, in imitation of the sufferings of Christ: "Through the suffering of one hour they inherit eternal life for themselves" (*Martyrdom of Polycarp*, cited by Pagels, p. 143).

    > Whether martyrs are to be viewed as heroes or neurotic masochists has been a controversial question since time immemorial. Their shouts of joy in the face of the death that they could have avoided by a simple profession of loyalty to the State have been transmitted in abundance. Ignatius, the Bishop of Antioch, is said to have welcomed his death sentence with jubilation as a possibility "for imitating the Passion of my God." "Allow me to be devoured by the wild beasts who will permit me to reach my Lord. I am God's wheat and when I am ground by the teeth of the wild beasts I will be able to become the pure bread of Christ." (Quoted from Pagels, p. 133)

31. Not even in Jerusalem had he achieved more than preliminary indications of success. He had found applause; a somewhat larger public had taken note of him. But he was really looking to win over all Jerusalem through his teaching. (See Goguel, p. 409 ff.; Matt. 23:37: "Jerusalem, Jerusalem . . . how often have I longed to gather your children as a hen gathers her chicks under her wings, and you refused!")
32. Küng (p. 334) draws a comparison to founders of other religions: Moses, Buddha, and Confucius: "All died at a ripe old age, successful despite many disappointments, in the midst of their disciples and supporters. . . . Muhammad, after he had thoroughly enjoyed the last years of his life as political ruler of Arabia, died in the midst of his harem and in the arms of his favorite wife."
33. Flusser, *Die letzten Tage Jesu in Jerusalem*, p. 81 f.

34. Whether Jesus throughout used the form of address "Abba" when praying to or invoking God is disputed in exegeses. This word is all too evocative of childish stammering, like the English "Papa." Haenchen, who deals comprehensively with this complex problem (p. 492 f.), cites John 17:1–26 as an example: "The prayer of a high priest cannot begin: 'Papa, the hour is come.'"
35. What is meant is the fifth glass of the Seder meal, a contested part of the ritual. It is the chalice of bitterness and of death (Ben-Chorin, *Bruder Jesus*, p. 182 ff.).
36. Cf. also the Letter to the Hebrews 5:7: "During his life on earth, he offered up prayer and entreaty, aloud and in silent tears, to the one who had the power to save him out of death."
37. P. 467
38. P. 315
39. The description in John's Gospel is altogether different. There is no trace of fear and doubt: "Am I not to drink the cup that the Father has given me?" A similar dichotomy is evident in Jesus' last words on the cross: the sorrow-laden outcry in Mark and Matthew, "My God, my God, why have you deserted me?" contrasts with John's resoundingly triumphant "It is accomplished!"
40. P. 392
41. P. 541
42. Ben-Chorin, *Bruder Jesus*, p. 182
43. P. 521
44. Goguel, quoted in Blinzler, p. 31, footnote 41

Twelve

1. Pesch points out (p. 413) that Mark 14:2 (as with Matt. 26:4–5) should not be translated "It must not be during the festivities." A more correct translation would be "among the crowd celebrating the feast." Hence the expression is to be understood to refer to locality (cf. also Schmithals, p. 588).
2. Küng (p. 329) highlights that the distinction between the Jewish Temple and its leaders was originally important. The expression "the Jews" as given a negative meaning appears in John's Gospel seventy-one times, and "only" eleven times in all the other Gospels put together.
3. P. 467
4. Here we are faced with a truly terrifying illogicality. It is on the same level as the terrorist outcry shouted by Christian Negroes in the revolt that broke out in San Domingo during the French Revolution, "The whites killed Christ, kill the whites!"

5. Quoted from Flusser, *Jesus in Selbstzeugnisse*, footnote 223 on p. 141. Cf. also Fiedler, p. 12.
6. *Wer war schuld an Jesu Tod?*, p. 72, with citation of sources
7. Claude Aziza, in *Journal für Geschichte* (March 1986), p. 52 ff.
8. *Antiquities of the Jews*, Book viii, 3:42
9. Bishop Eusebius invented the legend that Pilate, tormented by pangs of conscience, committed suicide by throwing himself into the Tiber (see Craveri, p. 408).
10. Lapide, "Jesu Tod," p. 242
11. Pesch (*Der Prozess Jesu*, pp. 69, 71) introduces an original insight, though it is not fully developed: "The communities of the evangelists still knew that all were responsible for the death of the Messiah, to the extent that they gave room to the hostility against God. . . . 'The Jews' in this sense can also be Christians who among the people of God do the work of God's adversaries."
12. Lapide, *Wer war schuld an Jesu Tod?*, p. 79
13. Trilling, *Das wahre Israel*, p. 72
14. Trilling, *Das wahre Israel* (p. 70 ff.), citing sources and texts, points out that this sentence might reflect a cultural legacy rooted in the Old Testament. Unfortunately, he overlooks clearly contrary texts. 2 Kings 14:6; Ezekiel 18:19–20; and especially Deuteronomy 24:16. Gübler (p. 29) shares Trilling's opinion. Another opinion, put forth by Klaus Haacker, holds that Matt. 27:25 is a Christological interpretation in the light of the Jewish generation that rose up in A.D. 66–74, and that "children" refers specifically to this generation.
15. Quoted in Lapide, "Jesu Tod," p. 239. Origen was condemned by the Church as a heretic not, of course, because of the commentary cited here, but because he did not believe Jesus was biologically the Son of God.
16. Thomas Aquinas, *Super Evangelium S. Matthaei Lextura* (Turin-Rome: Marietti, 1951), p. 2343 [on Matt. 27:25]
17. Mayer, p. 256
18. Quoted in Deschner, p. 458, with documentation
19. Pp. 98, 101
20. P. 314 f. In the footnote to p. 314, Blinzler cites a sentence from Ben-Chorin's *Bruder Jesus* to give the impression that he and Ben-Chorin are in complete agreement on this point. The sentence from Ben-Chorin (p. 205) reads, "It will never be possible to demonstrate that this loud and angry cry [Matt. 27:25] ever really went up. Nevertheless I consider it possible, although the formulation is unusual." Blinzler knowingly skips what Ben-Chorin writes a few sentences later (p. 209):

> But even if there actually were some savage bawlers or even if some creatures in the pay of the high priests had howled in this

manner, this explosion of an organized popular fury could in no way even remotely be blamed indiscriminately on the Jews of Jerusalem, even less so on the pilgrims from the other countries and the Diaspora who had come for the festivity, particularly those from the communities of Alexandria and Rome, none of whom had the slightest awareness of what had transpired. And least of all can the guilt be dumped on the Jews of later generations.

21. Pp. 333, 430 f.
22. Quoted from Lapide, "Jesu Tod," p. 240. Kolping *(Theologische Revue)*, p. 274: "Oberammergau, on the other hand, sprang from a historically narrow horizon, whose painful consequences are also to be found in Blinzler and Stauffer."
23. A classical case of the imputed indirect guilt is Peter's so-called Pentecostal sermon in Acts 2:22–23: "Men of Israel, listen to what I am going to say: Jesus the Nazarene. . . . This man . . . you took and had crucified by men outside the Law." Several verses later the reproach of indirect guilt is heightened: "This Jesus whom you crucified" (Acts 2:36). The author of Acts (Luke) continues a polemic begun by Paul already forty years before in the first Letter to the Thessalonians 2:15: ". . . the Jews, the people who put the Lord Jesus to death."
24. Mussner wrote an article that appeared in the official organ of the Passau diocese on March 21, 1985, in which he tellingly exposed the way stubborn theologians (and certainly many other persons who call themselves Christian) still reason:

> The Jews are guilty of killing Jesus for without the Jews the trial against Jesus of Nazareth and without the trial the Passion of Jesus would not have taken place. Because of the trial of Jesus the Jewish perpetrators provoked punitive consequences for themselves, above all the destruction of the Temple and the Holy City of Jerusalem. The punitive consequences for the killing of Jesus apply also to the "children" of the Jews, the enemies at the trial of Jesus, hence all Jews unless they make a profession of faith to Jesus. A "collective guilt" weighs upon the Jews! . . . All Jews, unless they convert to Christ, are excluded from salvation. The Jews themselves with their cry, "His blood be on us and our children" renounced their salvation in Christ. . . . With that cry the Jews abandoned God who, in turn, for that reason, repudiated them. . . . Every Jew has crucified Christ. Only when the Jew converts and submits to Baptism, hence when he gives up his Judaism, frees himself from the fetters of the fathers, from the collective guilt in the death of Jesus. . . . All this presupposes that Matthew (27:26) reflects a historical fact, hence that the Jews really uttered this shout, and that, moreover, according to the evangelist

Matthew, "the people to a man" thus shouted. The Jew C. G. Montefiore has observed, "A terrible verse, a monstrous invention. A bitter hatred makes the evangelist write 'and the people to a man' . . . This is one of the sentences that bear the guilt for seas of human blood and an unbroken stream of suffering and despair."

25. It could also be a rather late interpolation; the statement as such is unhistorical. Kolping (p. 662): "In the history of Jewish martyrdom the martyr never prays for his tormentor."
26. Quoted from Lapide and Lutz, *Der Jude Jesu*, p. 60
27. P. 169
28. *Dogmatik* IV, 3, 1007, cited by Lapide and Lutz, *Der Jude Jesus*, p. 19
29. Quoted from Lapide, *Wer war schuld an Jesu Tod?*, p. 90
30. P. 99
31. Trilling, *Das wahre Israel*, p. 73
32. The time discrepancy in Mark certainly cannot be explained by stating that in the ancient world time was estimated roughly, clocks not yet having been invented.
33. Goguel, p. 523
34. The theologian Gaechter (cited in Blinzler, p. 277, footnote 3) has developed his own theory on this matter: Caiaphas, when he initiated Jesus' arrest, asked Pilate for military protection. Pilate assured him, more or less conclusively, that Jesus would be put to death as a rebel, so the Sanhedrin hoped that they could put Jesus on the cross without a new trial proceeding. To their disappointment, Pilate was in no mood to accommodate them at that early morning hour. The French theologian Kohler even goes so far as to state that Pilate took back his given word because his wife (Matt. 27:19) intervened on Jesus' behalf. (Cf. Blinzler, p. 316, footnote 45.)
35. P. 314
36. Strobel, p. 111; "That Pilate expected the Galilean tetrarch to handle the troublesome case, as Blinzler assumes, seems questionable to the highest degree." Strobel, however, considers it possible that Pilate had expected a kind of legal opinion from the tetrarch.
37. The Italian scholar Lazzarato, in his book *La passione di Cristo* (1963), put forth the view that Herod Antipas's "sentence" had read "incapable of reasoning" (source in Blinzler, p. 27, footnote 32).
38. What happened to the rich cloak? According to Luke 23:34, Jesus was wearing his own clothes when they were divided among the soldiers of the execution detail. According to Matthew 27:28 it was not Herod and his soldiers who removed Jesus' clothes but the members of the Roman cohort who then derisively dressed him in a scarlet cloak.
39. Thus Pilate says neither that he considers Jesus to be the Messiah nor that Jesus considers himself as such. All he says is that other people say that Jesus is the Messiah.

40. Nestle-Aland, *Novum Testamentum Graece* (Stuttgart, 1979)
41. Oxford University Press, Cambridge University Press, 1970
42. He is called *lestes*, which can be translated as both "brigand" and "rebel."
43. Grant, p. 220, with documentation
44. Kolping never says that he considers an identity between Jesus and Barabbas as probable, but nevertheless lends the episode an air of skepticism (p. 654):

> The Barabbas episode is burdened with a certain improbability. Above all else, it is most improbable that the Romans presented Jesus to the crowd as though asking for a plebiscite on him "as King of the Jews." Nor can the occasion that introduced the Barabbas episode as *topos* in the passion story have been completely invented. It may be assumed that it results from a combination of circumstances within a political climate in Jerusalem that Pilate knew had to be taken into account.

45. The Greek *episemos* which usually means "well-known" in a good or bad sense, can also be rendered as "notorious."
46. *Das neue Testament, Deutsch*, "definitive edition," 1545–46 (Stuttgart: Deutsche Bibelgesellschaft, 1982), p. 61
47. P. 420 ff.
48. Friedell (p. 12) is critical in this regard.
49. Strobel, p. 120, with source notes
50. *Cod. Theol.*, ix, 38:3 ff.
51. Meanwhile it has been generally acknowledged that many falsifications were contained in the Christian reportage, even long before the so-called Donation of Constantine.
52. Only John depicts the scourging as a way of inclining the mob to pity. Luke merely refers to Pilate's intention to have the accused flogged and then release him. According to Mark and Matthew, the scourging took place after the death sentence was pronounced. Victims were harassed and tormented before being affixed to the cross, just as later the victims of the Christian inquisition often ended on the stake already half dead. Blinzler (p. 294): "Pilate was led to order that Jesus be scourged because . . . he was convinced by the failure of the attempts to grant him a pardon that Jesus could no longer escape punishment in some form."
53. Only John mentions the crown of thorns, but even the Johannine Gospel does not make it clear whether he still wore it on the cross.
54. The fact that the evangelist here lets the "chief priests" speak has only literary importance, inasmuch as "the Jews" remain in the context. On this point Fiedler (p. 13) comments, "The Jewish side is reproached with the historically unimaginable words in [John 19:15]

for renouncing its faith, its hope of salvation. That is a reference to Matt. 27:25."
55. Kolping (p. 657): "The Messiah is his [God's] deputy!"
56. P. 337
57. Blinzler, p. 332
58. Mussner argues totally misleadingly, "Although he was convinced of Jesus' innocence... he nevertheless condemned him to die on the cross for fear of the Jews" (*Die Kraft der Wurzel,* p. 135).
59. Blinzler (p. 313) complains "Some have found it strange that Pilate did not resort to a postponement of the case in order to deepen the investigation, an expedient that Roman trial proceedings permitted him. But he had denied himself this way out by his unfortunate tactic of asking the people's opinion."
60. Blinzler provides an explanation (p. 216 f.): "A very likely guess is that Pilate deliberately borrowed a Jewish custom since most of the Jews had not understood his words spoken in Greek and he wanted every one of them to understand him."
61. The so-called Gospel of Gamaliel (see Craveri, p. 408), a manuscript in the Ethiopian language, discovered in the 1970s, ends with these words:

> Now Pilate was in his garden, talking of the miracles of Jesus with his wife, Procula, and behold a voice came out of the clouds and said to them: "Pilate, knowest thou the souls of those who ascend to Paradise on this cloud? They are the resurrected thief and the centurion. Thou too, in thine own time, shalt be beheaded in Rome. Thy soul and thy wife's soul shall ascend together into the heavenly Jerusalem."

62. The feast day is on October 27.
63. *Apologeticum,* 21:24: *Et ipse iam pro conscienta Christianus* ("Already a Christian in his innermost heart"). A certain change of attitude toward Pilate emerged in the fourth century after the Roman Empire embraced Christianity. Since then many writings have condemned him.
64. Among others Roger Chaillos, *Pontius Pilate;* Michael Plaueli, *Sache Jesu*

Epilogue

1. Levinson (pp. 45–57):

> Christians react with an incredible astonishment and, often, also irritably to a simple historical fact: namely that Christianity without its Jewish roots, hence the New Testament without the He-

brew Bible, remains incomplete, whereas Judaism is very sufficient to itself even without Jesus and Christianity. Many Jews feel closer to the crucified Jesus than ever before. They think that the Christians are responsible for the deep rift which has so often arisen between Jesus and his people; and not only because they have persecuted these brothers and sisters of Jesus with fire and sword in the name of Jesus. Their theologians have repeatedly attempted to prove, and they do so to this day, that Jesus was so entirely different than this people, almost as if it must have been an oversight on God's part that he was born in the midst of this people.

2. Lapide, "Jesus Tod," p. 252
3. Printed in Heer, Foreword

BIBLIOGRAPHY

Aufhauser, J. B. *Antike Jesus-Zeugnisse.* Stuttgart, 1925.
Augstein, R. *Jesus, Son of Man,* translated by H. Young. New York: Urizen Books, 1977.
Bätz, K., and Mack, R. *Sachtexte zur Bibel.* Munich: Lahr, 1985.
Ben-Chorin, S. *Bruder Jesus.* Munich, 1985.
———. *Mutter Mirjam.* Munich, 1971.
———. *Paulus.* Munich, 1981.
Benz, E. *Der gekreuzigte Gerechte bei Plato, im Neuen Testament und in der alten Kirche.* Wiesbaden, 1950.
Bleicken, J. *Verfassungs- und Sozialgeschichte des römischen Kaiserreichs,* Vol. 2. Paderborn, 1981.
Blinzler, J. *Der Prozess Jesu.* Regensburg, 1968.
Bloch, E. *The Principle of Hope,* translated by N. Plaice, S. Plaice, and P. Knight. Cambridge, MA, 1986.
Bornkamm, G. *Jesus von Nazareth.* Stuttgart, 1977.
———. *Paulus.* Stuttgart, 1977.
Braun, H. *Jesus der Mann aus Nazareth und seine Zeit.* Stuttgart, 1969.
Bultmann, R. *Jesus and the Word,* translated by L. Pettibone and E. Huntress. Lantero, 1958.

Burckhardt, J. *Die Zeit Constantin des Grossen.* Stuttgart, 1970.
Carmichael, J. *The Death of Jesus.* New York: Macmillan, 1962.
Cohn, C. *The Trial and Death of Jesus.* New York, 1971.
Conzelmann, H. *Grundriss der Theologie des Neuen Testaments.* Munich, 1971.
———, in *Die Religionen in Geschichte und Gegenwart.* Tübingen, 1959.
Craveri, M. *The Life of Jesus,* translated by Charles Lam Markman. New York: Grove Press, 1967.
Dautzenberg, G. *Der Jesus Report und die neutestamentliche Forschung. Eine Auseinandersetzung mit Johannes Lehmanns Jesus-Report.* Würzburg, 1970.
Deschner, K. *Und abermals kräht der Hahn.* Düsseldorf, 1980.
Dibelius, M. *Jesus.* Berlin, 1980.
Doerff, F. *Der Prozess Jesu in rechtgerichtlicher Betrachtung.* Berlin, 1920.
Drews, A. *Die Christusmythe.* Jena, 1909.
Edwards, O. *Chronologie des Lebens Jesu und das Zeitgeheimnis der drei Jahre.* Stuttgart, 1978.
Encyclopedia Judaica, "Jesus." Vol. 10. Jerusalem, 1973.
Fiedler, P. "Die Passion und die 'Juden'—Last und Chance der Glaubensvermittlung." *Katechetische Blätter* 110 (1985): 10–17.
Flusser, D. *Die letzten Tage Jesu in Jerusalem.* Stuttgart, 1982.
———. *Jesus in Selbstzeugnissen und Bilddokumentationen.* Reinbeck, 1978.
Friedell, E. *Der historische Jesus Christus.* Salzburg, 1947.
Gibbon, E. *The History of the Decline and Fall of the Roman Empire.* 7 vols. New York: Macmillan, 1909–1913.
Gnilka, J. "Der Prozess Jesu nach den Berichten von Markus und Matthäus." In *Quaestiones Disputatae.* Freiburg, 1988.
Goguel, M. *The Life of Jesus,* translated by Olive Wyon. New York: Macmillan, 1933.
Goldschmidt, H. L., and Limbeck, M. *Heilvoller Verrat? Judas im Neuen Testament.* Stuttgart, 1976.
Gollinger, H. "Prozess Jesu." In *Praktisches Bibellexikon.* Freiburg, 1977.
Grant, M. *Jesus.* Bergisch Gladbach, 1979.
Guardini, B. *Juden und Christen: die fremden Brüder.* Stuttgart, 1981.
Haacker, K. "Sein Blut über uns, Erwägung zu Matthäus 27:25." *Kirche und Israel,* no. 1:47 ff., 1986.
Haarenberg, W. [ed.]. *Was glauben die Deutschen?* Munich, 1968.
Haas, K. "Standesrechtlich gekreuzigt." *Verwaltungsblätter für Baden-Württemberg* 6:322 ff. (1988).
Haenchen, E. *Der Weg Jesu.* Berlin, 1968.
Harnack, A. v. *Das Wesen des Christentums.* Stuttgart, 1903.
Heer, F. *Gottes erste Liebe.* Munich, 1967.
Hengel, M. "Mors turpissimi crucis." In *Rechfertigung: Festschrift für Ernst Käsemann.* Tübingen, 1976.
Holl, A. *Jesus in schlechter Gesellschaft.* Stuttgart, 1971.

Holtz, T. *Jesus aus Nazareth.* Zurich and Cologne, 1981.
Jens, W. *Der Fall Judas.* Stuttgart, 1975.
Josephus Flavius. *The Works of Flavius Josephus,* translated by William Whiston. Philadelphia: J. Grigg, 1835–1840.
Jüdisches Lexikon. "Jesus." Vol. 3. 1927.
Käsemann, E. *Das Problem des historischen Jesus.* Vol. 1. Göttingen, 1960.
Kastning-Olmesdahl, R. "Die Juden und der Tod Jesu: Antijüdische Motive in evangelischen Religionsbüchern." In *Juden, Judentum und Staat Israel im christlichen Religionsunterricht in der Bundesrepublik Deutschland.* Paderborn: H. Jochum & H. Krem, 1980.
Klausner, J. *Jesus von Nazareth.* Jerusalem, 1952.
Klein, C. H. *Theologie und Anti-Judaismus.* Munich, 1975.
Knoch, O. "Standesrechtlich gekreuzigt." *Anzeiger fur Seelsorge,* no. 6:220 ff., 1987.
Koch, W. *Der Prozess Jesu.* Munich, 1968.
Kolping, A. *Fundamentaltheologie.* Vol. II. Regensburg, 1974.
———. "Standesrechtlich gekreuzigt: Neuere Überlegungen zum Prozess Jesu." *Theologische Revue,* no. 4:265 ff., 1987.
Kremers, H. "Die Juden und der Tod Jesu als historisches, theologisches und religionspädagogisches Problem." In *Juden, Judentum und Staat Israel im christlichen Religionsunterricht in der Bundesrepublik Deutschland.* Paderborn, 1980.
Kroll, G. *Auf den Spuren Jesu.* Leipzig, 1964.
Kümmel, W. G. *Dreissig Jahre Jesusforschung: 1950–1980.* Bonn, 1985.
Küng, H. *On Being a Christian,* translated by Edward Quinn. New York: Doubleday and Company Inc., 1976.
Landmann, S. *Jesus und die Juden.* Munich, 1987.
Lapide, P. *Ein Flüchtlingskind.* Munich, 1981.
———. *Er predigte in Synagogen.* Gütersloh, 1985.
———. *Er wandelte nicht auf dem Meer.* Gütersloh, 1984.
———. "Jesu Tod durch Römerhand?" In *Gottesverächter und Menschenfeinde?* Düsseldorf: Goldstein, 1979.
———. *Mit einem Juden die Bibel lesen.* Stuttgart, 1982.
———. *Paulus, Rabbi und Apostel.* Stuttgart, 1981.
———. *Wer war schuld an Jesu Tod?* Gütersloh, 1987.
Lapide, P., and Lutz, U. *Der Jude Jesus.* Zurich, 1980.
Lehmann, J. *Das Geheimnis des Rabbi J.* Hamburg, 1985.
———. *Jesus-Report.* Düsseldorf, 1970.
Levinson, M. P. "Nicht anders als Jude." In *Gottesverächter und Menschenfeind?* Düsseldorf: Goldstein, 1979.
Limbeck, M. *See* Goldschmidt.
Lutz, U. *See* Lapide.
Maccoby, H. *König Jesus, die Geschichte eines jüdischen Rebellen.* Tübingen, 1982.

Mack, R., and Volpert, D. *Der Mann aus Nazareth: Jesus Christus.* Stuttgart, 1981.
Mackey, J. P. *Jesus, the Man and the Myth: A Contemporary Christology.* New York: Paulist Press, 1979.
Mayer, A. *Der zensierte Jesus.* Olten and Freiburg, 1983.
Mendelssohn, H. v. *Jesus: Rebell oder Erlöser.* Hamburg, 1981.
Mommsen, T. *Das Weltreich der Römer.* Reprint Stuttgart [undated].
Müller, K. "Möglichkeit und Vollzug jüdischer Kapitalgerichtsbarkeit im Prozess gegen Jesus von Nazareth." In *Quaestiones Disputatae.* Freiburg, 1988.
Mussner, F. *Die Kraft der Wurzel.* Freiburg, 1987.
———. *Traktat über die Juden.* Munich, 1979.
Pagels, E. *The Gnostic Gospels.* New York: Random House, 1979.
Pesch, R. *Das Markus-Evangelium, II Teil.* Freiburg, 1980.
———. *Der Prozess Jesu geht weiter.* Freiburg, 1988.
Pöhlmann, H. G. *Wer war Jesus von Nazareth?* Gütersloh, 1987.
Renan, E. *Life of Jesus.* Translation of 23rd edition. Boston: Little, Brown and Company, 1903.
Ritt, H. "Wer war schuld am Tod Jesu." *Biblische Zeitschrift* 31 (1987) [Special edition].
Ruether, R. *Nächstenliebe und Brudermord: Die theologischen Wurzeln des Antisemitismus.* Munich, 1978.
Schillebeeckx, E. *Jesus: Die Geschichte von einem Lebenden.* Freiburg, 1975.
Schlotheim, H. H. v. *Der Prozess gegen Jesus von Nazareth.* Hamburg, 1959.
Schmaus, M. *Der Glaube der Kirche: Handbuch der katholischen Dogmatik.* 2 vols. Munich, 1969–70.
Schmithals, W. *Ökumenischer Taschenbuchkommentar zum Neuen Testament.* Vol. 2, no. 1. Würzburg, 1979.
———. "Wer war verantwortlich für den Tod Jesu?" *Tagesspiegel,* December 22, 1987.
Schnackenburg, R. *Das Johannes-Evangelium, III. Teil: Kommentar zu Kap. 13–21.* Freiburg, 1979.
Schneider, G. *Geistesgeschichte des antiken Christentums.* Vols. 1 and 2. Stuttgart, 1954.
———. Jesus vor dem Synedrium. In Bibel und Leben II. 1970.
———. *Ökumenischer Taschenbuchkommentar zum Neuen Testament.* Vol. 3, no. 2. Würzburg, 1977.
Schoeps, H. J. *Das Judenchristentum: Untersuchungen über Gruppenbildungen und Parteikämpfe in der frühen Christenheit.* Dalp Taschenbuch, 1964.
Schonfield, H. J. *Der lange Weg nach Golgatha.* Bergisch Gladbach, 1978.
Schweitzer, A. *Geschichte der Leben-Jesu-Forschung.* Vol. 1. Gütersloh, 1977.
Simonis, W. *Jesus von Nazareth.* Düsseldorf, 1985.
Speidel, K. A. *Das Urteil des Pilatus.* Stuttgart, 1976.
Stauffer, E. *Jesus, Gestalt und Geschichte.* Bern, 1957.

Strobel, A. *Die Stunde der Wahrheit: Untersuchungen zum Strafverfahren gegen Jesus.* Tübingen, 1980.
Swidler, L. *Der Jude Jesus. Theologische Implikation fur Christen.* Transcript of the broadcast series *Begegnung mit dem Judentum.* Südwestfunk, 1980.
Tacitus. *The Annals of Imperial Rome,* translated by M. Grant. New York: Dorset Press, 1984.
Trilling, W. *Fragen nach der Geschichtlii chkeit Jesu.* Düsseldorf, 1966.
———. "Gegner Jesu: Wideracher der Gemeinde-Repräsentanten der 'Welt.' " In *Gottesverächter und Menschenfeinde?* Düsseldorf: H. Goldstein, 1979.
———. *Das wahre Israel.* Leipzig, 1975.
Vardimann, E. E. *Die Frau in der Antike.* Düsseldorf, 1982.
Wilcken, R. L. *Die frühen Christen-Wie die Römer sie sahen.* Graz-Vienna-Cologne, 1986.
Wilckens, U. *Das Neue Testament* (Wilckens' Bible). Hamburg, 1971.
Winter, P. *On the Trial of Jesus.* Berlin and New York, 1974.
Wolff, H. *Jesus der Mann: Die Gestalt Jesu in tiefenpsychologischer Sicht.* Stuttgart, 1975.
Zahrnt, H. *Es begann mit Jesus von Nazareth.* Stuttgart, 1960.

INDEX

Abraham, 84, 141, 219
Acta Pilati (Acts of Pilate), 51
Adar, 102
adultery, 46, 86, 89, 112
Agrippa I, King, *see* Herod Agrippa I
Agrippa II, King, *see* Herod Agrippa II
Ahaz, King, 63
Ahithophel, 123
Alexander (Herod's son), 69
Alexander the Great, 9, 64, 112
Alexandria, 45, 47, 172, 191
alien superstitions (*superstitio externa*), 115
Ambrose, 65, 110
amnesty, 215–16
Ananias, 113, 150
Ananos, 48
Anatolia, 31
Andrew, 194
Annals (Tacitus), 44–45, 148
Annas, 122, 131, 132, 150, 152, 204
Anthony, Mark, 191
anti-Judaism, *see* anti-Semitism
Antioch, 45, 47
Antioch IV, King of Syria, 183
Antiquities of the Jews (Josephus), 46–49, 112, 117, 138
anti-Semitism, viii, 140
    Christian Church and, 5, 19, 25, 32–34, 51, 124–25, 140–43, 206–9, 219–22
Antonia Fortress, 67, 106, 121, 128, 191, 205
aphedron, 23
Apocrypha, 13, 72, 79–80, 145–46
Apostles, 14, 23–24, 30, 34, 96, 122–24
    see also disciples
Apostles' Creed, 39, 148, 172
Arabia, 33
Aramaic language, 11, 17, 23, 175
Archelaus, Tetrarch, 67, 72
archeology, 110, 191
Aristobulus (Herod's son), 69
Arius, 171–72
Arminius the Cherischian, 67
asceticism, 43, 74–75, 85

284 Index

Asia Minor, 25, 29, 31, 47
astronomy, 69–70, 105
Athanasius, Bishop, 172
Augustine, 86, 206
Augustus Caesar, Emperor of Rome, 9, 39, 66–67, 69, 193, 204, 211
Auschwitz, 220

Babylon, 191
Babylonian captivity, 168
Balfour Declaration, 25
baptism, 43, 48, 58, 85
baptismal mandate, 20
Baptist sects, 57, 79
Barabbas, 116, 117, 213–16
Bar Giora, Simon, 179
Bar Kochba, 132, 179–80
bar Sarapion, Mara, 45
Barth, Karl, 15, 172, 209
Bauer, Bruno, 54
Bea, Augustin Cardinal, 209
Ben-Chorin, S., 20, 31, 32, 76, 82, 87, 99, 100, 124, 125, 134, 164, 175, 200
Ben Dinseus, Eleazar, 179
ben Matitjahu ha-Kohen, Joseph, *see* Josephus, Flavius
ben Zadok, Eleazar, 113
Bethany, 86, 121
Bethlehem, 25, 67–73, 204
Bethlehem-Ephrata, 71
Bethsaida, 96
Bingerbrück, 46
Bithynia, 43
Blank, J., 161
Blinzler, J., 106, 129, 131, 182, 208, 211, 216
Bloch, Ernst, 55, 163
Bonhoeffer, Dietrich, 172
Bornkamm, G., 40, 100–101, 103, 149, 161
Braun, H., 161
Bultmann, R., 15, 40, 75, 136–37, 161, 162, 168, 179, 192
Burckhardt, Jacob, 48–49
burial customs, Jewish, 137–38, 139

Caesar, Gaius Julius, 9, 111–12
Caesarea, 67, 114, 191
Caesarea Philippi, 162
Caiaphas, 17, 31, 104, 131–36, 150–52, 155, 160, 166–68, 173, 176–78, 180, 182, 203
calendar, Jewish, 102–5
Caligula, Gaius Caesar, Emperor of Rome, 42, 204

Calvary, 139
Cana, wedding at, 82
Cantabrians, 204
Capernaum, 70, 76, 74, 95–96
Capri, 135
Carthaginians, 111
Celsus (Kelsos), 46
census, imperial, 66–68, 72–73, 193
Cephas, 34
Chalcedon, Council of, 17, 172
chiliarchos (commander in chief), 128, 129
Chorazin, 96
Christian Church:
    anti-Semitism and, viii, 5, 19, 25, 32–34, 51, 124–25, 140–43, 206–9, 219–22
    central beliefs of, 5, 52
    common tradition in, 29, 86
    doctrinal opinion and controversy in, 13–15, 38
    faith vs. historicity in, 53
    New Testament selected and defined by, 13–15, 17, 53
    Paul as founder of, 38, 86
    Pauline influence vs. other sources in, 86, 88
    state religion status of, 13, 48–49, 51, 64, 139
    see also Eastern Orthodox Church; Protestantism; Roman Catholic Church
Christianity, early, 11–13, 16, 19, 27
    asceticism and, 74
    centers of, 45, 47
    Gnostic branch of, 29, 75, 172, 211
    growth and development of, 44–45, 47, 48, 49, 52, 106, 139
    Hebraic/Hellenic split in, 34, 142–43
    historical accounts of, 42–48, 49
    Judaism and, 35–36, 45, 140
    Pauline vs. Judaic theology in, 19–20, 32–34, 37–38, 142
    Pharisees and, 106, 142–45, 174
    role of Simon Peter in, 108, 123
    Roman Empire and, 44–45, 47, 139
    sects in conflict with, 57
    symbolism in, 60
    tenets of Essenism and, 43
Christian-Jewish dialogue, 149, 222
Christmas story, 27, 62–76
    birth date in, 65–70, 76
    birth place in, 70–74, 76
    cave vs. manger in, 73

political background of, 66–69, 72–73, 193
see also Holy Family; Jesus of Nazareth, birth of; Star of Bethlehem; Wise Men
Chur, 120
Church Fathers, 13–15, 33, 38, 48–49, 65, 141, 171
Church of the Holy Sepulchre, 139, 191
Cicero, Marcus Tullius, 111
Cilicia, 31
Claudia of Procula, 211, 217
Claudius, Emperor of Rome, 45
Codex laurentianus, 84
Cohn, Chaim, 187
communism, 27
Constantine the Great, 48–49, 60, 64, 66, 112, 139, 172
Constantinople, Council of, 20
Conzelmann, Hans, 29, 108, 161
Coponius, 67
Coptic Church, 217
Corinth, 12
Counter-Reformation, 27, 64
covenants, 43, 141
Craveri, M., 46, 99, 200
cross, 40, 60, 105, 110, 111, 119, 139
crucifixion, 51, 58–60, 73, 109–12, 179
 breaking of legs and, 110–11, 116
 cause of death in, 110
 history of, 111–12
 Jewish victims of, 111, 179, 205
 methods of, 110–11
 Roman use of, 109–12, 115, 205
 widespread use of, 111
crucifixion of Jesus, 18, 31, 58–59, 73
 contemporary Jewish view of, 18–19, 58
 date of, 102–6, 134
 Gospel accounts of, 50–51, 58
 historical accounts of, 44
 inscription on the cross at, 119
 Jesus' age at, 66, 68, 70, 105–6
 Paul's account of, 12, 36–37
 prominent theories on, 4
 redemption and, 15, 16–17, 37, 59, 60, 95
 survival theories and, 39–40
 two others crucified at, 111, 117–18, 138
 tying vs. nailing in, 110
 unique occurrences associated with, 50–51, 102
 witnesses to, 18, 106–7

see also Passion of Jesus; Pilate, Pontius
crurifragium, 110–11
Crusades, 139
Cumanus, 191
currency, 120
Czestochowa, vii–viii

Damascus, 33, 35–36, 67
Damascus I, Pope, 14
Damnaus, 150
Dautzenberg, G., 9
David, King, 10, 123
 House and lineage of, 17, 25, 30, 67, 71, 72, 76, 77–78, 119, 163, 169–70, 173, 180
Dead Sea, 43, 67
Dead Sea Scrolls, 15
death penalties, 109–10, 112–15, 138, 152
December 25th, 65–66
Deschner, K., 88
Diaspora, 29, 31, 34, 142, 190–91
Dibelius, M., 51
Dionysius Exiguus, 66
disciples, 9–12, 23–24, 75
 of Emmaus, 132–33, 170
 humble origins of, 10–11, 13
 Jesus' relationship with, 81, 85–88, 96, 101, 103–4, 106, 107, 108, 125–26, 129, 130
 marital status of, 87
 women as, 18, 27–28, 81–82, 86–88, 107, 108
 see also specific disciples
Drews, Arthur, 54

Easter amnesties, 216
Eastern Orthodox Church, 66, 211, 217
Easter Sunday, 36, 123
Ebionites, 19
Edessa, 45
Egypt, 25, 46, 184
 flight of Holy Family into, 68, 72
 Jewish exodus from, 98, 103
Egyptian language, 14
Egyptian mythology, 64
Eighteen Petitional Prayers, 40, 199
Eleazar, 179
Eli, 78
Elijah, 173
Emmaus, 40, 132–33, 170
Enlightenment, 14–15, 53
Ephesus, Council of, 172
Essenes, 43–44, 105, 142, 184, 194

Eusebius, Bishop, 48–49, 64, 75, 139
evangelists, 4, 9–13, 15–17, 19, 22–41, 56, 79; *see also specific evangelists*
Ezekiel, 14, 76

Feast of Tabernacles, 71, 98–100, 191
Feast of Weeks, 98
Felix, Marcus Antonius, 179
Festus, 114
Fiedler, Peter, 147, 178
"final solution," 32
First Vatican Council, 15
fish symbol, 60
Flusser, David, 18, 181, 184, 199
Fragments of H. S. Reimarus (Lessing), 53–54
France, Anatole, 51–52
Frederick the Great, 52
Freiburg assize court, vii–viii
Freisler, Roland, 153
Friedel, Egon, 40

Gabriel, 27
Galba, 58–59
Galilee, 4, 11, 22–23, 35–37, 49, 67–68, 71–74, 76, 95–97, 180, 193, 198–99
Gamaliel, Rabbi, 32, 50, 51, 133–34, 142
Gandhi, Mohandas K., 196
Gaul, 52, 205
Gennesaret, Lake of, 60, 70, 95, 204
Gentiles, 31, 49
German Bible Society, 213
Germany, 46, 52, 206–9
Gessius Florus, 191
Gethsemane, 30, 84, 103, 123, 125, 127–30, 198, 200
ghettos, Jewish, vii–viii
Gibbon, Edward, 115
Gnosticism, 29, 75, 172, 211
Goethe, Johann Wolfgang von, 52, 53
Goguel, M., 52, 108, 113, 117, 129, 193, 200, 201
Golan Heights, 67
Golgotha, 4, 37, 51, 106, 116, 132, 139, 191
Good News (eu-angelion), 15, 20, 24
Good Samaritan, 16
Good Shepherd, 29, 30, 83
Gospel of Philip, 86–87, 88
Gospels:
　anti-Jewish bias of, 4, 18–19, 26–27, 28–29, 124–25, 130–32, 140–42
　apocryphal versions of, 13, 72, 79–80, 145–46
　authors of, 4, 9–13, 15–17, 22–41, 56, 79
　catholic vs. heretical content of, 14
　chronology of, 12, 22, 23, 25, 28
　contradiction in, 18–19, 20
　error and discrepancy in, 13, 14
　historical and political settings in, 30–31, 56, 140
　historical background of, 9–21, 140
　history vs. legend in, 56
　intellectual and theoretical content in, 30–31, 43
　interdependence of, 17–19, 26
　interpolation into, 24–25
　oral transmission of, 13–14, 16
　pro-Roman tendencies of, 4, 18–19
　selection and elimination process and, 13–14, 17–18
　sociocritical elements in, 23, 26–27
　as testimonials of faith, 15–16
　translations and transcriptions of, 11–13, 14
Greece, 25, 45, 111
Greek language, 11, 23, 34, 60, 63, 73, 74, 79, 98–99, 112–13, 117, 119, 163, 167, 192, 213
Greek mythology, 64, 68
Gregory the Great, Pope, 220
Guevara, Che, 196

Habbakuk, 162
Haenchen, E., 120, 131, 146–47, 178–79
Haman, 204
Handel, George Frederick, 167–68
Harnack, Adolf von, 175
Hasmoneans, 116
Hebrew Bible, *see* Old Testament
Hebrew language, 11, 14, 47, 63, 76, 78–79, 119, 167, 175, 191–92
Helena, 139
Hellenism, 19, 26, 29, 31, 34
　Christianity and, 34, 59
　Jewish tradition vs., 34, 42, 134
　Paul and, 19, 26, 31, 34, 142
　Roman Empire and, 64
Hengel, M., 58–59
Herder, Johann Gottfried, 15, 129, 213
Herod Agrippa I, 24, 28, 113, 204
Herod Agrippa II, 48

Herod Antipas, Tetrarch, 67, 68, 72, 144, 145
   John the Baptist and, 48, 81, 98, 112, 135, 190
   trial of Jesus and, 48, 116, 212–13
Herod the Great, 150
   death of, 67, 68, 72
   infanticide charged to, 68–69, 72, 106
Hezekiab, 63
Hieronymus, 14, 43
high priests, 107, 115, 121, 131–32, 133, 142, 150
Hillel, Rabbi, 97, 144
History of the Jewish Wars (Josephus), 46–47, 111, 113
Hitler, Adolf, 208, 209
Holl, Adolph, 83–84
Holocaust, vii–viii, 207–8, 209
Holtz, T., 149
Holy Family, 68, 72
"holy lies," 38
Holy Sepulchre, 139
Holy Spirit, 14, 15, 20, 23, 53

Ignatius of Loyola, 38, 57
Immaculate Conception, 64
India, 39
Indo-European languages, 11–12
I.N.R.I., 119
Ireneus, 40
Isaac, 141, 219
Isis cult, 64
Israel, 19, 20, 25–28, 32, 43, 60
   modern state of, 25, 148, 184
   religious and political establishment in, 132–37
   Roman conquest of, 12, 19, 22, 47, 50, 111, 142, 179, 193
   Roman occupation of, 4, 25, 43, 58, 73, 114–15, 116, 119, 133, 134, 146, 168, 197

Jacob, 141, 170, 219
Jacob's Well, 28, 86
Jaffa Gate, 191
James (Jesus' brother), 10, 19, 33–34, 48, 55, 75, 113, 142, 149, 173
James (Joseph's father), 78
James (son of Zebedee), 24, 28, 64, 113, 173, 194
Jaubert, C., 116

Jericho, 67, 69, 78
Jerome, 14, 43
Jerusalem, 26, 27, 31, 32, 33, 35–36, 67
   Jesus' triumphal entry into, 95–101, 117, 120, 144, 192–93
   Roman conquest and destruction of, 12, 19, 22, 47, 50, 111, 142, 179, 193
Jesse, 76
Jesus, as name, 47–48
Jesus (son of Ananos), 47
Jesus (son of Damnaus), 150
Jesus Barabbas, 213–14
Jesus cult, modern, 83
Jesus in Bad Company (Holl), 83–84
Jesus Justus, 47
Jesus of Nazareth:
   anger of, 100, 120–21
   artistic portrayals of, 60, 84–85, 86, 110
   ascension into heaven of, 26, 39
   asceticism of, 74, 85–86
   attributes of, 16, 17, 19, 20–21, 23, 25, 29–30, 37, 56, 59, 60, 83–91
   baptism of, 23, 30, 57, 71, 75
   birth of, 25, 27, 36, 46, 62–76
   burial of, 50, 88, 105, 106, 116, 137–39
   as carpenter, 78, 79, 80, 84, 133
   childhood of, 62–63, 72–74, 79, 80, 83
   Christian vs. historical view of, 5, 12, 15–17, 21, 34–35, 40, 50–51, 53–55, 56, 73, 76, 82, 107, 120–21, 123
   circumcision of, 72
   circumstantial evidence of, 55–61
   clothing of, 85, 110, 212
   conception of, 62–65, 66, 79–80, 82, 171
   contradictory sources on, 20, 52, 79–80, 105
   disreputable associates of, 83, 86, 89
   divinity of, 17, 19, 23, 29–30, 53, 56, 60, 63, 86, 119, 170–71
   doubts on historicity of, 4, 52–53, 54–55
   enigmatic image of, 84, 88
   family of, 10, 19, 27, 36, 48, 55, 68, 72, 77, 78–82, 84, 98
   fasting of, 85
   genealogy of, 17, 25, 30, 77–78, 119, 170, 173
   healing powers of, 20–21, 26, 80
   height of, 84
   historical-critical research on, 4, 52–55
   historical evidence of, 4, 5, 9–21, 42–61

Jesus of Nazareth (cont'd)
  humanity of, 55, 56, 57, 60, 63, 84, 86–88, 125, 170–72, 199, 221
  illegitimacy question and, 78–79
  Jewish compassion for, 18, 57
  Jewish vs. pagan mission of, 20–21, 49
  Judaism and, 16, 18, 19, 20–21, 24, 28, 31, 37, 57, 60, 80, 98, 142, 144, 167, 221
  as "King of the Jews," 118–19, 173, 201, 202, 210–11
  lack of biographical sources on, 4, 9, 15, 16, 17, 30, 42–44, 46–47, 48, 52
  last words of, 15–16, 30, 102, 116
  lifestyle of, 83, 85–88
  literary-critical research on, 53–61
  love preached by, 125, 126, 198
  marital status of, 87–88
  as Messiah, 19, 25, 30, 37, 44, 48, 49, 54, 58, 60, 65, 71, 101, 118, 119, 131, 136–37, 141, 155, 161–70, 171–76, 192–93
  miracles of, 80, 82, 86, 96
  names and epithets of, 16–17, 23, 25, 36, 44, 47, 48, 55, 63, 74–75, 87, 104, 118–19, 163, 176
  non-violence of, 189–90, 194–95
  physical appearance of, 84–85
  premonition of death by, 121
  proletarian origin of, 23, 46
  prophecies fulfilled in, 19, 25, 37, 49, 56–57, 63, 71, 72, 75–76, 100–102, 107, 118, 120, 123, 124, 127, 192–93
  as prophet, 133, 137, 141
  public ministry of, 10, 20–21, 25, 44, 54, 56, 57–58, 63, 70, 78, 80–82, 85–91, 96–101, 107, 120–22, 127, 131
  radicalism of, 81–82, 83–84, 88–89, 117–20, 127, 132, 137
  as rebel, 117–20, 127, 132, 156, 198, 214, 217
  rhetorical style of, 10, 15–16, 23, 29, 85, 89, 144
  risk-taking of, 97–98
  sayings of, 10, 11–12, 14, 15–16, 18, 20, 24–25, 29–30, 37, 80–82, 89, 108, 116, 131, 144, 163, 187
  sexuality of, 86–88
  social justice and, 88–91
  symbolism and, 54, 60
  Talmudic slanders on, 46
  teaching and beliefs of, 60, 63, 70, 80, 88–91, 96–97, 100, 121, 122, 131
  tolerance and leniency of, 86, 89, 112
  tomb of, 88, 139
  virgin birth of, 19, 23, 36, 62–65, 77, 80, 82
  women and, 18, 27–28, 56, 64, 86–88, 198, 199
  see also crucifixion of Jesus; Passion of Jesus; resurrection of Jesus; trial of Jesus
Jewish law, 19, 28, 31, 33, 34, 37, 46, 78, 84, 98, 119, 142, 181–88
  on blasphemy, 187
  death penalties in, 109, 112–15, 138, 182, 183, 187
  on diet, 69, 186, 187
  on purification, 72, 185–87
  on Sabbath, 104, 105, 111, 138, 144, 153, 183–85
Jewish War, 19, 47, 49–50, 140, 152, 193
John (disciple), 10, 11, 13, 24, 28, 173, 194
John (evangelist), 10, 28–31
John the Baptist, 23, 43, 57, 68, 79, 135, 157, 173
  asceticism of, 74–75, 85
  execution of, 48, 58, 98, 112, 190
  Jesus and, 57, 74–75, 96, 98, 190
  repentance preached by, 168, 190, 196
John XXIII, Pope, 220–21
Jordan, 19, 67, 71
Jordan River, 23, 67
Joseph, 27, 62, 73, 77–80
  as carpenter, 46, 62, 84
  Mary's relationship with, 46, 65, 71, 72, 79–80
Joseph of Arimathea, 39, 50, 106, 135, 137, 138–39, 156
Josephus Flavius, 46–50, 68, 69, 74, 114, 150, 190, 191, 192, 205
  forgeries attributed to, 49, 51
  Jewish background of, 49–50, 152
  Roman allegiance of, 49–50, 117
  works of, 46–49, 51, 111, 112–13, 117, 138
Jotapata fortress, 50
Judah, 71
Judaism, 4, 16, 18, 20
  early Christianity and, 35–36, 45, 140
  Holy Days of, 18, 71, 98–100, 103–5, 115, 191; see also Passover
  modern, 25
  monotheism of, 38, 157
  Nazarene sect of, 47, 74–75

opposition to Jesus and, 25, 28–29, 51, 57–58, 96–97, 100
  see also Jewish law
Judas Iscariot, 101, 108, 122–129, 134, 194
  interpretations of betrayal by, 125–26
  Jesus' relationship with, 125–26
  Judaism associated with, 124–25
  motives of, 101, 123, 127
  Satan's possession of, 124–25, 126
  suicide of, 108, 122, 123
Judas of Gamala, 73, 193
Jude, 10
Judea, 23, 32, 35–36, 44, 67–68, 71, 73, 115, 204
Julian, Emperor of Rome, 174
Jupiter (planet), 70
Justin, 38
Justus of Tiberias, 43

Käsmann, Ernst, 55–56
Kastning-Oldesdahl, Ruth, 143
Kepler, Johannes, 69–70
King, Martin Luther, Jr., 196
Klausner, J., 49, 199, 204
Kolping, A., 52, 79, 143, 149, 161, 164–65, 177, 194
Küng, Hans, 15, 16, 40, 51, 53, 63, 76, 83, 144, 149, 172, 175, 182, 185, 195–96, 199, 209

lambs, sacrificial, 72, 103, 104
Landmann, Salcia, 11, 46, 82
Lapide, Pinches, 28–29, 38, 73, 147–48, 169, 194, 204, 205
Last Judgment, 37, 96
Last Supper, 36, 95, 101, 103, 105, 122–23, 125
Lateran Council, 65
Latin language, 11, 14, 119
Lazarus, 86, 121–22
Lehmann, J., 172, 184
Lessing, Gotthold Ephraim, 53–54
Limbeck, M., 122
Livia, 39
Lohse, E., 120
Lord's Prayer, 126, 199
Lucerne, 218
Luke (evangelist), 25–28
Luther, Martin, 30, 43, 82, 87–88, 104, 108, 128, 206–7, 215
Lutz, U., 147

Macarius, Bishop, 139
Maccabees, 168
Machaerus Fortress, 98, 112, 190
Magnificat, 27, 170
Malchus, 194
Mandaean Gnostic sect, 29, 75
Man of Sorrows, 207
Marcion, 14, 40
Marian cult, 27, 64–65, 78, 82
Mark (evangelist), 22–23
Mary:
  attributes of, 64
  betrothal of, 46
  at crucifixion, 39, 107
  divorce of, 46, 79
  Immaculate Conception of, 64
  Jesus' relationship with, 27, 62, 63–64, 81–82, 87
  Joseph and, 46, 65, 71, 72, 79–80
  pregnancy of, 46, 62–65, 68, 72, 73, 79–80, 170
  sexual life of, 46, 65, 78, 79–80
  virginity of, 19, 23, 36, 62–65, 77, 80, 82
Mary Magdalene, 28, 39, 86, 87, 88, 107, 175
Mary of Bethany, 86, 121
Masada, 179, 193
matzo (unleavened bread), 103
Matthew (evangelist), 23–24
Maundy Thursday, 115, 122
Mayer, Anton, 23, 26
Menachem, 179
Messiah (Handel), 167–68
Middle Ages, 84, 125
missionary mandate, 20
monotheism, 38, 157
Mosaic Law, see Jewish law
Moses, 10, 58, 68–69, 103
Mount Heron, 67
Mount of Olives, 24, 103, 128
Mount Pilatus, 218
Müntzer, Thomas, 196
Muslims, 66

Napoleon I, Emperor of France, 52
Nazarene sect, 47, 74–75
Nazareth, 5, 12, 17, 37, 42, 67, 70, 71, 72–76
Nazarites, 74–76, 142
Nazi People's Court, 153n
Nazi war crimes, vii–viii, 206–7

290 Index

Nero, Emperor of Rome, 12, 24, 44–45, 142, 191
New English Bible, 213
New Testament, viii, 4, 13–15, 36
  Gospels accepted into, 14
  historical events in, 56
  human vs. divine origins of, 14–15, 53, 55
  Old Testament link to, 25, 43, 101–2, 141
  Qumran scrolls parallels with, 43–44
  spiritual intent of, 15–17
Nicaea, Council of, 17, 20, 40, 172
Nicene Creed, 39, 148, 172
Nicodemus, 50, 51, 135, 138
Nisan, 102–3, 104, 105
Nuremburg trials, 206–7

Oberammergau Passion Play, 208
Old Testament, 19, 58, 69, 80, 181
  fulfillment legends in, 101–2
  New Testament link to, 25, 43, 101–2, 141
Origen, 14, 146, 171, 206, 213–14
Overbeck, 37

pacifism, 19, 43
pagans, 20–21, 22, 25, 26, 32, 59, 66
Palestine, 11, 17, 29, 35, 46, 47, 52, 85, 97, 115
palm branches, 98–99
Palm Sunday, 98–99
Pandera, 46
Papias, Bishop, 13, 38
papyrus, 12
parables, 10, 12, 20, 26–27, 29–30, 54, 85, 87, 89–90, 91, 141
parchment, 12
Parousia, 60
pascal lamb, 103, 104, 111
Passion of Jesus, 17–19, 36–37, 40, 95–108
  abuse and mockery in, 107, 116, 118, 146, 156, 178, 212
  arrest in, 18, 71, 88, 102–8, 115–17, 120–22, 127–30, 189, 201
  betrayal in, 36, 101, 108, 122–28
  carrying of the cross in, 40, 105, 111
  dates of events in, 98–106, 134, 210
  duration of, 115–16, 210
  prophecies fulfilled by, 100–102, 107, 118, 120, 123, 124, 127

scourging in, 102, 109–10, 116
  will to live vs. acceptance in, 198–201
  see also crucifixion of Jesus
Passover, 18, 98–100, 101, 103–5, 106, 115, 116, 134, 190–91
  Preparation Day for, 104, 105, 111, 137, 153
Paul, 9, 16, 31–38, 47
  anti-Jewish attitude of, x, 32–34, 140–42, 178
  bachelor status of, 88
  background and education of, 31–32, 34, 50, 51
  character and personality of, 88
  Christian Church and, 38, 86
  Christian conversion of, 33–34, 35–36
  communities founded by, 13, 35, 142
  controversy surrounding, 38, 74
  epistolary style of, 32, 101
  Hellenism of, 19, 26, 31, 34, 142
  Jewish background of, 32–34, 40, 59, 114, 142–43, 167
  letters of, 11, 12, 14, 24, 26, 31, 32–33, 34, 36, 142
  missionary travels of, 20, 35, 36, 142
  preaching and message of, 15–17, 19–21, 34–38, 40–41, 45, 55, 59, 60–61, 64, 70, 71, 86, 101, 140–42, 170–71, 186, 192
  Roman citizenship of, 31, 34, 114, 142
  Sanhedrin and, 32, 33, 112, 114, 132, 142
  Simon Peter and, 33–34
Paulus, H. E. G., 39
Pella, 19
penitential baptism, 57, 58, 85
Pentecost, 40
Perea, 67
Persians, 111
Pesch, Rudolph, 79, 215
Peter, *see* Simon Peter
Petrine Letters, 10, 11
Pharisees, 25, 32, 49, 85, 133–34, 140, 142–45
  conservative vs. liberal factions of, 97, 193–94
  early Christians and, 106, 142–43, 174
  Jesus and, 16, 46, 57, 97, 122, 135, 143–45, 151–52, 162, 174
Philip II, King of Macedonia, 64
Phillipus, Tetrarch, 67
Philo of Alexandria, 42, 204
Phoenicia, 46

Pilate, Pontius, 45, 150, 171
　anti-Jewish bias of, 4, 18, 201, 205
　character of, 4, 18–19, 42, 47, 120, 136, 178, 192, 204–5, 209–10
　Christian sympathy for, 217–18
　crucifixion role of, 4, 17, 37, 44, 49, 51–52, 101, 102, 109, 111, 113–20, 130, 136, 137, 145, 155, 156, 189–93, 197–98, 201, 209–13
　Roman mandate of, 67, 105, 135, 204
　washing of hands by, 102, 217
Pius IX, Pope, 64
Pius XI, Pope, 220
Pius XII, Pope, 220
Pliny the Elder, 42
Pliny the Younger, 42–43
Pöhlmann, H. G., 90
Pompey, 183
Poppaea Sabina, 45
Porphyrius, 174–75
poverty, ideal of, 19, 43
Power of the Keys, 24–25
Praetorium, Roman, 104, 116, 131, 191, 201, 210–11
Procurator of Judea, The (France), 51–52
prodigal son parable, 26
prophets, 14, 19, 25, 37, 58, 69, 84
Protestantism, 14–15, 208
"Pseudo-Matthew" Gospel, 72, 79–80
purification rituals, 43, 57, 72, 185–87
Pythagoras, 45

Quinisextum Synod, 60
Quintilius Vara, 67
Quirinius, 66–68, 193
Qumran, 43, 44, 63
Qumran scrolls, 43–44, 63

Rabbis, 87–88
Rahab, 78
Rahner, Karl, 51, 172, 209
Rama, 69, 71
resurrection of Jesus, 5, 12, 13, 15–17, 22, 95, 221–22
　appearances of Jesus after, 34–35, 36, 49, 88, 123, 175
　Pauline teaching of, 34–37, 40–41, 61, 123
　spiritual vs. personal reality of, 40–41
　witnesses and theories on, 38–41
Robertson, John M., 54

Roman Catholic Church, 14, 15, 34
　calendar of, 34, 65–66
　dogma in, 19, 20, 38, 53, 64–65, 80, 172
　ecclesiastical censorship in, 14, 15, 17, 60–61
　Gospel of Matthew and, 24
　Holy Days of, 34, 66
　Marian cult and, 27, 64–65, 78, 82
　sexuality and, 64–65
Roman Empire:
　anti-Jewish bias of, 18, 51
　crucifixion role of, 4, 18, 19, 23, 44, 50, 57, 58, 60, 105–7, 108–48
　holidays of, 66
　Jewish resistance to, 117–18, 140
　military presence of, 4, 23, 33, 46, 49–50, 58, 67, 110, 111, 114–15, 127–32
　occupation of Israel by, 4, 25, 43, 58, 73, 114–15, 116, 119, 133, 134, 146, 168, 197
　persecution of early Christians by, 44–45
Roman Missal, 220*n*
Rome, 13, 22, 24, 44
　Christian community in, 45, 47, 142
Rosenzweig, Franz, 38

Sabbath, 104, 105, 111, 138, 144, 153, 183–85
Sadducees, 97, 133, 142, 143, 152, 179, 194, 203
Salonika, 12
Samaria, 20, 73
Samaritans, 16, 86, 205
Samson, 74
Sanhedrin, 32, 33, 35–36, 128, 129, 143
　authority and power of, 35–36, 48, 102, 112–15, 150–51
　Jesus' hearing before, 17, 49, 50–51, 101, 106, 115–16, 123, 130–32, 138, 149–80, 212
　Paul and, 32, 33, 112, 114, 132, 142
　Supreme Council, 95, 106, 130, 135–36, 138, 140, 151
Saturn (planet), 70
Scarf, Bishop, 196
Schammai, Rabbi, 97
Schillebeeckx, E., 97
Schlotheim, H. H. V., 160
Schmithals, W., 140
Schweitzer, Albert, 54–55, 74
scourging, 102, 109–10
scribes, 97, 107, 121

Second Vatican Council, 220–21
Seders, 103, 104, 105, 115, 153, 154
Sejanus, 134–35, 204
Semitic languages, 11–12
Sermon on the Mount, 43, 90–91, 96, 126, 176, 181, 196–97
Shakespeare, William, 16
Shavuoth, 98
shepherds, 73
Sidon, 46, 96
Simon, Akiba, 180
Simonis, W., 26, 123–24
Simon of Cyrene, 40, 105, 111
Simon Peter, 10, 11, 64, 142, 162, 173
  Christian leadership of, 108, 123
  confession of, 108
  denial of Jesus by, 107, 108, 151
  divine authority of, 24–25
  guard's ear mutilated by, 130, 194–95
  Jesus' reprimand of, 24–25, 108
  martyr's death of, 24
  Paul and, 33–34
  preaching of, 40, 55
Simon the Pharisee, 86
Sinai, 141
Six Day War, 25
Slaughter of the Innocents, 68–69, 106
Smith, William Benjamin, 54
Socrates, 45
Sodom, 96
solar eclipse, 51
Solomon, King, 10, 78
Spain, 58
Star of Bethlehem, 69–70, 106
Stauffer, E., 79, 85, 128–29, 131, 134–35, 159–60, 182, 208, 209–10
stellar constellations, 69–70
Stelter, Johannes, 114
Stephen, 34, 112, 114
stoning, 34, 86, 112, 113, 114, 138
Strauss, David Friedrich, 54
Streicher, Julius, 206–7
Strobel, A., 182, 193
Stürmer, Der, 206–7
Suetonius, 45, 58–59
Sumerians, 45
synagogues, 63, 70, 78, 122, 131
Synoptic Gospels, 12, 17, 18, 25, 29, 30, 50, 95, 98, 100, 102–6, 127, 141, 170, 181
Syria, 23, 52, 66–67, 73, 150

Tacitus, 44–45, 51, 148
Talmud, 46, 113, 207
Tarsus, 31
tax collectors, 23, 68, 73, 89, 90
Temple, 97, 112–13
  Jesus and, 26, 62–63, 72, 79, 98, 100, 101, 107, 120–21, 122, 131, 157–59, 166
  offerings and sacrifices in, 72, 98, 120, 168
  pilgrimages to, 98, 106, 115, 120, 190–91
  plunder and destruction of, 12, 22
  police of, 120, 121, 130
  Portico of Solomon in, 100
  torn curtain of, 50–51
Tertullian, 14, 20, 38, 65, 171, 217
Testimonium Flavianum, 49
Teutoburg Forest, 67
Theodotus of Byzantium, 171
Thielicke, Helmut, 15, 84
Thomas Aquinas, 57, 146, 206
Tiberius, Emperor of Rome, 44–45, 50, 67, 135, 205, 216
Tiberius Julius Panther, 46
Tillich, Paul, 15
Titus, 111, 113, 208
Tower of David, 191
Trajan, Emperor of Rome, 43
trial of Jesus, 3–4, 49–50, 71, 101–8
  blasphemy charge in, 176–80
  charges against Jesus at, 153–66, 176–80, 212
  historical-juridical approach to, 3–5
  lack of historical sources on, 4, 17, 50, 106–7
  near acquittal in, 157–61
  political context of, 112–20, 132–37
  Roman vs. Jewish responsibility in, 4, 50, 57, 106, 109–48, 152, 202–18
  summary court-martial nature of, 3–4, 110, 115–16, 118, 120
  transgressions not addressed in, 181–88
  witnesses to, 106–7, 123, 158, 159
Trilling, W., 124, 186–87
Trinity doctrine, 20, 175
Tyre, 96

Valerius Gratus, 150
Vespasian, Emperor of Rome, 50
Via Dolorosa, 191–92
Vita Claudi (Seutonius), 45

Vitellius, 67, 150, 205
Vulgate Bible, 14, 73

washing of feet, 86, 105
West-East Divan (Goethe), 53
Wilcken, R. L., 174
Wise Men, 68, 72
Wyszynski, Stefan Cardinal, 64

Yom Kippur War, 184

Zacchaeus, 90
Zahrnt, H., 37, 53, 161
Zealots, 4, 24, 28, 127, 142, 147
    uprising and rebellion by, 73, 118, 149, 189–90, 193–96
Zebedee, 24, 28, 113

INDEX OF BIBLICAL VERSES

OLD TESTAMENT

Amos, 102

Daniel, 110, 163
Deuteronomy, 58, 98, 138, 154, 157, 160, 188, 206

Esther, 204
Exodus, 81, 111
Ezekiel, 14, 76, 206

Genesis, 66, 78, 171

Isaiah, 20, 38, 63, 71, 76, 84, 101–2, 118, 138, 167–68, 169–70, 174

Jeremiah, 69, 76, 120, 158
Joshua, 78
Judges, 74

Kings, 20, 78

Leviticus, 72, 99, 114

Micah, 71, 76

Psalms, 10, 37, 72, 84, 99, 101–2, 107, 123, 126, 169, 173, 174, 205, 217

Zechariah, 110, 192

NEW TESTAMENT

Acts of the Apostles, 10, 11, 12, 19, 23–24, 26, 27, 31, 34, 35, 39, 40, 47, 55, 63–64, 74, 75, 106, 112, 113–14, 123, 126, 128, 133–34, 138, 142, 146, 173, 193, 209, 215

Colossians, 26, 47
Corinthians, 15, 31, 36, 41, 55, 59, 75, 88, 104, 170, 186

Ephesians, 220

Galatians, 31, 33, 34, 36, 38, 59, 63, 75, 221

Hebrews, 59

John, viii, 10, 12–13, 16, 17, 28–31, 39, 50, 56, 59, 63, 70, 71, 75, 76, 77, 79, 82, 84, 86, 88, 96, 97, 98, 99–100, 102, 104, 105, 106–7, 111, 112, 113, 121–22, 124–25, 128, 130–32, 134–36, 138, 152, 156–57, 171, 175, 187, 191, 197, 203, 205, 210–11, 213, 216, 217

Luke, 12, 15–16, 17, 18–19, 21, 23, 25–28, 36, 39, 50, 62–63, 65, 66–68, 69, 70–73, 77–78, 79–81, 84, 85, 86, 87, 89, 90, 91, 96, 97, 99, 100, 102, 103, 105, 106, 107, 110, 118, 120, 125, 126, 128, 132–33, 141, 144, 146, 155–57, 162, 163, 170, 189, 190, 193, 194, 197, 199–200, 203, 210, 212–13, 214

Mark, 10, 12, 13, 15, 17, 18, 20, 22–23, 24, 26, 30, 36, 37, 39, 59, 63, 70, 71, 77, 78–79, 80, 81, 84–85, 89, 97–99, 100, 101, 102, 103–5, 106, 107, 108, 116, 117, 118, 120, 121, 128, 137, 138, 142, 146, 151, 153, 155, 156, 157, 158, 160, 162, 163, 164, 165, 169, 177, 184, 185–86, 196, 197, 199, 203, 208, 210, 211

Matthew, viii, 12, 15, 17, 18, 19, 20, 21, 23–25, 30, 37, 39, 50, 57, 62–63, 65, 68, 69, 70, 71–72, 75–76, 77–78, 80, 81, 84, 85, 86, 87, 88, 89, 90, 96, 98–99, 100, 101, 102, 103, 104–5, 107, 108, 117, 120, 121, 122, 123, 125, 128, 138, 142, 144, 145, 151, 153, 155, 156, 158, 162, 163, 164, 165, 173, 176, 178, 181, 184, 189, 190, 194, 196, 197, 199, 206, 208, 210, 211, 213, 214, 217

Philemon, 31
Philippians, 31, 36, 38, 142

Romans, 31, 33, 36, 38, 45, 141, 142, 167, 170–71, 221

Thessalonians, 12, 31, 32, 141
Timothy, 37, 171–72